LANDMARK COLLECTOR'

Peakland Air (

The Central Area

Pat Cunningham DFM

'Remember when you simply used to go out walking?'
Wies

'Pat, you've got a Distinguished Flying Medal. Just for a change, how's about letting us see
some distinguished effing flying?'
Me regular nav, Squadron Leader Roy Gibbard, No.114 (Argosy) Squadron

Landmark Publishing

Published by

Ashbourne Hall, Cokayne Ave
Ashbourne, Derbyshire DE6 1EJ England
Tel: (01335) 347349 Fax: (01335) 347303
e-mail: landmark@clara.net
web site: www.landmarkpublishing.co.uk

ISBN 13: 978-1-84306-220-2

ISBN 10: 1-84306-220-8

British Library Cataloguing in Publication Data: a catalogue record for this book is available from the British Library.

Printed by Gutenberg Press Ltd, Malta

Front Cover: Handley Page Heyford K6898 (courtesy of Stockport Express)
Back cover top: Handley Page Harrow K6989 (courtesy of Derbyshire Times)
Back cover bottom; left: Data plate from P-47 Thunderbolt 41-6628.
Right: A P-47 pilot's parachute minutes after excavation from forty-six years in a crater.
(both by courtesy of Mr Martin Glover, Thorncliffe)
Page 1. The author, with obligatory coffee, at the controls of a British Midland DC-9

CONTENTS

AIR-CRASH MYTHS

DETAILS OF THE AIRCRAFT INTRODUCED IN PEAKLAND AIR CRASHES: THE CENTRAL AREA

CONTENTS: CRASH SITES BY GEOGRAPHICAL LOCATION

Chesterfield

Blenheim V6078, Spitewinter (north-east of Matlock)	31
Harrow K6989, Barlow	57
Master M7836, North Wingfield	178
Meteor Mk.8 WE904, Millthorpe	74
Phantom 64-1018, Unthank	100
Unidentified type, Flash Dam (area), Screetham	155
Unidentified twin-engined type, near Gladwin's Mark	155
Wellington X3941, Screetham	144
Wellington Z8491, White Edge Moor	148

Derby (Addendum to *The South*)

Harvard KF570, Postern Hill Farm, Hazelwood, Belper	172
Magister L8227, Long Lane, Lees	174
Magister L8277, Hollybush Farm, Alfreton	177
Magister N3813, Roston, Rocester	176
Magister N3876, Culland Hall, Hollington	176
Master Mk.1 T8685, Denby Common	180
Oxford N4597, Elm Farm, Little Eaton	181
Tiger Moth, de Havillard DH82A, Morley Lane, Little Eaton	186
Wellington DV435, Shottle Hall, Belper	188

Dronfield

Auster, Toad's Mouth	18
Auster, Owler Bar	19
Battle K9221, Dore	28
Blenheim Z5746, Ox Stones, Ringinglow	34
Wellington Z8980, Burbage Moor, Rud Hill	135

Foolow

Harvard FX306, Foolow	60
Shackleton WR970, Foolow	110
Wellington DV732, Eyam Moor	140

Matlock

Bristol Fighter Mk.3 J8432, Matlock Moor, 'Golf Club'	35
Magister N3811, Snitterton, Matlock	69

Monyash

Blenheim L6800, Tagg Lane	33
Canberra WT207, Monyash	41
Oxford V3626, Fawside Edge, Longnor	92
Wellington L7811, Conksbury Bridge, Youlgreave	139
Wellington BJ652, Smerrill Grange, Middleton	146

Rotherham

Bristol Fighter Mk.3 J8458, Treeton Grange	38
Meteor Mk.8 VW267, Todwick	80
Meteor Mk.8 WB108, Treeton Colliery	82

Special Personal Acknowledgements

In addition to those acknowledged to the rear of this Central book of the Peakland series, I owe an especial debt to the following:

Ron Collier and Roni Wilkinson, the pioneering authors whose two volumes of *Dark Peak Aircraft Wrecks* (1979 and 1982) have carved an enduring niche for themselves in the field. And particularly to Roni, of Pen & Sword Books Ltd, for assistance, and for details of their association.

John Woodside, for his expertise in the areas of Air Traffic Control, airfield procedures, aircraft operating, and aircraft handling. Retired from a career in Air Traffic Control but in 2006 still a professional pilot – and of over thirty years standing –, his insightfully analytical input has been of great value.

Alan Clark, and Mark Sheldon, whose fieldwork results were shared so generously with me, and particularly to Mark, an aerospace engineer by profession, who nobly proof-read the crash-site element in the early drafts of all three books.

Veteran crash-site researchers John Ownsworth, and Alan Jones (an aviation artist, in addition), both of whom were helpful throughout and especially so in furnishing extra-archival details of several northern and central sites. This also applies to Arnold Willerton, of Hyde, similarly a researcher since boyhood.

Malcolm Barrass, whose superlative website, *Air of Authority* (www.rafweb.org), is only a pale reflection of his encyclopaedic knowledge of Aviation and RAF historical organisation. Throughout the writing and researching of the Peakland series his experience as a college lecturer in technology, as a pilot, and as an officer with a lifelong commitment to Youth and the Air Training Corps, has been a never-failing source of archival facts and dependable personal opinion. Despite the inestimable assistance I have received any errors remaining, and all opinions expressed, are my own.

Pat Cunningham DFM, June 2006

10

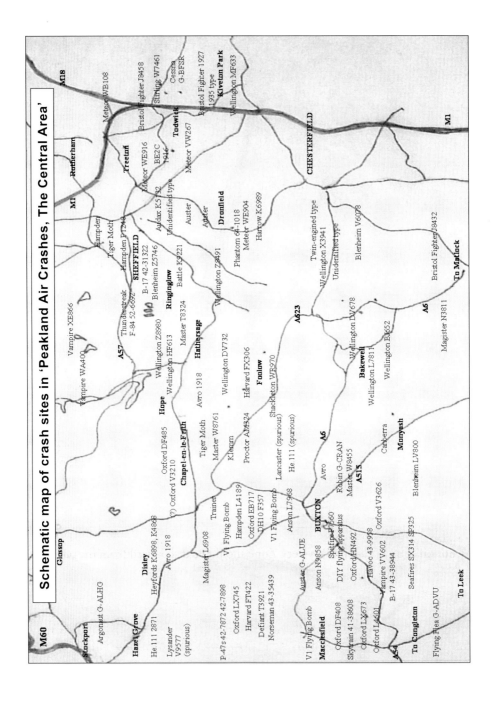

Schematic map of crash sites in 'Peakland Air Crashes, The Central Area'

The primary aim of the *Peakland Air Crashes* series is to supply walkers with the provenance of the aircraft wreckage they chance upon in the area. 'Peakland' is the resurrected term for a Pennine swathe embracing the White and Dark Peaks of Derbyshire and the adjacent parts of Staffordshire, Cheshire, and South Yorkshire. Essentially, Peakland embraces that part of ancient Mercia, including modern Sheffield, into which the Danish influence was slow to intrude, being hampered in the north by the high ground once inhabited by the eponymous *Pecsaeton* people, and in the south by the lowland forests.

A secondary aim of the series is to enable the walker to confidently plan visits to other wreck-sites. To which end *Peakland Air Crashes*, written from the professional flier's point of view, focuses upon where the crash happened, why it happened, and the appearance of the site in 2006.

Yet although the series deals with air crashes, it should be borne in mind that the vast majority of flights are carried out in perfect safety. As was the case with the author's first flight in 1947, a seven-and-sixpenny (35.5pence!) twenty-minute joy-ride in a Dragon Rapide at the embryo Heathrow. The lady pilot took off with her eight passengers, climbed to altitude, overflew swathes of dolls'-sized houses, returned to align herself with the tents paralleling the Bath Road, and landed. A very sedate performance. And for the author, the precursor of nearly twenty thousand hours of flying during forty years of RAF and civil aviation, as crew and as pilot, and in both peaceful and operational settings. Widening the aspect, it epitomised, in fact, the gratifyingly prosaic pattern for virtually all flights undertaken since the dawn of heavier-than-air flight.

Viewed against such a backcloth it can be seen that the 296 crash sites, and the 305 individual aircraft, to be encountered in this Peakland series, are very much at variance with that pattern. Indeed many of the aircraft concerned had been dispatched in company with other machines which, although encountering essentially identical flight conditions, subsequently returned to safe landings. Certainly each of the Peakland crashes serves to illumine the celebrated remarks of Captain A.G. Lamplugh:

'*I am convinced*', he wrote, concluding his 1931 paper on civil air accidents, '*that aviation in itself is not inherently dangerous ... but I do personally feel that the air, to an even greater extent than the sea, is terribly unforgiving of any carelessness, incapacity or neglect.*' He explained that by '*unforgiving*' he meant that '*carelessness, neglect or overconfidence are paid for more quickly and more dearly than in other forms of transport*'.

His conviction notwithstanding, the Peakland was often to prove surprisingly forgiving to aviators, largely because for every crag edging the several massifs there are many miles of relatively flat moorland.

Yet the notion of any Peakland Mystery Zone should be discounted from the outset, for many areas of Britain, both highland and low, have garnered their crops of aircraft, some equally as bountiful. And there is nothing mysterious about any of these crashes.

Nor is it surprising that the majority of them occurred during the years encompassing the Second World War. For that was a period in which hurriedly trained aircrews were sent off with pitifully little experience, in virtually all weathers, by night and day, to European destinations three and four hours distant; and then left to find their way back to often blacked-out airfields, navigating largely without radio aids, and therefore relying on meteorological data that, at best, had been an estimate, and by any token was by then hours out of date. And so, as in a fatal *leitmotif*, courts of inquiry would report, 'Pilot descended below cloud when uncertain of his position', and commanders would first fulminate, and then despair, as the tenets of good airmanship were seen to be so frequently cast aside.

For RAF regulations abounded with admonitions against descending blind: 'Cloud must never be entered in the neighbourhood of and below the level of high ground.' And the RAF's *Air*

Navigation manual, with the original 1941 emboldening of the text reproduced here, further stressed: 'Above all do not descend below cloud unless **absolutely sure there is no high ground nearby**.' But then many operational crews whose aircraft crashed in a cloud-shrouded Peakland were convinced that they were letting down over their Lincolnshire bases, where the four-hundred foot Wolds presented the only obstruction. In similar fashion, many others on innocuous-seeming training exercises were flying tracks as far as fifty miles from where they imagined themselves to be.

And if it is hard to credit that trained, or even trainee, aircrew could stray so far off track, it has to be remembered that they had few of the modern aids which now more nearly make air navigation a precise science. All too often, with radio silence imposed to obviate hostile intrusion, the only navigational aid was dead reckoning – deduced reckoning – which depends upon up-to-date winds for its accuracy. So that for two and three hours on end a navigator might have to rely on nothing but a forecast wind that had been suspect from its conception.

For it has to be appreciated that an aircraft's flight is constantly affected by the wind. Given details of the wind, then a course for a destination can be calculated, and a time determined for reaching it. Let that wind alter, however, whether in speed or direction, and both the course and the lapse time will be affected.

Further, should an aircraft stray just one degree from its compass course, then having travelled sixty miles it will be a full mile to one side of its planned track. So a typical Second World War aircraft flying at two hundred miles an hour, but inadvertently steering one degree off heading, would be over twelve miles astray after returning from certain European targets. Then again very few pilots, or indeed automatic pilots in the 1940s, would have been capable of flying so accurately for that length of time, a heading error of some four degrees being much more likely. This alone would put the machine nearly fifty miles off track.

In practice, by the time the navigator's watch showed them to be overhead their base, many returning crews had been totally unable to fix their position. Clearly luck – given due recognition even in the RAF's *Air Navigation* manual, which styled it, 'that undefinable element'– had some part to play, for just a glimpse of the ground might have allowed any crew member to update the navigator's plot.

But failing that, if the best navigational information obtainable held that the aircraft was over its base, then the machine could be descended in the hope of breaking cloud while still at a safe level above the local high ground. Only what if, approaching that safe level, no break in the cloud was forthcoming?

In that case the captain had four alternatives: to fly out to sea, and then descend towards the coast; to fly to another airfield which might be clear of cloud; to gingerly descend below the safe level in the hope that, on finally breaking cloud, the airfield would be close at hand; or to circle at a safe height, hoping for a weather clearance until the fuel was low, and then bale out. Except that the last would mean abandoning a perfectly good aeroplane.

In this context the psychological drives acting upon the crews must be considered; and not only the mindset of a nation at war. For although most wartime fliers who came down in the Peakland area had less than five hundred hours' flying experience and few as much as one thousand, yet all were volunteers, and being both young and dashing were, therefore, decidedly 'press-on', in the parlance of the day.

All these are very relevant factors when related to flight safety. And each merely sketched in. But far too sketchy nonetheless, without mention of the aircraft altimeter, and without at least a skeletal description of contemporary altimeter practice.

For the altimeter is nothing but a barometer which indicates height against the datum to which it is set. Accordingly, a Lincolnshire-based crew would be provided with the datum by the meteorological section at their near-sea-level airfield. This would cause their altimeter to read zero when the aeroplane was on the runway. And, in contrast to modern practice, this was how the altimeter was left throughout the sortie. But wherever the machine flew, the altimeter would show only the height above that datum. So if the aircraft climbed to 2,100 feet overhead, it would truly have that much clear air below it. But let it move over Kinder Scout, at its 2,088 feet above sea level elevation, and although the crew would still see 2,100 feet on their altimeter the aircraft would be skimming the rocks by only twelve feet.

And every crew member was well cognisant of that. Therefore, if the decision was made to descend blind through cloud, then as the throttles were eased back and the nose lowered, it would be as if a relative silence had fallen, as every eye strained uneasily downwards through the cloud-filled night.

But of course, for the great majority, the calculated risk paid off, and on breaking cloud the grudgingly-lit lights of the flare path flickered into sight. The *Peakland Air Crashes* series deals only with the unlucky few – the very few – for whom it did not pay off.

THE CRASH SITES

As late as 2006 a fair number of the aircraft crash sites featured in this Central volume and the forthcoming Northern book of this series were still marked by débris. Many of these, however, lay on high, trackless moorland where water channels and rock-strewn heather often made the débris difficult to distinguish even at the range of a foot or two. In contrast, on the relatively low-lying, often cultivated, ground covered, in particular, by the Southern volume, there was frequently nothing to see. In all cases, however, the provision of a dependable grid reference aims to afford the walker a frustration-free visit. To accomplish this every location was verified by repeated site visits, initially determined by a Global Positioning System (GPS), and then re-plotted against the Ordnance Survey map, the references being expressed in the increasingly-familiar ten-digit GPS form.

The GPS-equipped walker will have heeded well the maker's warnings regarding this wizardly aid's limitations; and have reflected, perhaps, on what close kinship they bring the walker and the aviator. For, historically, at least, the aviator has always flown in the full knowledge that none of the instruments upon which the exercise of his craft depends ever tells him the unvarnished truth: that his airspeed indicator lies about his speed, his altimeter about his height, and his compass about his direction. So that his competence has always been measured by his sensible use of the tools at his disposal.

Just the same, although the walker is furnished with a proven reference, some sites may still require a patient cast-about in order to locate them on the ground. However, in this series the visitor is assured that each incident really did happen at the reference shown, or in the immediate area indicated, whether surface débris remains or not. To further assist location, the photographs portray the general area of the site, with a few showing the débris – mostly re-interred – by which the site was positively identified.

Yet any walker may legitimately ask why such piles of aircraft wreckage still litter our countryside. For the Ministry of Defence, if they so wished, could clear the sites within a matter of hours. But then in the course of time souvenir hunters seem set to do the job for them.

Given that crash sites do exist, however, then what is likely to be found varies. For the most part there will be a sparse heap of metal fragments, globs of molten aluminium, a bare patch amidst flourishing heather, and powder-blue corrosion beneath the peat. Often the metal will have been gathered into a circle of rocks, although this is often indicative of an impact point elsewhere. Similarly, salvage teams habitually tumbled the wreckage into a convenient gully and burnt or buried it in order to obviate its distracting any future search-and-rescue undertaking.

On occasion there may be an unofficial – albeit Service-related – memorial, and not infrequently, a Remembrance-Day cross, with scarlet poppies to give a touch of colour. But for all the wide conception that the sites are officially viewed as war graves, there is no indication yet that Authority will one day furnish suitable markers.

Not that all these crash sites garnered by the Peakland are graves of any sort, if the insensate aircraft themselves are discounted. For several airmen survived unexpected encounters with its flat moorland, while others were permitted to live after their aircraft had been flown directly into its cliffs. Then again a few aircraft crashed after being abandoned, their crews having very properly saved themselves by taking to their parachutes.

Regarding the visiting of crash sites in general, the walker should be aware that Service sites are held to be under the protection of the Ministry of Defence. Of more practical moment, however, is that, despite the September 2004 'Right to Roam' legislation, many sites are on private land, from which it follows that the normal courtesies should be scrupulously observed. And this is of particular importance when sites are on working farms. This notwithstanding, it became gratifyingly clear in the course of research that every landholder courteously approached, whether owner or tenant, was not only accommodating, despite the intrusion, but keenly interested in the circumstances surrounding the accident associated with their property.

On the subject of the appropriation of aircraft débris found on site, there is little enough worth saying. In the past, enthusiasts have removed many parts, ostensibly to positively identify the aircraft. And of these parts, some have been lodged in museums and private collections. Many others, however, have been scavenged as souvenirs, and very often discarded on the return journey from the site: after all, few sitting rooms are enhanced by lumps of corroded metal. But as the RAF commanders found in their day, crews continued to descend blind, no matter how many appeals were made, or strictures issued. Similarly some people will scavenge. Pragmatically viewing the problem then, all that can be done is to determine a location for each crash site before the last evidence disappears: reason enough in itself, perhaps for this series.

THE CRASH-SITE NARRATIVES

Each entry is introduced by the aircraft type, its registration, and a descriptive locality of the crash site. This is followed by the precise ten-figure map reference – or in a few, unavoidable, cases merely by 'area of'– and the more tentative height of the site above sea level. Next comes the unit or organisation, together with the date of the crash. All available details of the crew, or occupants, are then given, and finally a Crown Copyright photograph of the type of aircraft concerned upon its first appearance.

The narratives are derived, in the main, from the Air Ministry Form 1180s which summarise RAF crash investigations; from the War Department Form 14s for American aircraft; from Air Accidents Investigation Branch Bulletins for civil aircraft; and from witness accounts taken at first hand.

Over the years various enthusiasts have made lists of crash sites, with some entries proving either doubtful or downright spurious. As this series aims to set a benchmark the most persistent not only of these are included not only to save the walker wasting time in fruitless visits but also to record the suspect entry for a posterity in which it might be validated.

Each narrative concludes with a description of the site in mid-2006.

The author, throughout, has unashamedly adopted the dedicated aviator's view that anything to do with Flight Safety demands critical evaluation; for criticism – and most especially, self-criticism – underpins aviation just as surely as does the heartfelt relevance of 'There, but for the Grace of God ...'

But first, just one of the many who 'got away with it':

C-47A ('Dakota') 42-93683, Hathersage area

United States Eighth Army Air Force, 9th Tactical Control Center,
2nd Troop Carrier Pathfinder Squadron, AAF465 (RAF Chalgrove), Oxfordshire
21 January, 1945

Crew: United States Eighth Army Air Force, uninjured:
Second Lieutenant Lloyd E. Beckman, pilot
Second Lieutenant Ronald E. Humpherys, co-pilot
Flight Officer Robert G. Simpson, navigator
Staff Sergeant Albert S. Beck, radio operator
Corporal Albert D. Caswell, dispatcher

On 21 January, 1945, Second Lieutenant Lloyd Beckman and his crew were part of a five-'Dakota' formation on a roundabout route from their base at RAF Chalgrove. As the flight progressed the weather deteriorated, causing the formation leader to call off the exercise and direct a dispersed return to base. Left to his own devices Second Lieutenant Beckman decided to maintain contact flight below cloud. 'We were flying at 1,500 feet indicated', he wrote in his accident report, 'and the visibility was fairly good at this time.' But as he proceeded, and approached the Hathersage area, so conditions grew worse. 'I now came to the conclusion that we could no longer continue contact and upon checking the terrain with the navigator, I realized we were in a very dangerous position. I started to climb immediately … [but] saw an obstruction … looming directly in front of us. I pulled up but not in time to clear it and we heard the trees scraping the bottom of the aircraft. On returning to Chalgrove I dragged the runway [made a low pass] so the tower could note the extent of the damage and was advised to land.'

The aircraft had damage on its right wing and tailplane with dents down its belly and radio aerials torn away. The investigation attributed the accident to pilot error with weather as a contributing factor but recommended that a repeater altimeter, airspeed indicator and air-temperature gauge be supplied to the navigator's station.

One of who knows how many crashes, then, that never actually happened.

Hawker Audax K5132, Coal Aston/Norton, Greenhill, Sheffield

SK 35473 81352 179m
No.11 Flying Training School, RAF Shawbury, Shropshire,
No.23 (Training) Group, RAF Flying Training Command
7 February, 1939

Occupant: solo pupil pilot:
Corporal William W. Thompson, shocked

On 7 February, 1939, pupil pilot Corporal William Thompson, a trainee with some 128 hours' flying experience overall, which included sixty hours on the Audax, was dispatched on a solo night cross-country flight from RAF Shawbury, in Shropshire. In the course of this flight he went off track but eventually relocated himself over Sheffield. By that time, however, his fuel was running low, so, realising that he was some sixty-five miles from his base, he decided to make a precautionary landing on a former World War I landing ground maintained as an aerodrome by Sheffield Corporation. During the First World War the landing ground had served No.2 Northern Aircraft Repair Depot which, situated between Coal Aston to the south and Norton to the north, was confusingly designated as both Norton and Coal Aston. The depot had been centred upon the crossroads of Norton Lane and Dyche Lane, and in the 1914–18 war its landing strip had been equipped with a flare path. By 1939, however, this aid, and indeed the greater part of the site buildings, had long gone, presenting Corporal Thompson with the daunting task of setting down with only his wingtip flares for illumination, a light source nowhere near as effective as modern landing lights.

Part of No.2 Northern Aircraft Repair Depot in its heyday, by courtesy of the Sheffield Local Studies Library archives

Fortunately, Mr Cedric Rotchell, the motor mechanic in charge of the night shift at nearby Messrs Newboult and Sons Garage, on Meadowhall Crossroads, realised that the pilot circling low overhead wanted to set down. As he told the *Sheffield Telegraph* later that night, 'I drove my car to the airfield which was only some hundreds of yards away and put my headlights on to assist him to land. I was then joined by Mr R Neale, of Overstones, Norton Lane, who switched on his headlights too.'

It seems that the additional lights gave Corporal Thompson the visual reference he required, for he now made his third approach. Seeing a tree looming up, however, he hastily banked aside but in doing so hit the ground short of the strip, his aircraft overturning and catching fire. As Mr Rotchell saw it, 'He seemed to lose height suddenly, and dropped like a stone. The plane's nose struck the ground and it turned right over. A Verey light set fire to the wing and at the same time the engine burst into flame. I climbed up onto the wing and shouted to the pilot. At

The Audax crash site

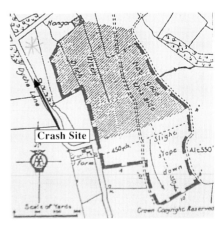

AA Register of landing grounds, 1930s: Norton

first he did not answer. Then his head came out of the cockpit and he said he was all right. He climbed out and fell semi-conscious to the floor. Aided by Mr Beale and PC Price, I dragged him away from the flames. I asked if there was anyone else in the plane but he replied that he was alone. He was badly shaken, but didn't appear seriously hurt.' Fellow rescuer Mr Neale expressed his admiration for the selfless way in which Mr Rotchell had gone about helping the pilot. 'He deserves a medal', he told reporters.

In 2005 Mrs Sheila Gilmour, of the Norton History Group, was able to detail the changes the locale had undergone in the interim, explaining that Norton College stands at the intersection of Dyche Lane and Norton Lane, and that the broad dual carriageway of the Bochum Parkway which actually parallels Norton Lane now swallows the actual crash site. Just the same, the area beyond the Parkway, and to the front of Norton College, will represent a close-proximity site for the suburban walker.

Auster Autocrat G-ALUE, Axe Edge Moor, near Buxton

SK 02224 70424 480m, as recalled by two 1952 witnesses
Private ownership
20 September, 1952

Occupants: pilot and passenger, unhurt:
Mr Kenneth Stockfis, pilot
Mr Charles Kitchen, passenger

The crash of non-radio equipped Auster Autocrat G-ALUE on Axe Edge Moor in September 1952 shows the pertinence of the contemporary RAF flight-safety poster whose exhortation began, '*If, on route from A to B, you change your mind and land at C ...*', and went on to spell out the desirability of letting the originally-proposed destination know of any change of plan. For when the Auster did not reach its destination the pilot, Mr Kenneth Stockfis, having inadvertently flown into the ground in low cloud, would have known that his non-arrival would not necessarily spark off any immediate search-and-rescue operation.

He and his passenger, Mr Charles Kitchen, had already been fortunate in coming down on a relatively level area of moorland, for cloud-mantled ridges reared two hundred feet above them. They were even more fortunate in having found themselves uninjured when they had scrambled from their inverted and badly damaged aircraft. So, shocked and disorientated, with the fog drastically reducing visibility and the evening light fading, Mr Stockfis made the always problematical decision to leave the wreck and set off to seek help.

Had they known it they were less than half a mile from the main Buxton to Congleton road, but unaware of this, they began ploughing their way further into the moor. Just the same their relative good fortune held, for when Mr Kitchen found himself floundering, soaking wet, in a bog, they turned back to the relative shelter – and the more easily located bulk – of the wreck.

As they were later to relate, they endured a long and uncomfortable night, only to find, as dawn broke, that the fog was even thicker. Upon which, deciding that there was still little chance of anyone happening upon them, they set out to seek succour once again. Yet for the second time they headed south-westwards, away from the nearby roads, and therefore further into the moor. Fortune, however, continued to mellow towards them, for after some considerable time they stumbled into the remote holding of Orchard Farm, one-and-a-half hard moorland miles from the crash site. Here they found hot drinks, and food, but no telephone, although before long the news was carried to the local policeman at Quarnford, Constable Frank Gardner. His daughter, Brenda, later to become Mrs Farlam, of Wallnook Farm, Brand Side, speaking in early 2005, remembered that summons.

'I would often accompany Dad on call-outs,' she smiled, 'indeed he'd have me take down the

Orchard Farm in 2005

Mrs Brenda Farlam, née Gardner

details in shorthand. So we biked over to Orchard Farm – no car in those days, of course – to find that Joe and Lizzie Wardle had taken good care of the two men. Then, in company with Mr Edwards, an Automobile Association patrolman, we set off over Bareleg and Cheeks Hill to keep an eye on the aircraft. It was smashed, and I don't suppose it was much use. But I can't remember what happened to it after Dad passed over the responsibility. After all, it was all such a long time ago.'

As indeed it was. Nevertheless, farmer John Bowler, of Tor Gate Farm, Wildboarclough, remembered the aircraft on the moor with gratitude. Because, for safety's sake, its fuel tank had to be emptied of its relatively low-octane contents. Which was serendipitous, for his

The area of the crash site of Auster G-ALUE, looking north-west, over the Congleton Road, towards the Cat and Fiddle Inn

motorbike, parked on Thatch Marsh Lane, only 300 yards distant, had a tank with plenty of spare capacity.

Despite Mrs Farlam's dire assessment of its condition, the Auster was subsequently recovered from the moor, after which, rebuilt and re-registered, it flew happily on at Barton for several years until it was eventually destroyed in a mid-air collision. Back on Axe Edge Moor, there was no visible sign of the 1952 crash in mid 2005, and even the location given here is, at best, a remembrance from many years past.

Taylorcraft Auster, Toad's Mouth, Hathersage

SK 25803 80805 320m
Club aircraft
1950s–60s

This incident was recorded in a generally dependable list compiled by crash-site enthusiasts in the 1970s. It is not even known whether the machine was set down due to bad weather, or because it was lost and short of fuel, or whether it actually crashed. Lack of detail notwithstanding, the occurrence is included here in the hope of something more coming to light in the future. Certainly there would have been coverage in the local press.

The area of the crash site near Toad's Mouth

Taylorcraft Auster, Owler Bar, south-west of Sheffield

SK 29402 77921 299m
North-East Airways
8 January, 1951

Pilot: unhurt after a precautionary landing:
Captain G.S. Pine

On 8 January, 1951, when Captain Pine of North-East Airways was flying from Brough, near Hull, to his base at Blackpool, he was caught out by bad weather in the vicinity of Sheffield. Well aware of the high ground he would have to overfly, he judiciously put his Auster down at Owler Bar. The field he chose, directly opposite the Peacock Inn, and paralleling the elongated roundabout, was adequate to the purpose, but a slightly undulating surface caused his propeller to strike the ground, breaking off one of the tips. The aircraft remained on the ground for a day or two until the engine was checked for internal damage due to the impact, but once reassured on that score, and after a replacement propeller had been obtained and fitted, Captain Pine then flew the aircraft onwards to his base.

The incident was duly reported in the *Sheffield Independent* newspaper on 9 January, 1951, together with a photograph of the downed aircraft and its pilot. Unfortunately the original plate was not retained by the paper and the newsprint copy is too obscure to usefully reproduce.

In 2005 Mr Howard Fisher, of Pewitt Farm, near Owler Bar, had to reflect for a moment or two in order to recall the incident. Then he observed, 'That's going back a bit, and I was only a kid. But it came down in the field opposite the Peacock. There wasn't much wrong with it. And after a day or so, it flew off again.'

An innocuous enough incident. But one imbued with the flavour of the new, post-war attitude to flight safety, the captain setting his machine down rather than risk low-level flight through cloud-obscured hills.

Mr Howard Fisher, of Pewitt Farm, witness

2005, the field utilised by Captain Pike for the setdown

Avro Anson Mk.1 L7968, Moss House Farm, Combs Moss, north-west of Buxton

SK 04615 75097 446m
Central Navigation School, RAF Cranage, No.25 Group,
Flying Training Command
15 October, 1942

Crew: four, all killed:
Sergeant Paul Joseph Woodcock, RAF Volunteer Reserve, staff pilot
Sergeant Richard James Reay, Royal Canadian Air Force, pilot
Sergeant James Munro Matheson, RCAF, pilot
Sergeant William Gordon Dale, RAFVR, staff wireless operator/air gunner

When operational bombing over Germany commenced with the advent of the Second World War, the RAF soon realised that its aircrews were woefully lacking in the navigational skills called for. To remedy this the Central Navigation School (CNS) was set up and tasked with improving navigational standards overall. Indeed, in part because of the excellent job this establishment did, it has been held that by 1944 navigational accuracy, and following on from that, bombing accuracy, had increased fivefold.

From the outset the School set itself high standards, for notwithstanding such exceptions as Donald Bennett, who was to become the pilot-founder of Bomber Command's Pathfinder Force, and whose 1936 *The Complete Air Navigator* had become the RAF's *Air Navigation* manual, most pilots – and many observers – had received only the basics of navigational training. This despite navigation being an adjunct of pilotage, rather than the separate field it was to become under pressure of war requirements: in 1942 the by-then time-honoured aircrew speciality of Observer was to be restyled Navigator. CNS aimed to change the generally low standard of navigating practice, to which end its first priority had to be to train specialist navigators in the way that the Central Flying School had always trained pilots to be qualified flying instructors.

From the outset, of course, it was necessary to have staff pilots who were more than navigationally adept; accordingly, on 15 October, 1942, when Sergeant Paul Woodcock, a pilot on the staff of the CNS, was dispatched from RAF Cranage on a night navigational exercise, his Anson carried two Canadian pilots in addition to the staff wireless operator. At 2215 hours, however, while in the course of homing towards Cranage on its return leg, it clipped the top of a ridge just to the north-west of Buxton, and sixteen miles from base. The aircraft was destroyed, and all on board were killed.

The court of inquiry submitted that the crew members carrying out the homing must have mistaken the Cranage occulting beacon for the Cranage pundit. This deduction was based upon the position of the crash in relation to the airfield, and also upon the fact that neither the captain nor the operating pilot had felt it necessary to call for a course to steer for Cranage; the implication being that, having the airfield-identifier light signal in sight, they had felt no need for any other assistance. The Air Officer Commanding (AOC) concurred with this conclusion, while his superior, the AOC-in-Chief, put it on record that as a result of this accident No.25 Group had been directed to ensure that all their aircrews were aware of the difference between occults and pundits.

Yet to the writer, the whole premise appears specious. To support this jaundiced view it is necessary to set out the differences between pundits and occults.

The pundit, or airfield identification beacon of the day (although still in use in 2006; red at RAF airfields, green at civil), was a mobile beacon which flashed a two-letter characteristic in morse code appropriate to that airfield: so that, for example, Shawbury's pundit flashed 'SY'. In peacetime operation pundits are invariably positioned within the airfield boundaries, but in wartime a pundit actually on the airfield would act as a guide to hostile intruders, therefore it might be positioned up to five miles from the airfield, with operating crews being briefed on its current location for any given night.

The contemporary aerodrome beacon, in contrast – alternatively known as an aerial lighthouse, or occult – showed a periodically-shaded (that is, occluded) white light coding a single identifying letter.

However, of more relevant significance, albeit rather theoretical, is that while pundits were designed to be visible at a range 'not exceeding fifteen miles in good weather', the occulting searchlight – whose beam could be redirected to point the way towards an active airfield – was designed to be visible for 'up to thirty miles'.

The court's premise then, was that the aircrew had seen the occult at a range of something just under thirty miles, mistaken it for the pundit, and assuming that they were at only fifteen miles range, had begun to let down. Yet the writer, at least, is left bemused at the suggestion that fliers would ever base their range upon a light, whatever its source. Direction, of course, but hardly range. So the most likely scenario is that the crew relaxed when they saw an identifying light and began to descend without taking the basic precaution of double-checking their position. That is, over a blacked-out land they complacently let down blind into high ground as so many had done before them, and so many more were still to do, pundits or occults notwithstanding.

In early 2006 neither the Moss Bank ridge impact site, nor the grassy, south-western slope onto which the Anson then tipped, bore any scars from the tragedy, but in 2004 a metal-detector search by a crash-site researcher, re-determining the location, resulted in the recovery of an Anson cowling clip.

Cowling clip found by a researcher in 2004

The terminal crash site on the Cranage side of the ridge, near Moss Bank Farm and Buxton

Avro Anson Mk.1 N9858, Dane Bower, Wildboarclough

SK 00311 69926 501m
No.10 Flying Training School, RAF Ternhill (south-west of Market Drayton, near Stoke-on-Trent), No.21 Group, Flying Training Command
14 November, 1940

Pilot: killed:
Leading Aircraftman Martin James Walton Taylor, pupil pilot

The Avro Anson, always steady and reliable, became the standard twin-engined trainer for many of the flying training schools, not least those operating overseas under the Empire Air Training Scheme. In the United Kingdom one of the many units equipped with the type was No.10 Flying Training School, based at RAF Ternhill, near Stoke, one of whose Ansons, N9858, was lost on 14th November, 1940.

The pupil pilot flying N9858, Leading Aircraftman Martin Taylor, was relatively advanced in his pilot training, having logged 109 hours total flying, with twenty-two dual and thirty-six hours solo on the Anson. His duty on this flight was to carry out a navigational test. Unfortunately he got himself lost, strayed from his assigned route into an area of high ground and bad visibility, and flew into a hill at 1,600 feet above sea level, thirty-five miles from Ternhill. Leading Aircraftman Taylor was killed on impact, even though there was no fire.

No record is now available of the route Leading Aircraftman Taylor had been set to fly but the court of inquiry, who would have had those details to hand, found that he was badly off track when he crashed, noting that the weather on the correct route had remained perfectly suitable for the exercise.

In seeking to determine what had caused him to stray so far from track the court looked, among other things, at the possibility that this inexperienced pilot had incorrectly set his directional gyroscope – basically a dead-beat compass repeater. They would also have had to consider spatial disorientation leading to loss of control in poor visibility. But with so many sources of navigational, and indeed piloting, error to choose from, they finally had to submit that they were unable to attribute the accident to anything but faulty navigation, which in turn, had to stem from inexperience.

The crash site lies some way up a long-established, and in 2006 private, farmland track which would have furnished easy access to the recovery team, allowing them to do a thorough job. For although in 2004 some scraps of canvas were found in the molehills at the foot of the slope, no trace of this accident was found during an early-2006 search.

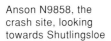

Anson N9858, the crash site, looking towards Shutlingsloe

Canadair Argonaut C-4, G-ALHG, Stockport

SJ 89896 90076 61m
British Midland Airways, Castle Donington, Derby
4 June, 1967

Occupants:
72 passengers and two crew members died. 13 persons survived.

Crew:
Captain Harry Marlow, survived
First Officer Christopher Pollard, killed
Flight Engineer Gerald Lloyd, killed
Stewardess Miss Julia Partleton, survived
Steward Tony Taylor, survived

Passengers (official list; but sources vary):
These were killed:
Mrs Dorothy Ackroyd; Mr and Mrs Ayland; Mr William and Mrs Eliza Booth; Mrs Catherine Brooks; Mr Herbert, Mrs Phyllis, and Miss Christine Denton; Mr Ronald and Mrs Annie Cowgill; Mr Philip Cruse; Mr Bernard and Mrs Jane Down; Mrs C Gill; Mrs Goodwin; Mr and Mrs Harland; Mr Alan and Mrs Kathleen Hughes; Mrs Elsie James; Mr Arthur and Mrs Elsie Kemp; Mr Roy Latham and Mrs Margaret Latham; Miss Mabel Mellor; Mrs and Miss Nolan; Mrs Owen; Mr and Mrs Reynolds; Mr, Mrs, Master and Infant Shaw; Mr Harry, Mrs Joan and Master John Stansfield; Mr and Mrs Smart; Mr Brian and Mrs Ann Stott; Mr Alec and Mrs Gwen Smith; Mr and Mrs Arthur Smith and Master David Smith; Mrs Taylor; Mr Royston and Mrs Nancy Taylor; Mr and Mrs Raymond Tomlinson and Master Michael and Miss Ann Tomlinson; Mr Phillip, Mrs Jean and Master Thorne; Mr Thomas, Mrs Jean, Master William and Miss Jeanette Walsh; Mrs and Master Williams; Mr Ivan, Mrs Marjorie and Miss Wilshaw; Miss Joan Wood; Mr Ruben and Mrs Sonia Woolfson; Mr and Mrs Joseph Nicholson; Mr Alan and Mrs Jean Taylor; Mr Raymond; Mr Frank Thompson; Mrs Phyllis Elsie Thompson.

These survived:
Miss Fiona Child; Miss Mary Green; Miss Susan Howarth; Mr Allan Kee Johnson; Mr Albert Owen; Miss Lilly Parry; Mr David Ralphs; Miss Vivian Werrett; Master Billy and Master Harold Wood.

Derby-based British Midland Airways acquired five ex-BOAC Argonauts in September 1961, on the demise of Overseas Aviation Ltd. However, although purchased cheaply they proved to be an expensive investment, being costly to run and less technically sophisticated than other types that had been considered. Indeed it was soon realised that the decision to buy had been a bad one. Just the same the company kept the aircraft until late 1967 when, following the disastrous crash of G-ALHG on the fourth of June, the two then remaining were withdrawn from service.

On the fatal day, G-ALHG was returning from Palma and about to make an approach into Manchester. Suddenly its right-outer engine (No.4) failed, and shortly afterwards the right inner (No.3) lost power. A right-hand circling turn was initiated while trying to resolve the problem and restart the failed engines, but in the process so much height was lost that Captain Harry Marlow had no option but to set the machine down. For this, he chose the undeveloped area at the junction of Waterloo Road and Hopes Carr, the only uncluttered space to present itself. On his approach he overflew many twelve-storey blocks of flats, but then struck a car-packed garage, an electrical substation and a warehouse. On impact the Argonaut broke into three sections, the cockpit finishing up in the garage forecourt, the cabin on the substation, where it burst into flames, and the tail on the steeply sloping bank of a ravine.

A young enthusiast, who had been tuned into the Air Traffic Control (ATC) frequency, was able to repeat the poignant final radio exchanges to the *Stockport Express*.

ATC: 'Go around, at 2,000 feet: what is your height?'
Aircraft: 'One thousand feet.'
ATC: 'Say again?'
Aircraft: '800 feet, and falling.'
ATC 'You have gone off the radar screen. Hotel Golf? Hotel Golf?'

Another witness, Mr Derek Outram, of Cheadle Heath, was later to tell the inquiry, 'The plane just seemed to flop.' He also testified that as he helped police remove twenty-five persons from the burning wreck he found many who had survived the impact itself but had died having been trapped by their seatbelts, and by the collapse of the restraining bars of their seats.

Among causal factors considered by the three-man Board of Trade Inquiry were the age of the aircraft, error by the captain, and poor maintenance, but Sir Elwyn Jones, QC, the Attorney General, concluded, 'I think it right that I can say that shortcomings in design is probably the main cause.' Effectively, an open verdict completely exonerating both the crew and British Midland itself.

It transpired that, due to a peculiarity in the Argonaut's fuel-system switchery, an engine could be starved of fuel. Further, that short-statured pilots could not reach the appropriate control in order to remedy the situation. Yet the type had been in service for twenty years, and although at least three other operators were aware of the problem, warnings had not been passed on. As just one of the positive outcomes of this tragedy, dissemination of such known hazards became an aviation requirement.

In June 2002 a memorial was raised at the site commemorating the seventy-two people on board who died, to be supplemented later by a similar memorial to the many rescuers who gave aid.

One such rescuer, early on the scene, had been able to tell the inquiry, 'The captain was trapped in the cockpit in the now-burning plane but asked continuously, "How many passengers got out?" and said he had been "trying to find somewhere to put the aircraft down".' Clearly, it was with this in mind that, when the second memorial was unveiled, Captain Marlow's sons received a bravery award on his behalf.

The memorials at the Waterloo Road and Hopes Carr site.

'In memory of the seventy two passengers and crew who lost their lives in the Stockport Air Disaster 4th June 1967'

'This memorial is dedicated to those involved in the rescue and who gave aid at the Stockport Air Disaster 4th June 1967. All were faced with the true horror of tragedy and did not turn away. Their courage saved twelve lives.'

The crash scene (courtesy of the *Stockport Express*)

Boeing B-17 42-31322, '*Mi Amigo*', Endcliffe Park, Sheffield

SK 32857 85899 138m
United States Eighth Army Air Force, 305th Bombardment
Group, 364th Bombardment Squadron, AAF105 (RAF
Chelveston), south-east of Kettering
22 February, 1944

Crew: ten, United States Army Air Force, all killed:
First Lieutenant John Glennon Krieghauser, pilot
Second Lieutenant Lyle J. Curtis, co-pilot
Second Lieutenant John W. Humphrey, navigator
Second Lieutenant Melchor Hernandez, bombardier
Staff Sergeant Robert E. Mayfield, radio operator
Staff Sergeant Harry W. Estabrooks, engineer/top turret gunner
Sergeant Charles H. Tuttle, ball-turret gunner
Sergeant Maurice O. Robbins, tail gunner
Sergeant Vito R. Ambrosio, right waist gunner
Master Sergeant George U. Williams, left waist gunner

Once combat experience with the RAF had shown the advisability of operating the Boeing B-17 Flying Fortress in interdependent defensive formations, it became a formidable adversary. Bolstered by this strategy, and although it had a relatively small bomb load, it formed the mainstay of the United States Eighth Army Air Force's striking force when the Americans began their European bombing campaign in August 1942. Accordingly, on 22 February, 1944, eighteen months into the campaign, it was B-17s that were dispatched to raid Ålborg airfield in Denmark.

Among these was '*Mi Amigo*', First Lieutenant John Krieghauser's aircraft. The Danish target was obscured by cloud, however, and the raiders turned back from overhead. Only by that time they were under fierce air attack, with '*Mi Amigo*' being one of those singled out. Having been seen to suffer damage to its fuselage and engines, it then fell out of formation, subsequently jettisoning its bombs into the North Sea.

First Lieutenant John Krieghauser's crew would have been aiming to return to their base at Chelveston, to the south-east of Kettering. But they evidently had navigational problems, for they drifted north of track and were next seen circling over Sheffield, some eighty miles to the north-west of their Northamptonshire base. The machine was clearly in difficulties, and as an engine cut out so one wing dropped in an auto-rotation that first rolled, then spiralled '*Mi Amigo*' into the ground in a Sheffield park. Just one airman survived the impact, poignantly pleading with a young boy, 'Can you save me, kid?' only to be engulfed in the conflagration moments later.

Among those who found their way to the park was Mr Gordon Taylor, by 2006 long domiciled in Connecticut, United States, but then a lad of 13 living in Abbeydale, Sheffield, who wrote, 'By the time I cycled over to the scene, the park had already been sealed off by the army, and all that I could see from the distance was that very distinctive Boeing tail sticking up among the débris. But even after the army had cleared the site there was still a lot lying around, and kids were fighting over their souvenirs. I picked up a piece of an exhaust and saved it for years until my mother threw it out as morbid.'

It is not known why First Lieutenant Krieghauser did not order at least some crew members to take to their parachutes before the situation got critical. But in view of his aircraft's battle damage, evidenced not least by the failure of some of its navigation and communication aids, it is probable that he had some casualties on board who could not jump.

Witness accounts make it quite clear that the aircraft had gone totally beyond control, both rolling and gyrating before diving heavily into the ground. But, perhaps inevitably, the years have brought embellishments, notably one that has First Lieutenant Krieghauser attempting to

The impact site of B-17 42-31322, '*Mi Amigo*'; ten American oaks were planted in commemoration

avoid children playing on the football ground. Indeed, although contemporary accounts show that this has no substance, the American authorities, in awarding First Lieutenant Krieghauser a posthumous Distinguished Flying Cross, and an Air Medal with Oak Leaf Cluster, saw fit to have the citation speak of his avoiding 'an English home' by manoeuvring 'the crippled aeroplane over the dwelling'. Which seems a shame, for he and his crew deserve much better, the ten of them swelling the total of American aircrew lost over Europe that day to 430, and with '*Mi Amigo*' bringing the day's toll of American bombers downed to 43.

Yet perhaps they have been better served by the memorial that was erected on the crash site in 1969 by the Sheffield Branch of the Royal Air Force Association; by the ten American oaks that fringe the riverside knoll; and by the annual homage paid each February not only to them, but through the memorial, to all American aircrew who died while operating from British airfields in the course of the Second World War.

Boeing B-17G 43-38944, Birchenough Hill (East), Parks Farm Moor, Wildboarclough

SJ 99460 67766 457m impact site and nearby memorial
SJ 99545 67797 456m terminal site
United States Eighth Army Air Force, 398th Bombardment Group, 603rd Bombardment Squadron, AAF131 (RAF Nuthampstead), north-east of Stansted
2 January, 1945

Crew: five, United States Army Air Force, all killed:
First Lieutenant Donald James DeCleene, pilot
Second Lieutenant Maynard Stravinski, co-pilot
Flight Officer Thomas Manos, navigator
Technical Sergeant Howard F. Ayers, radio operator
Technical Sergeant Frank E. Garry, flight engineer

The B-17 Flying Fortress had an operational crew complement of ten men, but fewer might well be carried on non-operational flights. As was the case on 2 January, 1945, when Fortress B-17G 43-38944 had to be ferried to one of the American squadrons occupying RAF Nuthampstead, near Stansted. In fact, First Lieutenant Donald DeCleene elected to take just five crew members when he was detailed to collect the new B-17 from the United States Army Air Force's Base Air Depot at Burtonwood (near Liverpool), a unit whose function was to supply new and modified bombers to combat groups.

The weather forecast was satisfactory, promising a light scattering of cloud with a base lifting from an already generous 1,500 feet to 3,000 feet as the route progressed. The visibility, too, was to be fine, generally five miles, and even downwind of industrial areas not expected to fall lower than 3,000 yards: conditions which meant that it was perfectly proper for First Lieutenant DeCleene to elect to fly the direct-track route over the intervening high ground, even though darkness had fallen by the time he got airborne, at 1904 hours.

The distance the crew had to fly was 150 miles which, at the B-17's cruising speed, and in the existing light-wind conditions, would have taken them under fifty minutes. It must be assumed, therefore, that before actually setting course they carried out a few 'shaking down' exercises, because it was already 1925 hours when they were seen overflying the hills at Wildboarclough, just twenty-nine miles down the route – or only ten minutes' flying time out from Burtonwood.

Farmer Wilf Massey, of Berry Bank Farm, was alarmed when he saw the course the aircraft was taking, while farmer Thomas Smith, at Hammerton Knoll Farm, and farmer Alan Waller, at Blaze Farm, adjoining it to the east, both testified to their own concern, reporting that the aircraft had passed very low over their high-moorland holdings with its engines roaring steadily and without any indication that it was in difficulties. What all three had feared, it was plain, was that, with the evening so dark, the aircraft might fly into either Tagsclough or Birchenough Hill. And only seconds later each of them saw a flash as the bomber did indeed fly into the ground, Mr Smith actually seeing wreckage thrown up into the glare.

Striking flat-topped Birchenough Hill at 1,500 feet above sea level the aircraft burst into flames and slid on in an easterly direction, disintegrating and throwing clear the bodies of some of the crew before burning itself out.

The Accident Investigation Committee, noting that the aircraft had cruised into Birchenough Hill in a west–east slide, considered the possibility of an engine failure having caused it to turn east and fly four miles off its direct south-easterly track to Nuthampstead. No evidence was found of such a failure, however, and the investigators were forced to the opinion that 'the plane was operating normally but the pilot was in error due to the extremely low altitude over which he was flying the direct route'.

The Committee then went on to record that, in the opinion of the flight-controlling authority in the area, American pilots used to operating from the flat fenlands of East Anglia had consistently shown themselves reluctant to accept routings around the 'rugged terrain' of the Pennines, exercising their prerogative to fly directly across it. Which meant, in Flight Control's view, that such accidents would continue to occur, even in good weather.

The Accident Committee also noted that, since becoming a pilot ten months earlier, First Lieutenant DeCleene had flown some 187 hours, with about 58 hours on type, but that in the six months before the crash he had done just one hour's flying at night.

Ultimately, however, having considered all the facts elicited, the lieutenant-colonel chairman of the Accident Committee was unable to find any reason that could excuse First Lieutenant DeCleene from having elected to fly at such a low altitude.

By early 2006 the crash site, on the northern lip of Birchenough Hill quarry, and bypassed to the west by a low-routing public footpath, had been marked by a standing stone, and by a commemorative board around which scraps of wreckage had been collected. Of the true impact point, slightly to the north, nothing was to be seen. But 100 yards to the east of the impact point, where the bulk of the bomber burnt out, débris was still much in evidence, while between the two, burnt shards of metal beneath the turf still marked the path of the aircraft's slide to destruction.

2006, the memorial, slightly south of the actual impact site of B-17G 43-38944

2006, the terminal site of B-17G 43-38944

Debris found along the line of flight (re-interred)

Fairey Battle Mk.1 K9221, Dore, south of Ringinglow

SK 28939 82668 351m
No.16 (Polish) Flying Training School, RAF Newton (near
Nottingham), Polish Air Force under RAF Command
28 August, 1941

Pilot: successfully forced-landed, uninjured:
Leading Aircraftman Leon Pszeniczka, pupil pilot, Polish Air
Force under RAF Command

When the Fairey Battle was proposed in 1933 the concept of a single-engined, metal-constructed, monoplane light-bomber was very advanced. Indeed, even when it entered RAF service in 1937 the Battle was ahead of its field in both range and bomb load. However, an extra crew position and other modifications had added to its weight, and when matched against modern fighters and ground anti-aircraft defences it proved disastrously slow. Following a series of debacles, each a harrowing saga of gallantry, the type was withdrawn from operations in September 1940 and relegated to the training role.

One of the many units to receive the Battle was the Polish flying training school at RAF Newton, in Nottinghamshire, among whose pupil pilots was Leading Aircraftman Leon Pszeniczka. On 28 August, 1941, with a total of just fifty hours of flying behind him, Leading Aircraftman Pszeniczka, airborne on a solo navigation and map-reading cross-country, was transiting the Parkhead area in the south-west of Sheffield when his engine caught fire: an unenviable situation for any pilot, and one in which many might have taken to their parachutes without further ado. Indeed the contemporary training manual urged personal safety as the first consideration, with loss of the machine very much secondary. Notwithstanding which the young Pole put his aircraft first, and decided to do his best to save it.

Ruddering into a descending spiral he evidently followed the recommended drill, turning off the fuel, pushing the throttle fully open until the engine stopped, then, in turn, flicking off the ignition switch and operating the fire extinguisher. 'Evidently', for at that point Fortune, having had her little jest, favoured him, and saw to it that the drill killed the fire.

The procedure necessarily cost him height, but with no more flames to menace him he came out of his skidding turn and banked towards a suitable-looking area of open moorland, just beyond the closely-walled pastures of a farm. Then, still sticking to the approved procedure for the tailwheel aircraft of the day, he carried out a neat, wheels-up belly landing, the upward slope and the rough ground bringing the aircraft to an abrupt, but safe halt.

Among those who witnessed the drama was Mr Noel Hancock of Sheephill Farm, Ringinglow. 'He came from the direction of Sheffield,' he recalled in 2005. 'He was on fire, I could see. But he made two circles, and then came down on his belly onto Houndkirk Moor, just beyond our boundary.' And Mr Hancock smiled, remembering how he, his slightly older brother, Roy, and their dog, had run to the scene. 'Our mother was frantically calling us to come back. Telling us that the pilot might be a German. But we took no notice, and just ran faster.' His smile broadened. 'Mind you,' he confessed, 'while we ran we did agree that if he really turned out to be a German we'd turn and run straight back again.'

How quickly they would have returned to mum had they heard the Polish guttural is a matter for speculation, for when they reached the boundary wall they stopped, all three, and merely peered over, the dog on its hind legs.

'The pilot was standing by the aeroplane,' Mr Hancock continued, 'all covered in what looked to be oil, but was probably smoke. We were the first on the scene. But then lots of people began arriving.'

Another resident, to whose cottage Leading Aircraftman Pszeniczka was led for succour, remembered the aircraft remaining on the moor under guard for some time before it was removed. 'It was hardly damaged, so there was little enough left once they'd gone,' the lady said. However, the locally-proffered story of a subsequent romance between a girl from the cottage and the young Pole was strongly denied …

To explain Leading Aircraftman Pszeniczka's presence in Britain it is necessary to remember that Britain and France had given guarantees to Poland. Accordingly, when on 1 September, 1939, Germany invaded Poland, the guarantee was called into play, and two days later both Allies declared war on Germany. Swamped by superior forces the Poles resisted bravely, and when the hoped for – and it must be said, trustingly expected – help from their Allies did not materialise, they told themselves that at least they were holding down one front of the common fight. But when Russia treacherously launched its own pincering invasion two weeks later, the Poles knew the end had come. Acting on orders from their government, as many servicemen as possible crossed into then-neutral Romania. From there, after a nominal period of internment, they were moved to France, and when France fell, on to England, clamouring to be allowed to fight alongside the British armed forces. For expediency, the airmen among them were enlisted into the RAF Voluntary Reserve, but swiftly-constituted legislation soon sanctioned the setting up of 'The Polish Air Force under RAF Command'.

Before the invasion of Poland Leading Aircraftman Pszeniczka had been serving with the Polish Sixth Air Force Regiment, and on arrival in Britain had continued his interrupted pilot training. However, despite the aptitude he showed in handling the fire-in-the-air situation and the subsequent forced landing, things evidently went awry at some later stage of his flying training, for he failed to gain his pilot's wings, and in 1943 remustered to become a Radio-Telephony Operator.

The site, rough moorland, showed no sign of the incident in 2006, and although on one occasion Mr Hancock personally directed searchers to the area of the slope where evidence of the setdown might have been found, metal detectors turned up no sign of the crash.

Left: Area of the crash-site of Fairey Battle K9221, looking towards Sheephill Farm

Bristol BE2C, near Coal Aston (or Norton) Aerodrome, Sheffield

Exact site undetermined
A Flight, No.33 Squadron, Royal Flying Corps Station Coal Aston
24 September, 1916

Pilot: solo, slightly injured:
Captain E.N. Clinton, RFC

On 24 September, 1916, Captain E.N. Clinton was detailed to carry out a night patrol, the duty of RFC Coal Aston being to protect Sheffield's manufactories from air raiders. After flying for some thirty minutes in poor visibility, he attempted to put down – what necessitated this is not recorded – but crashed into high ground and was slightly injured. It has not proved possible to identify whereabouts he came down.

Biplane type, Lydgate Farm, Eccles Pike, near Chapel-en-le-Frith

SK 04056 81370 260m
RAF
3 December, 1918

In her book, *Except the Lord Build the House*, Rose Hannah Swindells related how, on 3 December, 1918, when she was a pupil at Bugsworth school – a modern restyling makes it Buxworth – an aeroplane came down in a field belonging to Lydgate Farm, halfway up the slopes of Eccles Pike, and that at lunchtime many of the scholars absconded to go and see it. Not her, though. 'Not for one moment did I consider going to look at it then,' she wrote. However, that evening she was to ruin her Goody Two Shoes image. 'My mother', she continued, 'had asked me to get half a pint of vinegar and two pennyworth of barm [a form of yeast used aerate dough in breadmaking] on my way home from school that afternoon, so at four o'clock when school finished I … made my purchases, put the barm which was in a triangular toffee bag in one pocket of my coat, the bottle of vinegar in the other, and set off to have a look at the aeroplane. The latest information was that it was still on the ground and likely to be there at least until the following day. I did not see a Zeppelin high up in the air which happened to pass over Bugsworth, but I resolved to see an aeroplane.'

2005, the site of the December 1918 setdown at Lydgate Farm, Eccles Pike

Mrs Swindells then gave a detailed description of the route she took to the field, eventually crossing Goodman's New Road [Back Eccles Lane] and following a cart track [redundant, with the public footpath having been re-routed long before 2006] to the field, 'where the aeroplane was stranded, or more correctly, grounded.' She went on, 'The light was fading. I was not very big and there was a thorny hedge bordering the field and ditch in front of it. I strode over the ditch and could just see over the hedge … to see the wing of the aircraft and pilot standing by it. He … turned his head and looked at me and I looked at him, and then clambered back on the track and set off home.'

On the way back she felt hungry and, feeling for the packet of barm, 'pinched out some of the contents and ate it', an act which mystified the writer but one which was endorsed by Mrs Margaret Martin, of Whitehough, who recalled, 'I always used to beg my granny for "just a pinch" of the barm when we'd been shopping.' Supplementing which Mr Maurice Hobson, of Rawmarsh, advised, 'It tasted sweet – and was satisfyingly claggy in texture.'

Although the field was re-identified in early 2006, no one could be found who knew anything more of the event.

'He looked at me …'

Biplane, Avro, Colt Croft Farm, Buxton

SK 06885 72310 325m
15 January, 1919

Enthusiast sources, some using the above date, have a biplane coming down at Colt Croft Farm, on Duke's Drive, Buxton. However, enquiries through into 2006 lent no substance to the report. The incident is recorded here against future research shedding more light.

Of possible relevance, records do exist of *de Havilland* biplanes coming down in the Buxton area: a DH60X Moth, registered G-EBWA, on 11 October, 1934, and a DH60M, registered K1112, on 18 July, 1938. Newspaper searches, however, proved negative, suggesting that the G- registration notwithstanding, the Buxton referred to might not be the Derbyshire spa, but a town in the Commonwealth. In the same way, nothing was found in the press concerning De Havilland DH82A T7749, become G-AKXD, which is recorded as having been damaged on 10 February, 1960, as a result of a forced landing 'in Derbyshire'. It could well be, of course, that more diligent research might turn up something on any of these.

Biplane, Avro, Sparrowpit

15 January, 1919

In similar fashion to the preceding entry, enthusiast sources record that an Avro biplane came down near Sparrowpit on 15 January, 1919, but nothing more was discovered during press searches, or in the course of enquiries made between 2004 and 2006. This incident, again, is recorded for posterity.

Bristol Blenheim Mk.4 V6078, Spitewinter (north-east of Matlock)

SK 34332 66203 277m
No.42 Operational Training Unit, RAF Ashbourne, No.70 Group,
Army Co-operation Command
7 April, 1943

Crew: three, all killed:
Pilot Officer John Barry Welton, pilot
Sergeant Leslie Harold Redford, navigator/bomb aimer
Sergeant Eric Desmond Murphy, wireless operator/air gunner

At the start of the Second World War it was generally accepted that the RAF had a world beater in the Blenheim. Accordingly the light bomber received its full share of publicity, carrying out both the first reconnaissance and the first bombing raids on German territory. In truth, however, technical development had been so swift that the type was effectively redundant from the outset. Just the same the Blenheim continued to give good value as a trainer, and it was in that role that Blenheim V6078, of No.42 Operational Training Unit, was dispatched from RAF Ashbourne on 7 April, 1943.

Pilot Officer John Welton and his two-man crew were tasked to carry out a night navigation and wireless-telegraphy (W/T) cross-country. This meant that the wireless operator/air gunner, Sergeant Eric Murphy, was expected to play a key part in the conduct of the flight by furnishing weather information, directional bearings, and fixes. The court of inquiry, however, was to establish that the aircraft had set course without having done either a ground or an airborne check on W/T equipment which subsequently proved to be unserviceable.

The corollary of this was that when, during the course of the flight, the inexperienced crew realised that they had became totally lost, the pilot took up the pre-planned heading for base and descended through cloud in an endeavour to fix their position. But such blind descents are always fraught with danger, and on this occasion he came far below the safety height for the area and struck the edge of Scout's Wood, at Spitewinter, north-east of Matlock, and some fourteen miles from Ashbourne. Losing a wing, the stricken machine rolled violently before plunging inverted into the field beyond and breaking up against a drystone wall. There was no fire, but disintegration was total, and none of the crew survived.

One of the earliest on the scene was Air Raid Warden Mr Bill Davis, who later declared that the only recognisable part of the machine had been the tailwheel. Indeed so widespread had the break-up been that long after the salvage teams had cleared from the region, farm workers found themselves retrieving human remains.

In 2005 both Mrs Edna Hawksworth (née Keeton) and her brother, Mr John Keeton, whose family farmed the area, and lived just beyond the débris trail, well remembered the night of the crash. 'It was a very stormy night,' recalled Mr Keeton, 'everyone was in bed, with the windows tightly closed against the wind and rain.' Mrs Hawksworth nodded agreement. 'The aeroplane had hit Scout's Wood, then exploded in the field. But the only person who heard a thing was our auntie, who had a room on that side, and she woke the rest of us. But there was nothing to be done, of course ... And they wouldn't allow us children near it.'

Mr Keeton shook his head sombrely. But then smiled. 'It didn't stop us, of course. For there were souvenirs to be had.' After which it came as no real surprise to learn that one of the offshoots of the tragedy was that each of them later fashioned shards of perspex into rings and pendants ...

Mr Peter Hawksworth, the 2005 incumbent of the farm, remembered his father, Mr Ernie Hawksworth, telling him that a part of a wing and one of the engines was left up in a tree. He himself had grown up with the site. 'For years afterwards,' he said, 'you could see the gap where the aircraft came through the trees, although they've grown up again now. Grandfather once found a human jawbone, which he placed in the wall. But I still find bits now and again: of the aircraft, that is ...'

And he produced two items found only months before in the vicinity of the drystone wall.

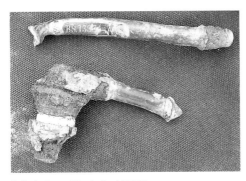

Débris from Blenheim V6078

The terminal site of Blenheim V6078 in 2005, looking towards Scout's Wood

Bristol Blenheim Mk.1 L6800, Tagg Lane, Monyash

SK 14310 66390 269m
No.2 School of Army Co-operation Flying (Operational Training Unit), RAF Andover, No.22
(Army Co-operation) Group with Command Status
17 November, 1940

Pupil pilot: survived forced landing:
Pilot Officer G. F. Kilburn

The Bristol Blenheim, whose 1935 forbear, the Bristol Type 142, had so impressed the Air
Ministry, had itself become obsolescent by the start of the Second World War and by 1940 was
generally used for training and for testing purposes. At No.2 School of Army Co-operation
Flying, located at RAF Andover, the type was used to liaise with army air defence units. On 17
November, 1940, however, one of the unit's aircraft, Blenheim Mk.1 L6800, was damaged in a
forced landing at Monyash, in Derbyshire.

Pilot Officer Kilburn, a trainee, had been dispatched on a detail which required him to fly to
and land at Desford (west of Leicester), then return to Andover. However, on the outbound leg
he encountered bad visibility and became totally lost. Despite his lack of experience he was
aware of the inadvisability of flying blindly on for too long, but even then, when he decided to
make a wheels-up precautionary landing, he was already at Monyash, some forty-six miles
north-west of Desford.

The pupil pilot planned his approach into a suitable-looking field, but what with the
unfamiliarity of the procedure, not least in judging an approach all the way down to touchdown
with the undercarriage up – the configuration recommended for forced landings with the tail-
wheeled aircraft of the day – it is evident that he overshot his initial choice, for the field he
actually touched down in was both narrow and restricted. Certainly he carried away some
overhead wires in the process of landing, and then, having touched down, ran on into a drystone
wall. Just the same, Pilot Officer Kilburn was uninjured, and the aircraft not too badly damaged,
although it was to be a matter of days before the recovery crew cleared the site.

The findings of the court of inquiry were passed to the Air Officer Commanding who, in
view of Pilot Officer Kilburn's inexperience – he had less than one hundred hours total flying
and only two hours solo on type – decided that no disciplinary action was called for.

In 2004 Mrs Molly Boam, a key member of a prominent Monyash-area farming and
landowning family, having by then retired to live in the village itself, well remembered being
taken to the scene by her grandfather.

'The aeroplane,' Mrs Boam recalled, 'one of those black bombers, was lying in a field of mine
called Sammy's Pringle: the one with the dew pond. It had run into the drystone wall but
stopped short of the field beyond, the long narrow one, which was my mother's.'

Termination point of
Blenheim L6800, looking
back along the approach

Mrs Boam remembered that she and her grandfather spent some time watching the RAF salvage party who had been billeted at another family property, Endmoor Farm, near the main Ashbourne–Buxton Road. She remembered too that sometime later, when a village maiden bore an infant, gossip had it that one of the airmen had fathered the child. However, as she confided, 'That was just rumour. In fact, it was old Farmer –'; she dropped her voice to murmur the name, 'as everyone knew, really ...'

To have the owner of the field as a witness who could vouch for the location was both fortunate and gratifying, for neither visual nor metal-detector searches turned up any evidence of the setdown. But then this was a precautionary landing that went only a little awry, and with an adjacent road so convenient for salvage operations, it is not really all that surprising that nothing seemed to have remained.

Bristol Blenheim Mk.4 Z5746, Ox Stones, Ringinglow

SK 27883 83214 420m
RAF Catfoss (near Hornsea), No.2 Operational Training Unit,
No.17 Group, Coastal Command
26 January, 1941

Crew: three, all killed:
Sergeant John Robson, pilot
Pilot Officer Ivor King Parry-Jones, navigator
Flight Sergeant Eric Brown, wireless operator/air gunner

By 1941 even the updated Mk.4 Blenheim had been withdrawn from active operations in Europe, although the type would continue as a first-line bomber in other theatres until 1943. Even before being superseded, however, many had been diverted to other roles, notably to that of training. One of the units which employed Blenheims was No.2 Operational Training Unit, whose function was to produce crews for Coastal Command. However, on 26 January, 1941, when Sergeant John Robson and his trainee crew got airborne from RAF Catfoss to carry out a navigational training exercise in the Midlands, they strayed from their course into an area of

high ground, and with their altimeter still set to register the height above their sea-level base, bellied into gently rising moorland at Ox Stones, near Ringinglow, all three dying from the impact.

The crash had been heard in Ringinglow, and consequently would-be rescuers were quickly on the scene. Yet even the earliest arrivals were to discover that nothing could be done. In the aftermath the recovery teams arrived with their Queen Mary trailers and took away the wreckage.

The investigation found that the cause of the accident lay in an error of navigation, and surmised that the aircraft had probably been in cloud when it crashed. The Air Officer Commanding, when the findings were passed to him, made the additional, and transparently political, point that the orders for the flight – issued on his authority, of course, by his subordinate commanders – had been adequate, and that the pilot had been specifically instructed to turn back if the weather became unsuitable.

In September 2005 farmer Mr Kenneth Wilson, of Hathersage, whose sheep were to range the Ox Stones area for many years, was able to verify the impact site. 'Peter Priestley,' he said, 'of Overstones Farm, who went to the scene, told me that the plane looked like a big bird on the snow, and seemed quite whole, although they'd all been killed. I

Mr Kenneth Wilson,
Hathersage

2006, the Ox Stones site

didn't bother walking over there until it had been taken away, for when Peter had tried to get closer he was stopped some distance short by a soldier who said he was a sentry. "Then tha's a long way off tha post," Peter told him, sure that the chap had crept off for a pint.'

Having bellied onto only gently rising, snow-covered moorland, the aircraft probably shed little débris on its slide; certainly there was no visible evidence in 2006, although the flourishing heather might well have concealed fragments.

Of additional interest, perhaps, to aviation-minded walkers, Mr Wilson, a wealth of local knowledge, was also able to point out the moorland site, off the Houndkirk Road (at SK 77700 81400), of one of the decoy-Sheffields, where piled motor tyres were set ablaze when German bombers were expected. 'But', he said, a little wryly, 'they never wasted a single bomb on Houndkirk.'

Bristol Fighter Mk.3 J8432, Matlock Moor, adjacent to the Golf Course

SK 31183 62224 222m
No.5 Flying Training School, RAF Sealand (near Chester),
Headquarters Inland Area
16 July, 1928

Pupil pilot: survived:
Pilot Officer Charles Lilburn Myers

In its Mk.2 version the Bristol Fighter F2B two-seater reconnaissance machine, after meritorious service during the First World War, became the standard army co-operation machine for the peacetime RAF. Unusually, the appellation 'Fighter'– as opposed to 'Scout'– had been attached to the type since its first flight in September 1916, and it was as the Bristol Fighter Mk.3 that the structurally-altered version delivered to the RAF in 1926 was designated.

Of the fifty machines so styled, construction number 6991, taken into the RAF's charge on 17 January, 1927, re-dubbed J8432, and employed as an advanced trainer, was to suffer major damage on 16 July, 1928, when its pilot attempted to take off again after making a successful precautionary landing on Matlock Moor, adjacent to the Matlock Golf Course.

Pilot Officer Charles Myers was a pupil on 'A' (Army Co-operation) Flight of the Advanced Squadron of No.5 Flying Training School at RAF Sealand, near Chester, and was on a cross-country to Woodford when he became lost. At length he found himself over a moderately-sized town, but despite the singular features it offered, not least the shell of an apparently slighted hill-top castle, he was still unable to locate himself. Sensibly, therefore, he decided to put down and determine his whereabouts: his topographical map might not have given such details as Riber Castle, but it most certainly registered the high ground so bleakly massed towards the north.

More immediately to hand, however, just to the north-east of the town, lay an area of reasonably uncluttered ground, so choosing the most suitable field, where a valley side levelled into a shoulder, he made his approach, and at some 45 mph, and aided by the braking effect of the tail skid on the long grass, soon came to a halt. To find, gratifyingly enough, that golf club members, and others, were already running to the spot.

2005, the eponymous Cuckoo Stone, apparently supporting Mr Barry Kay, ex-RAF Physical Training Instructor, and author of the centenary history of Matlock Golf Club

In 2004 Mr Fred Hole of Wayside Farm indicated the landing and take-off area: the arrows show the approach to touchdown, and the attempted take-off path. The 11th green, containing the Cuckoo Stone, runs parallel beyond the hedge

In fact, the town had been Matlock, in Derbyshire, and the valley the Cuckoostone Valley, even then largely occupied by Matlock Golf Club, the touchdown field being upslope of what, in 2006, was the club's eleventh green – and upslope too, of the eponymous Cuckoo Stone.

As the local newspaper of the day, *The Matlock Visitor* ('incorporating the *Matlock Guardian* and *List of Visitors*') reported in its next issue, 'At about 11 am on Monday morning a large RAF plane was noticed circling Matlock. It then dipped behind a hill in the direction of the golf course'.

One of the club members, a Mr Norman Travis, recorded, 'We were soon able to set the pilot's mind at rest regarding his whereabouts. Then, on his instructions, we swung the machine around to enable him to get airborne once again.'

A statement of no little import. For there is no mention of Pilot Officer Myers taxiing back to his touchdown point once again. Which implies that he had either landed downwind, or intended to take off downwind. In any event his take-off run – up or downwind as it might have been – was certainly slightly uphill.

Notwithstanding wind and slope – the wind on the day, like the slope, could well have been infinitesimal – and despite his inexperience, Pilot Officer Myers might easily have accomplished a safe take-off. Only he made another fundamental error.

'There was a fair distance before the walls of Martin's Path,' noted a bystander. 'But he tried to take off through mowing grass. So although he managed to lift, he couldn't clear the wall, and smashed over into the path.'

A fair assessment, for the high-grown, unmown grass dragging at the wheels prevented even the 275 horsepower of the Rolls-Royce Falcon engine from giving the machine adequate flying speed. Accordingly it ran out of space, impacted into one of the path-bordering drystone walls, and flipped ignominiously into the lane beyond. Fortuitously Pilot Officer Myers clambered from the cockpit with nothing more than bruises and some superficial cuts to his face.

One of those who viewed the wreckage on the Sunday after the crash, cutting across the fields after the Methodist Chapel's Sunday School to do so, was Mr Fred Hole, of nearby Wayside Farm, then in his early teens.

'The pilot', he remembered in 2005, 'had come down in Mr Bowler's "Cuckoo Field", which still belonged to Cuckoostone Farm. He'd knocked the wall down, shed his wings, smashed his propeller, and crumpled the nose.'

The wreckage was left in the lane for some days. But badly damaged though the aircraft was, it took a considerable time for its future to be decided, for it was 1929 before it was transferred to the Home Aircraft Depot at RAF Henlow.

The Bristol against one of the walls bounding Martin's Lane (Photograph by Mr Harry Gill, used by courtesy of his daughter, Mrs Phyllis Higton)

Bristol Fighter J8432 on Matlock Moor, looking westerly, up the Martin's Lane track, with Cuckoostone Farm off the picture to the right (Photograph by Mr Harry Gill, used by courtesy of his daughter, Mrs Phyllis Higton)

Mr Fred Hole, in July 2004, photo-matching the site from the picture, above right, after 75 years

Souvenir-hunting boys, identified as, left to right: Charlie Taylor, Henry Douglas (the son of Smedley's Hydro owner), Bob Walters (5th right, son Roger, a 2005 Golf Club Member), Jack Denny, Tom Emery (Photograph by Mr Harry Gill, courtesy of his daughter, Mrs Phyllis Higton)

As for Pilot Officer Myers, evidently the powers-that-be viewed his misadventure benignly, putting it down to lack of experience. For he gained his pilot's wings just weeks after the incident and, on 18 September, 1928, was posted to No.28 Squadron, at that time stationed at Ambala, India, 120 miles north of Delhi. Here he was reunited with the Bristol Fighter, this time in its F2B guise, and employed in army co-operation work on the turbulent North-West Frontier. He was not to survive that tour, however, being killed on 6 November, 1928.

The crash site is located on the wall-bordered Martin's Path, a favourite route for dog walkers. The path runs downhill to cross what has become the Golf Club's eleventh green. As for the Bristol's ground-manoeuvring area, to the south of the crash site, despite being drained it was still deemed unsuitable for a green in early 2006, and seasonally displayed the 'mowing grass' which proved the undoing of Pilot Officer Myers.

Clearly the young boys who thronged the site when the wreckage was in situ did a fine job. Consequently a 2005 metal-detector search along both sides of the walls gave no signals, leaving the site to be determined by photo-reference, cross-referring between the skyline contours to the west and the pile of Riber Castle to the south. But this was a task eased by the aid of two mentors: Mr Fred Hole, visiting the site for the first time in 75 years, and Mr Barry Kay, who as an ex-RAF Physical Training Instructor, and past captain and active member of 45 years' standing of the Matlock Golf Club, was the author of its centenary history.

Bristol Fighter Mk.3 J8458, Manor Woodlands Farm, Treeton, Rotherham

SK 44289 87326 87m (area of)
No.2 Flying Training School, RAF Digby (Lincolnshire), Inland Area
22 September, 1930

Pilot: solo pupil pilot, mortally injured:
Pilot Officer Alfred Cecil Sant

On 22 September, 1930, Pilot Officer Alfred Sant, a pupil pilot at an advanced state of his flying training at RAF Digby, was authorised for a solo return cross-country flight to RAF Upper Heyford, in Oxfordshire. The outbound leg was uneventful, but on his return flight Pilot Officer Sant's navigation went awry and he realised that he had progressed too far north. Ascertaining that he was near Sheffield, thirty miles off track, he calculated a new course, and turned onto a south-easterly heading. Unfortunately, at this juncture his engine began giving trouble.

The machine, a Bristol Fighter, had been air tested at Digby by instructor Sergeant L.C. Marks before Pilot Officer Sant had been allowed to take it up, but it is not known whether this had been a routine check, or whether it was to confirm that an engine fault had been corrected. As it was, the farmer at Manor Woodlands Farm, Treeton, Rotherham, was convinced that the approaching machine was in trouble. 'He came from the north-west,' he told the local newspaper, 'flying very low, with his engine misfiring. Indeed on one or two occasions it stopped altogether, at which the pilot decided upon landing in one of my fields. He made a good touch down, and when I reached him he told me that his magneto had begun missing. On finding that the nearest telephone was at the colliery, four hundred yards away, however, he began to examine the engine himself. Once he started it up again, though, it seemed to be running very slowly. Just the same, he got the people who had gathered to turn the machine into wind, and said he would "take it for a low run". He sat there with it going for about two minutes, then set off towards Aughton [to the south-east], getting up after about fifty yards and flying at fifty or so feet. But just as he reached the next field, the engine – which had been sounding very rough indeed – stopped short. Then the plane keeled sharply to the left, dived steeply, and burying its nose in the ground, spun about to face the way it had come. We rushed to it, to find the front badly damaged, the lower left wing totally destroyed, and the propeller yards off, stuck into the soil. The pilot was obviously in a bad way. Indeed we had to cut one of his shoes away from the rudder bar before we could free him. Even so he died two days later in Rotherham hospital.'

At the inquest, a Flight Lieutenant White, sent from RAF Digby to assist the coroner as a specialist witness, advised that the Bristol Fighter's fuel system had both a priming pump and a hand-operated pressure pump, and that having been on the ground for some time, it would have been necessary to employ the hand pump before take-off. He felt it only too likely that Pilot Officer Sant had not remembered to do this, and had, therefore, regardless of any other problem, starved his engine of fuel.

In 2006 Mr Hedley Frost, of Treeton, remembered that the detached propeller had stood in a local house for many years. 'Though it's long gone now, I suspect.' Again, by 2006, Manor Woodlands Farm had become a housing complex and the smaller fields of the day had been merged into a single enormous stretch, making it virtually impossible to determine exactly where the setdown and subsequent crash had taken place: even Mr Frost could only venture that it had been somewhere in the general area of Treeton Grange and to the north of Wood Lane. The reference given, however, does meet the additional criteria of being some four hundred yards from the colliery.

The area of the crash site of Bristol Fighter J8458, looking towards Treeton

Bristol Fighter, Little Wood, Thorpe Salvin

SK 52061 80369 107m
RAF
1927–8

Pilot unidentified: unhurt

This incident, in which the Bristol Fighter, short of fuel, merely put down, was refuelled, and then took off again, hardly represents a crash, but it is certainly evocative of the 'Golden Age' of flying of which H. Barber had written back in 1916 in *The Aeroplane Speaks* when he has his pilot observe: 'Well, it's a fearful bore, but the first rule of our game is never to take an unnecessary risk.' (A homily delivered as, standing close beside his aircraft, the pilot puffs at his pipe!) The setdown also forms one of the earliest aviation memories of Mr Bert Waller, in 2006, of Hardwick Farm, Todwick.

'It happened in 1927 or 1928,' he recalled, 'when we were at Moor Mill Farm. A Bristol with a great radial engine came down beside Little Wood. He'd been on his way to Nottingham and had run out of fuel. So they got four gallons of petrol in cans, and filled him up. I was very young, perhaps only three. But Jack Apple, who worked for us, took me along with him. I walked as far as I could, then Jack put me on his shoulders for the rest of the way. It had come down just beside Little Wood. And once it was refuelled it took off again.

'But seeing it so close', he continued, 'whetted my appetite, so that, in 1934, when Scott and Black won the Melbourne Air Race, there was an air show at Netherthorpe, and I took my savings, didn't tell anyone, and bought a ten-minute flight in a Bristol for five shillings [25p].'

Mr Waller smiled, then went on, 'I also remember helping push the first plane back onto Netherthorpe aerodrome: it's always been rather short.'

The Bristol Fighter's forced-landing site at Little Wood, Thorpe Salvin

English Electric Canberra BMk.6 WT207, Monyash

SK 16155 66133 263m, port mainplane
SK 16340 65895 276m, starboard mainplane
SK 15005 65376 329m, tailplane and rear fuselage
SK 15979 69304 280m, front fuselage
SK 14209 69960 362m, rocket motor
SK 15197 66508 271m, mainwheel
SK 16401 65420 296m, pilot parachuted
SK 16740 66740 288m, navigator parachuted

No.76 Squadron, detached from RAF Wittering (south of Stamford), Bomber Command
9 April, 1958

Crew: two, ejected successfully, both slightly injured:
Flight Lieutenant J. Peter F. de Salis, pilot, temporary physiological effects
Flying Officer Patrick Lowe, navigator, frostbite

In the mid-1950s, with the Cold War heating up, a primary concern was to develop an interceptor fighter capable of protecting United Kingdom airspace against any incursion by the bombers of the Soviet Union. One expedient investigated was a rocket motor which would enhance the high-altitude performance of the prospective machine, the English Electric P1, which in its production form would become the Lightning. Canberra bombers were used in developing the technology.

Indeed in August 1957 one trials Canberra with a Napier Double Scorpion rocket motor installed in its bomb bay set a new world altitude record of 70,310 feet. But not all trials returned such felicitous supplementary results, for on 9 April, 1958, a No.76 Squadron Canberra was lost when a malfunction in the volatile hydrogen peroxide fuel system of the test motor caused an onboard explosion.

Flight Lieutenant Peter de Salis, a graduate of the Empire Test Pilots' School, and his trials navigator, Flying Officer Patrick Lowe, both suitably kitted for high-altitude flight, had taken off from RAF Hemswell, near Lincoln, at 1500 hours, and climbed towards North Wales ready to begin the rocket-motor trial. At the planned height they turned about and settled on a north-easterly heading. Then, counting down, they switched on the rocket motor in their bomb bay.

As expected, the unit responded immediately, supplementing the Canberra's own engines and sending the machine soaring thousands of feet beyond its normal achievable ceiling. Having reached the planned altitude, the motor was switched off once more, at which the aircraft began to descend, its own unassisted engines being incapable of maintaining the extreme altitude. However, as the descent neared 56,000 feet the procedure called for the rocket motor to be restarted in order to use up the residual, highly-volatile fuel before landing. Only this time when Flight Lieutenant de Salis pressed the switch the motor exploded, effectively blowing the Canberra apart.

With the wrecked machine obviously beyond all control, Flight Lieutenant de Salis ordered Flying Officer Lowe to eject, moments later ejecting in turn. But to eject at 56,000 feet was to set another world record – for the highest emergency ejection yet – and neither man was in any doubt that in that rarefied atmosphere his life hung upon a thread.

The extreme altitude notwithstanding, the navigator, Flying Officer Lowe, had a remarkably trouble-free descent. However having previously removed his gloves in order to work, he suffered frostbitten hands, so that when he approached the ground he was unable to manipulate the parachute risers and landed heavily on his back.

Flight Lieutenant de Salis, for his part, had a far more traumatic ejection. He was already dazed by the explosion. Then the small drogue parachute that should have stabilised his ejection seat failed to operate, permitting the seat to spin with such violence that blood was not only forced into his limbs but also into his head, so that he believed he had lost his sight. And even when his seat separated and the main parachute was extracted, its cords were so twisted that for a time he feared that he would simply plummet onwards into the ground. Fortunately the canopy then deployed, but with the rigging lines so twisted that the rest of the descent passed in a series of windings and unwindings that caused him to vomit.

The navigator, Flying Officer Lowe, came to earth to the north of Lathkill Gorge, on the Monyash to Bakewell road. And his luck held, for almost at once he was picked up by Mr Raymond Brough, of Rake End Farm, Monyash, and taken to Bakewell Cottage Hospital where he received initial treatment for frostbite.

Meanwhile Flight Lieutenant de Salis had landed on the far side of Lathkill Dale, to be succoured by Mr Colin Slater, and by his brother James, both of whom had been rolling nearby fields. They took him to One Ash Grange Farm and passed him into the care of other relatives, Mr Frank Slater and his brother, Charlie, where, sipping hot sweet tea, Flight Lieutenant de Salis was able to direct messages to be sent to RAF Hemswell, and to his fiancée.

Examining himself, Flight Lieutenant de Salis found that one forearm was thickened, 'like Popeye's', as his report was to read, and that his reddened eyes were mere slits in his blood-engorged face. But his main concern at this time, the Salters recalled, was for the safety of his navigator. Accordingly he was to be hugely relieved when they were reunited some hours later in Chesterfield Hospital, whence they were transferred to the RAF Hospital at Halton, in Buckinghamshire, for more detailed checks.

Mr Frank Slater, in 2005, of Stanley Lodge, Hucklow, formerly of One Ash Farm

Despite their shared ordeal both were quickly reinstated to full flying duties, although in view of his more severe frostbite Flying Officer Lowe was placed under a three-month restriction limiting him to temperate-climate operations.

As might be expected with an aircraft breaking up at such an extreme altitude, the débris fell over a wide area; and, providentially, without causing damage to life, or even to property, on the ground.

The RAF set up a tented salvage camp alongside the Bakewell road, at the entrance to Lathkill Dale, one tent quickly blossoming with a legend pronouncing the site to be 'RAF Monyash'. Here, a picquet was maintained and débris pooled, while for some weeks other RAF parties scoured the countryside searching for a specific, but unspecified, item. Unspecified, that is, to the public, for a security blanket was placed over some aspects of the operation in view of the nature of the trial that had gone so disastrously wrong.

The tented camp set up beside the entrance to Lathkill Dale: in 2006, the site of the public toilets (Photograph by courtesy of Mrs Valerie Shipley (née Slater), via Crown Copyright)

The search parties had little trouble in locating much of the débris, as Mrs Eileen Slater, James Slater's wife, then working part-time at the village post office, was able to verify. 'It littered both the street and the gardens of the village,' she said. Only when she came out and viewed the wreckage she was not to know that one piece had hazarded her son, Brian, then aged ten, falling within feet of him as he played by a barn near the entrance to Lathkill Dale.

Cataloguing the larger components to fall, the complete tailplane and rear section of the fuselage came down beyond the copse fringing Summerhill Farm, to the south of Monyash. Meanwhile, long

2006, James and Eileen Slater, Monyash

minutes after the explosions that had alerted Mr Dennis Mycock to something going on above the clouds – in fact, after he had actually lost interest and recommenced work again – Dennis, busy near Rowson House Farm, at the east of the village, heard the organ whine of windmilling turbines and saw both wings spiralling down in the fashion of sycamore keys. One was to land beside the popular path to Lathkill Dale, the other within three hundred yards of it, upslope to the south-east, at the corner of the field locally known as Friezland.

The front fuselage fell into Deep Dale, a mile and a half to the north, just below Over Wheal Farm, where the 2005 incumbent, Mr Frank Allen, remembered it trailing smoke and spewing oil; he remembered too that a guard was set until the remains were dragged south, and up the dale to Wheal Lane, and the road.

For her part, Mrs Molly Boam, of Monyash, learnt of this section having fallen as she wheeled her son in his pram to visit at Over Wheal, when she was hailed by a former schoolfriend, working on a ladder. 'We used to call him "Barmy" at school,' she smiled. 'So when he shouted down that he had just seen an aeroplane going over with no wings I told him, "Don't be barmy, Barmy". But he was right, as it turned out.'

As the days turned into weeks so the pool of débris outside the temporary camp grew. But it was clear to all that one significant part had not yet been found, for the search continued unabated, with a helicopter scouring the area and even the gliders from the nearby club at Great Hucklow being asked to assist. The missing item was popularly held to be the aircraft's 'black box' or flight recorder, but it was subsequently known to have been a significant portion of the rocket motor. And throughout the period there were alarums regarding nuclear contamination: certainly warnings were issued from the start that wreckage should be merely reported, and never handled by the public …

The port mainplane and engine of Canberra WT207 in Lathkill Dale (courtesy of Crown Copyright)

The port-mainplane impact site, with corroded metal, 2006

As it happened, it was to be the Taddington postmistress, Mrs Dorothy Cooper, who was to finally bring the search to a halt, finding the unaccounted-for component nearly two miles north of Monyash. As Mr Frank Boam, of Nether Wheal Farm, but formerly of Rockfield House Farm, remembered: 'In those days she'd walk the footpaths from Taddington daily to deliver to Hubber Dale. And she found the bit they'd all been looking for on the rough pasture where the two paths cross.'

So the search ended. RAF Monyash loaded its assorted scrap metal onto Queen Mary trailers, folded its tents, then quietly faded from the scene. And the village returned to normal. But reflecting surely, upon just how blest it had been. Indeed, it had been good fortune all around. So not for nothing did Flight Lieutenant de Salis declare to photographers, six weeks later, 'I'm the luckiest man alive.' Although he did add, smiling down upon his brand-new bride, 'Because I've married Jane'.

The unheralded arrival of the Canberra débris meant that the Lathkill path became doubly rich in bale-out associations, memories of the abandoned Canberra bomber at its western end complementing those of the abandoned Wellington bomber which fell at its eastern end, just three hundred yards short of Conksbury Bridge. But by 2006 Lathkill had long since covered up its surface scars, as indeed it has done following so many of the despoliations man has visited upon this fair dale.

The starboard mainplane and engine of Canberra WT207, in Friezland (courtesy of Crown Copyright)

Above left: The starboard wing site in 2006, looking northwards across Lathkill Dale, towards Bole Hill

Above right: 2006, Deep Dale, where the fuselage section impacted

Left: Where the long-sought rocket motor was found by the Taddington postmistress, just off the Taddington to Hubber Dale footpath

Above left: Tailplane and rear fuselage of Canberra WT207 (courtesy of Crown Copyright)

Above: The field above One Ash Grange Farm into which pilot Flight Lieutenant de Salis parachuted

Left: The tailplane site in mid-2006, Summerhill Farm behind the coppice

The field on Organ Ground Farm where navigator Flying Officer Lowe landed

Monyash, which was littered with Canberra debris

Letters acknowledging Mr James Slater's assistance, from Flight Lieutenant de Salis and from Air Commodore Coles (courtesy of Mr James Slater)

From: Air Commodore W.E Coles, C.B.E., D.S.O., D.F.C., A.F.C., R.A.F

Dear Mr. Slater,
While studying the result of an investigation into a recent aircraft accident I note that you and your brother found Flight Lieutenant J.P.F De Salis soon after he had landed by parachute and took him to your home, ordered an ambulance, looked after his comfort until he was taken to hospital and also telephoned Royal Air Force Hemswell to inform them of the accident.

As a result of the help and sympathy which Flight Lieutenant De Salis received immediately following this accident I am pleased to say he has made a quick recovery. Please accept my thanks for the part you played.

Princess Mary's Royal Air Force Hospital, Halton

Sunday 20th *[April, 1958]*

Dear Mr James Slater,
I was the pilot of the Canberra that crashed on the 9th April and I am writing to you to thank you for the help you gave me when I landed by parachute. I don't think I would have been able to walk on my own and I could not see very well. I did not know where I was.

I have very nearly completely recovered. I have two red eyes left and that is all the evidence left. I luckily didn't break any bones.

I hope that in the future I will be able to come up to Derby to thank you personally.

Canberra WT207 port-wing site. Ahead, on the left, to Lathkill; upslope as if through the gate, to One Ash Grange, and the starboard-wing site

Wellington L7811 crash site, having left Conksbury Bridge for Monyash

Cessna 150, G-BFSR, Thorpe Common, Thorpe Salvin

SK 52687 79417 92m
Netherthorpe Aerodrome
9 December, 1978

Occupants: two, both unhurt:
Mr Paul Harrison, assistant flying instructor
Mr Phillip Waller, student pilot

On 9 December, 1978, Cessna 150 G-BFSR, engaged in flying training from Netherthorpe Aerodrome suffered an engine failure shortly after take-off and was badly damaged when it made an emergency landing in a ploughed field. Neither occupant was hurt.

The student pilot involved, Mr Phillip Waller, of Todwick, described the incident in early 2006.

Mr Phillip Waller, a student pilot in 1978

'Having done about twelve hours' flying,' Mr Waller recalled, 'I was at the post-first-solo stage of consolidating and was climbing through about 600 feet, having carried out the take-off, when the engine cut dead. Mr Harrison took over, and steering straight ahead, put the machine into a ploughed field – White's Field. The earth was soft, however, with just a light covering of snow, therefore the moment the nosewheel touched, it dug in, and the tail flipped over, leaving us inverted. Fortunately, although this particular Cessna was not approved for aerobatics, it had a four-point harness fitted, as opposed to a lap strap, and so we were held securely in our seats. Mind you, it took a very long minute and a half before we could release ourselves and climb out. The aircraft was very substantially damaged, particularly the wings, but after that I rather lost track of it. Certainly it was dragged from the fields, but whether it flew again I don't know. They suspected carburettor icing, but were unable to substantiate this.'

And how did Mr Waller feel, as a raw-enough student, having an aircraft let him down like that? 'We had a very good Chief Flying Instructor,' he explained, 'Wendy Mills, and she had me up again less than an hour and a half later.' After which, Mr Waller progressed very well and achieved his Private Pilots Licence. Later, with expense in mind, having got married, he had a lay-off for some years, but had returned to flying some time before. By 2006 he had done very nearly 400 hours, and carried out some interesting flying, not least what must have been a truly memorable sortie cruising down Monument Valley in the States.

With Netherthorpe aerodrome carrying out flying training in the vicinity it is hardly surprising that such incidents occur, albeit infrequently, so that occasions where two men escaped when their light aircraft crashed at Thorpe Salvin – but beyond the bounds of this series – are also on record for 10 May, 1991, and for 1 March, 1996. Beyond the bounds, for just to the east of this Cessna crash site is the Three Shires Stone, marking the boundary between Yorkshire, Nottinghamshire and Derbyshire. And significantly, the modern Derbyshire boundary matches with that of its forbear, ancient Mercia, so justifying the inclusion of this crash site, the most easterly of all those covered in this Peakland series.

The impact area, looking back towards Netherthorpe airfield

Boulton Paul Defiant T3921, Shining Tor, Cat and Fiddle Inn, Buxton area

SJ 99830 73581 517m
No.96 Squadron, RAF Cranage (south-east of Northwich, Cheshire), No.9 Group, Fighter Command
16 October, 1941

Crew: both injured:
Pilot Officer M.G. Hilton, pilot
Sergeant H.W. Brunckhorst, air gunner

Thanks to its airborne-interception (AI) radar, the Defiant proved far more successful as a night fighter than it had in its design role as a day fighter. However, the AI system required a ground radar station to guide the fighter to a range and position from which its airborne radar could make contact, and to perfect this technique both components required regular practice. So it was that on the night of 16 October, 1941, the crew of Defiant T3921 had been detailed for a Ground-Controlled Interception sortie.

With the liaison part of the exercise completed, Pilot Officer Hilton and his air gunner were descending towards Cranage. But as the crash site is far from the centre line of any runway, or from where any Standard Beam Approach facility ran, it is evident that they were homing on a bearing designed to bring the aircraft into a position from which a visual approach could be made. Moreover, as the undercarriage had been lowered it is clear that Pilot Officer Hilton thought he was far nearer the airfield than he actually was, and was intent on losing height rapidly. Only Defiant T3921 was still fourteen miles from Cranage when it was flown into the intervening eastern side of Shining Tor at an elevation of 1,700 feet above sea level. It was wrecked on impact, but did not burn, and although both aircrew were injured each survived to fly again.

There had been cloud above the hills and the night had been reported as one having very little horizon. Accordingly, having interviewed Pilot Officer Hilton, the court of inquiry was

Above: Débris removed and framed by enthusiasts; in 2006, held in the Old School, Wildboarclough

Left: Defiant T3921, Shining Tor, looking towards the Cat and Fiddle Inn

able to establish that, because he had been concentrating on instrument flying at his last-checked altimeter reading of 2,500 feet, he had not realised that he had emerged from cloud, still less that he was yet so far from the airfield and therefore over high ground.

Over the years doubts had arisen and some had questioned whether the site at this reference was that of the 1941 Defiant, or that of the American Norseman which crashed nearby in 1944. In 2005, however, retired shepherd Mr Albert Heathcote resolved the matter, confirming the existence of this site when he began working on the ridge in 1943.

In 2006 little evidence of the crash remained, just a scar in the heather, and the frosting of aluminium flakes left when the salvage party had finished reducing the residual wreckage by burning.

De Havilland DH10 Amiens F357, Burbage Edge, Derbyshire Bridge

SK 02354 71587 463m
National Aircraft Factory No.2, Heaton Chapel, Stockport, de Havilland assembly line, flown from Ringway, on delivery to the Royal Air Force
8 December, 1919

Although nearly 1,300 Amiens were ordered for the about-to-be-styled Royal Air Force following the machine's first flight in March 1918, only 260 were completed by the time the Armistice was signed in November 1918. And while it has been claimed that a No.104 Squadron Amiens, F1867, accompanied a raid on Sarrebourg airfield on 10 November, 1918, neither the RAF Communiqués nor the Independent Force (RAF) Diary record this, notwithstanding which the contemporary Jane's says the type saw active service.

F357 over Burbage, by courtesy of the artist, Alan Jones

DH10s in their Colonial role

DH10s certainly played their part in the post-war years both in the RAF's Colonial Policing role in India, and in the development of the mail routes between Cairo and Baghdad, and Bombay and Karachi. But regardless of such pioneering exploits the type was never to stand on terms with such designs as the DH2, DH4, and the DH9A from the same stable.

Normal practice at National Aircraft Factory No.2 at Heaton Chapel, Stockport – the site of Crossley Motors and later of Fairey Aviation – was to send new machines by rail to Ringway for assembly and flying off, although some were dispatched to such local airfields as Hooton Park, near Ellesmere Port. The main output was DH9s, but on 22 March, 1918, an order for two hundred DH10s was received, the first batch to be numbered F351 to F550.

In the end, a total of seven DH10s – some sources say twenty-two – is believed to have been completed before the cancellation of the larger order. Unpropitiously at least four from this batch came to grief before even reaching the Royal Air Force.

Of these, DH10 F351 lost an engine on take-off, stalled, went into an incipient spin ('sideslipped' was the contemporary term), and crashed with the loss of its crew during a demonstration flight at Dunham Massey, a country house at Altrincham, just south of Manchester.

Another, possibly DH10 F354, forced-landed at Hooton Park on 21 March, 1919. When taking off again, however, its wingtip was allowed to hit a tree and it crashed, seriously injuring the pilot, Major S.E. Adams.

DH10 F352, crewed by Flight Sergeants Moss and Ballard and one unidentified crew member, crashed on the aerodrome adjacent to the factory.

Finally, on 8 December, 1919, DH10 F357, the machine in question, got as far as Burbage Edge, ran into bad visibility, and was inadvertently flown into the ground.

One of the ill-fated DH10s from National Aircraft Factory No.2, Stockport, 1919
(photograph by courtesy of the de Havilland Trust)

Mr Bernard Minshull, Burbage

The Cat and Fiddle Inn

The crash site of DH10 F357, looking towards the Cat and Fiddle Inn

But at this remove even datings vary, and besides 8 December, 1919, 20 December, 1918, and both 18 and 24 February, 1919, have been put forward for this series of crashes.

Yet if knowledge at the time of writing was scanty, the remains at the site were even more so. Metal components found some years back were known to have been removed by enthusiasts, so that by 2004 all that had survived were a few dabs of doped fabric under rocks on the peaty soil.

Just the same, Mr Bernard Minshull, of Goslin Bar Farm, Burbage, approached in August 2005, had no difficulty in marking in the crash-site location on the map. 'It was', he explained, 'just up from the Derbyshire Bridge information station, but much lower down than the Oxford [EB717]. Only', he continued, showing his intimacy with the site, 'there's nothing now, just bits of canvas.' And he explained how he came to be so conversant with the crash. 'The head keeper on the Edge, Tom Bell, lived at Tunnel Farm and had taken the wheels from the plane to make a hand-cum-horse haycart. He and my Dad, although Dad was a lot younger than Tom, used it long before the war. Indeed Dad had a tale about the cart getting away, and running down the moor.' He paused. 'Again, according to Dad, mechanics from Park Garage — Hodgkinson's place in Buxton — took the Sopwith's engines, so possibly they're in their collection even now.'

Do–it-Yourself flying apparatus, Flash Bottom Farm, Quarnford; possibly Bosley; Congleton

SK 02300 66000 390m (area of)
1970–80

In 1993, while off-path walking past Flash Bottom Farm in the direction of Flash, and with no interest in aeroplanes that were anything but 100% serviceable (or very nearly so), the author remarked the rather battered fuselage of a Cessna-type machine among the junked cars and agricultural paraphernalia littering the farm's enclosure. Returning to the area in 2006 when researching this series, no trace of this aircraft could be discovered, but the probable answer to its presence was supplied by Mr and Mrs Frank and Margaret Parker, of Quarnford.

'Almost certainly,' they agreed, 'that would have belonged to Arthur Poulson, who had the place then — he's been dead a good ten years now — for while he turned his hand to many things his great passion was for aviation. He knew all the crash sites in the area, and after visiting them would bring back pieces to the farm.'

From their anecdotes it emerged that Mr Poulson's escapades were legion: his residing in a hollowed-out rabbit warren in order to evade National Service; his having done much the same when faced with fines regarding Poll Tax; and his being brought from custody in order to dispose of his store of lethally-unsafe dynamite. His inclusion in this series, however, is not based upon his standing as a larger-than-life character, or even as an early crash-site enthusiast, but as a pilot. Or as a pioneer aviator, perhaps. For it seems that on one occasion — just possibly when he lived in the Bosley area, before moving to Quarnford – he attached the propeller from a bomber to a Volkswagen engine, constructed a supporting frame, and having started the contraption, strapped himself in and released the restraints. The apparatus successfully carried him up above the trees, but it appears he had given no thought to controlling the craft once it was airborne: firmly allying him with many a pioneer would-be flier! Of course, he might have hoped the discing propeller would float him back to earth once the fuel lines had emptied themselves. If this was the case, however, he had evidently overrated the autorotative assistance his propeller would furnish when called upon to act as a windmilling rotor, so that when the engine stopped he was left to plunge into an elm tree, breaking some bones in the process.

After such a pioneering exploit, Mr Poulson simply has to be worthy of inclusion in this series as one of the many Peakland sons of Icarus portrayed herein. But certainly not as a modern Daedalus, for all that Mr Poulson was demonstrably innovative; for Daedalus, the very first aviator, carefully planned his flight beforehand, did not too nearly approach the sun, or take off too near an elm tree, and therefore not only successfully flew, but reached his destination safely.

Handley Page Hampden Mk.1 L4189, Black Edge, Dove Holes (north of Buxton)

SK 06389 76843 468m
No.106 Squadron, RAF Finningley (Doncaster), No.5 Group, Bomber Command
30 September, 1940

Crew: four: three killed; one survived, injured:
Sergeant John Gray Gow, pilot
Sergeant Charles Owen Cook, observer
Sergeant Eric Burt, wireless operator/air gunner
Sergeant N. Powell, air gunner, injured

Having been savagely mauled as a day bomber at the start of the Second World War, the Hampden, like other British bombers of its class, was quickly diverted to night operations. Its métier was to become minelaying, although by the end of 1940 twenty-one had already been lost on the task. Only, as so often occurs in aerial operations, the losses attributable to direct enemy action were significantly outweighed by those due to fundamentally non-operational causes, a statistic to be swelled on 30 September, 1940, with the loss of Hampden L4189 of No.106 Squadron.

At the outbreak of war No.106 Squadron had been one of those reserve squadrons tasked by Bomber Command's No.5 Group with training crews on the new bomber types; in their case, the Handley Page Hampden. By August 1940, however, No.106 had been raised to the status of an operational squadron. Just the same, although it was called upon to lay mines outside those French harbours housing the German invasion barges, its training commitment continued unabated. Which meant that it suffered the hazards of both operations and training. Indeed by February 1941, when it was restructured – with its 'C' Flight forming a cadre which would evolve into No.26 Operational Training Unit – it had lost six Hampdens, two of which crashed in the Peakland area.

One of the two, Hampden L4189, the one in question here, was lost during a night flight on 30 September, 1940, when it was flown into Black Edge, a ridge at an elevation of 1,660 feet above sea level, just north of Buxton.

On the night they crashed Sergeant John Gow and his crew were airborne on a navigational exercise from RAF Finningley, near Doncaster. It is not known how experienced the observer, Sergeant Charles Cook, was – the aircrew category 'Observer' was to be redesignated 'Navigator' in 1942 – but it seems that Sergeant Pilot Gow, with forty hours on type, was well advanced in his operational training, notwithstanding that he had less than 200 hours' total flying time. It also seems that certain restrictions had been imposed on the degree of outside assistance the crew were allowed to obtain during the sortie: presumably there was an exercise-imposed radio silence, designed to give a foretaste of operational conditions. What is known for certain is that there came a time during the exercise when the crew were forced to admit to being totally lost.

This was not a matter of great concern, despite the heavy cloud, provided they kept a safe altitude. A matter of frustration, rather. For it meant that their release to operational flying as a crew might be delayed while pilot and observer further honed their skills. But having exhausted all efforts to determine their own position unaided, both pilot and navigator submitted resolutely, directing the wireless operator to summon outside aid and call Finningley for a course to steer. (In the parlance of the morse brevity code, '*QDM IMI*' – 'What is my magnetic course to steer for your station?') In those days, however, the procedure took some considerable time. But the aircraft having transmitted the two ten-second dashes – separated by its call sign – that were required to enable a bearing to be taken by the Finningley direction-finder, the sanctuary-affording course-to-steer was duly passed.

Tragically, before an acknowledgement could be tapped out, let alone in time for Sergeant Gow to respond and turn onto the given heading, contact was lost, the Hampden having crashed into Black Edge, thirty-nine miles south-west of Finningley, where it had exploded and burst into flames.

Exactly why the crew had descended so low that they struck beneath the summit ridge at an elevation of just 1,530 feet is yet another unknown, although a fair assumption is that they had blindly let down through cloud in a determined effort to paddle their own canoe and re-establish their position visually.

As might be expected, having flown into the ridge at some 217 mph (189 knots) there was no hope for the three crew stationed forwards, but incredibly the gunner, Sergeant Powell, survived the crash, seriously injured though he was. Indeed, he was doubly fortunate, for although the weather had been too cloudy for those on the ground to actually see the aircraft, its engines had been heard heading for Black Edge, so that after the impact local farmers reached the scene in time to drag him clear of the flames.

In 2005 Mr Bill Hollinrake, who had been working at Black Edge Farm at the time of the crash, remembered, 'The plane had come down in what we call Coltsfield, and the gunner – I think he'd broken a leg – was brought down through the Hundred Acres field to the road.'

Notable among the early arrivals was Mr John Prince, of Brookhouse Farm, who secured a parachute, telling his friends that he intended to have his wife make handkerchiefs of the silk. Only when no handkerchiefs appeared it was widely held that the material had been commandeered by the lady for knickers instead …

In 2006 the impact site was still bare of vegetation, although only a few globs of molten metal remained, dispersed in the thin surrounding grasses. Débris very similar, in fact, to that to be found where the other No.106 Squadron Hampden crashed in the Peaklands, when X3154 flew into Rushup Edge, near Mam Tor, some three months later.

The crash site of Handley Page Hampden L4189, looking downhill

Handley Page Hampden Mk.1 P1248, Concord Park, Shiregreen, Sheffield

SK 38025 92781 100m, impact site
SK 37391 92002 144m, pilot landed, location subsequently a sports centre
No.25 Operational Training Unit, RAF Finningley (south-east of Doncaster, Yorkshire), No.7
Group, Bomber Command
19 April 1941

Crew: two: one survived, one killed:
Pilot Officer Ralph Athelsie Pole Allsebrook, pilot, survived, parachuted
Pilot Officer Jeffery Bohun Ranson, observer, killed

On the late afternoon of 19 April, 1941, Pilot Officer Ralph Athelsie Pole Allsebrook, a pupil at
No.25 Operational Training Unit, then located at RAF Finningley, near Doncaster, was briefed
to carry out an instrument-flying practice in Hampden P1248. The exercise would have involved
Pilot Officer Allsebrook flying eyes-down on his instruments while carrying out various flight
manoeuvres: cruising straight and level, and turning, not only while level but also while climbing
and descending, building up his experience against the occasions when he would be forced to
rely upon his instruments alone. It was necessary to have someone to act as lookout while the
pilot's attention was inside the cockpit, accordingly Pilot Officer Jeffery Bohun Ranson, his
observer – his navigator – was detailed to carry out this function. Because of the restricted
nature of the flight, however, the flight commander decided that it would not be necessary to
carry a wireless operator in addition, and accordingly that crew member was stood down.

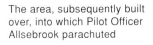
2005, the Concord Park impact site of Hampden P1248

The area, subsequently built
over, into which Pilot Officer
Allsebrook parachuted

Unfortunately, the observer must have been less attentive than the situation demanded, for Pilot Officer Allsebrook strayed from the local area and penetrated the Sheffield air defences, and in particular the balloon barrage, and failing to hear, or to be advised of, the automatic warning signals sent out by the balloons, flew into a balloon cable at 2,800 feet. The cable, in essence, cut deeply into the aircraft structure, and presumably killed Pilot Officer Ranson. The crippled aircraft then fell out of control to crash into a woodland fringe in Concord Park, on the north-western outskirts of Sheffield, catching fire and burning out. Pilot Officer Allsebrook parachuted to safety, and though injured, survived the crash.

The court of inquiry into the accident found that the crew had lost themselves and that 'the observer, who was also the "look-out", failed to keep check of the pilot's course on the map'. When shown the preliminary findings, however, the Air Officer Commanding (AOC) of the Group had more to add on the control and command issues involved. While conceding that the aircraft had become lost in poor visibility he found the root cause of the fatal crash to be the lack of explicit orders for the sortie, and went on to make the constructively political point that this was due to 'the inexperience of the instructional staff', observing further, 'a common failing in OTUs – an inherent defect due to [the] general lack of trained personnel'. He then made the specific charge that no wireless operator had been carried: another pair of ears to have listened for the balloon warning signals, at least, and a crew member who would have been able to furnish his colleagues with bearings throughout the flight. This error of judgement the AOC attributed scathingly to 'a misconception on the part of the flight commander', and ruled that in future, wireless operators would be carried on all flights, a stricture duly incorporated into the formal findings of the court.

Pilot Officer Allsebrook, having returned to flying duties and joined No.617 Squadron on Lancasters, was promoted to flight lieutenant and was to gain both the Distinguished Service Order and the Distinguished Flying Cross before being killed in action on 16 September, 1943. He was lost when the Coningsby-based squadron, mounting a return visit following a weather-aborted first attempt, raided the Dortmund-Ems Canal at relatively low level with the new 12,000lb bomb, the precursor of the 'earthquake' 12,000-pounder, and lost five out of the eight aircraft tasked.

The 1941 accident was not to be the only brush Sheffield's Concord Park was to have with Hampdens during the Second World War, for two years later another training bomber would put down, lost and short of fuel, but this time more innocuously.

Mr Gordon Taylor, in 1941 a schoolboy living at Abbeydale, Sheffield, but in 2006 domiciled in Connecticut, remembered visiting this crash in Concord Park. 'It had been caught by a barrage balloon cable and crashed,' he wrote, 'although I've always thought it was an Anson.'

Mr Terence Crooks in 2005; in 1941, 'thick ears rather than souvenirs'

Similarly recalling the event, Mr Terence Crooks, who still lived in the vicinity of the park in September 2005, described where the cable-stricken aircraft crashed. 'It was just inside Woolley Wood, not far from the Concord Road entrance. Or from where they later built some brick toilets, as if in commemoration.'

Mr Crooks went on: 'I was only about eight at the time, but we all wanted to get souvenirs. Only when we got close to where the wreckage was the police and the RAF chased us off.' He grinned. 'We wanted souvenirs, whereas all we got for our pains were thick ears.'

In 2006 there was nothing to mark the actual impact point, while the place where Pilot Officer Allsebrook had parachuted down had long been built over by the Concord Sports Centre. Both locations were vouched for, however, by Mr Patrick Flynn, of Preston, who knew the Park well during his late-1942 to 1944 tenure as a gardener's mate.

Handley Page Hampden, Concord Park, Shiregreen, Sheffield

SK 37606 92368 132m
RAF Bomber Command
8 July, 1943

Crew: probably four, survived a successful forced landing, uninjured

Sheffield's Concord Park, in the Shiregreen area, to the north-west of the city, is a generously open public space variously utilised by a golf course, assorted sports fields, a children's playground and woodland walks. Twice during the Second World War, Handley Page Hampden bombers came down within its bounds, one disastrously, in 1941, the other making an innocuous and successful forced landing in 1943.

Unlike the 1941 Hampden crash in Concord Park, very little is known of this second incident: merely that the aircraft, presumably lost and short of fuel, set down, and after a day or two under guard, was flown away again.

Mrs Maureen Bailey (née Rodgers), however, encountered by the author in September 2005 as she was dog-walking, was well aware of this second incident, responding at once, 'My older sisters, Sheila and Margaret, have often told me how they went to see it, and showed me where it happened – I was just a baby, of course. It had come down in what was then a cornfield not that far from the golf course. But it wasn't damaged and was flown off again just days later.'

As might be expected, in 2006 there was no indication in the park that the incident had ever occurred, nor was it reported in the press of the day, although a successful forced landing would hardly have given much 'comfort to the enemy', even had the wartime censorship allowed it to be reported. This must remain another site, then, to be recorded for a posterity which will hopefully be able to fill in the gaps. Just the same, Mr Patrick Flynn, of Preston, a gardener's mate in Concord Park from late-1942 to 1944, was able to indicate the area – still a wide space in 2006 despite the encroachment of the 1990s golf driving range – where both this Hampden, and a Tiger Moth, successfully put down.

The area in which the 1943 Hampden set down, and subsequently took off from again, diminished since the nineties, not least by a golf driving range

Handley Page HP54 Harrow Mk.2 K6989, Barlow (north-west of Chesterfield)

SK 34350 75192 109m
No.214 (Federated Malay States) Squadron, RAF Feltwell
(12 miles north-east of Ely), No.3 (Bomber) Group, Bomber
Command.
8 July, 1939

Crew: six, uninjured:
Pilot Officer M. F. Briden, pilot
Identities of the other pilot and three crewmembers presently undetermined

The Handley Page Harrow came into squadron service in January 1937 as a bomber and troop carrier. Although its design marked the heavy bomber's transition from biplane to monoplane the fixed undercarriage was retained, the Handley Page justification being that a streamlined design compensated for the weight penalty of a retractable landing gear. Production finished in December 1937, after one hundred had been built, when it was replaced by the Wellington bomber. Just the same the type flew throughout the war as a transport, twelve being stripped of turrets and renamed the Sparrow.

As a transport the Harrow, cruising at 163 mph (142 knots), was most notably employed in evacuating casualties during the battle for Arnhem when it was the only large aircraft capable of landing in such small fields. But although the design method of subcontracting components to many small firms simplified repairs, neither rough-field capability nor ease of repair had been able to save Harrow Mk.2 K6989 five years earlier, when on 8 July, 1939, it made an inglorious touchdown on its last outing.

On that occasion several Harrows of No.214 Squadron had been on detachment to RAF Aldergrove, Northern Ireland (in the course of time to become Belfast International Airport), and were returning in company to RAF Feltwell, their Norfolk base, some twelve miles north-east of Ely. While climbing through cloud, however, Harrow K6989, under the command of Pilot Officer M.F. Briden, lost the formation.

The weather was cloudy, and the visibility poor, the high-summer haze being exacerbated by some lingering low-level mist which blotted out much of the ground. Further, in this extremity the wireless operator reported that the communications equipment had stopped working, which meant that the crew was cut off from outside aid. As a result, the time came when Pilot Officer Briden realised that they were hopelessly lost.

While they continued to search for a ground feature with which to fix themselves, Pilot Officer Briden maintained a rough, south-easterly heading for base. As a pilot he was relatively experienced for the day with over three hundred hours on type, if under five hundred hours' total flying, and he put all those hours to good use. Eventually, however, with no ground features appearing that would allow the crew to locate themselves by their own efforts, he made the decision to put the machine down in order to ascertain their position before shortage of fuel robbed them of some measure of control.

With forward visibility so much reduced by haze it was, of course, no easy task. Indeed when he made his first attempt – into a field at the hamlet of Bole Hill, three miles north-west of Chesterfield – he misjudged his approach and lost his tailwheel to some trees.

Hastily going around, he remained in the area, where at least he could see the main layout of the land, finally choosing an upsloping field half a mile to the east, at Barlow, as it would transpire, ninety-eight miles from his base in Norfolk. Only here, in aiming to maximise the space available, he once again hit trees on the approach, this time denting the slipstreaming boots of his main wheels. Even so it seems likely that he feared running out of space after touchdown, for as the speed fell off so he swung the machine diagonally across the field in order to gain himself some extra distance. But any such fear proved groundless, and the machine came to rest with space in hand.

The aircraft's arrival was witnessed by Mr Horace Noble, destined to become a career engineer, but at the time a schoolboy to whom the visitor represented both a welcome break and an outstanding event.

Another witness was villager Mr Wilf Needham, farmer, special constable, and countryman of many other functions whose oral memories were recorded in the Barlow Social History Group's *c*.1997 publication, *Everybody is Somebody*. 'We were whitewashing the cowshed,' Wilf remembered, 'when this aeroplane dropped into William Needham's "Seven Acre" field. He had tried to drop at Bole Hill, but had taken off his back wheel. So then he came over the chapel and managed to land in the field opposite the back of David Granger's house. He had broken his undercarriage on some trees at the bottom, and finished facing Chris Holmes' house before turning towards Rutland Terrace.'

It was clear from the outset that it would not be feasible to safely take off from the field once more. Therefore, while the crew packed their belongings and were taken back to Feltwell, the aircraft was placed under guard, initially by police and special constables, and later by RAF personnel.

The recovery operation was handled by a team from No.9 Maintenance Unit, but although they officially took over responsibility for the task the next day, the shell of the machine was to remain in situ for some considerable time. Nor is the reason hard to deduce. For the accident report records that the aircraft landed heavily: one imagines that the upslope of the field proved deceptive. So that for all the machine appears relatively intact in the contemporary photograph of it on site, it had evidently suffered some significant structural damage. Accordingly, on 30 November, 1939, the decision was finally made to scrap what remained as being beyond economic repair.

'It stayed there for weeks,' Wilf told the history group, 'and drew more people that year than came for the well dressing. So that the hedge all along the lane – the gate, the lot – from Keeper's Cottage, down towards the church, was trampled under by visitors. But when the decision was made to scrap it on site we got some right good timber. In fact, one piece of three-by-two was used to make the roof of the well dressing.'

But he had apparently remembered with particular satisfaction the oil. 'I asked the sergeant about that, and he said, "If you want it, tek it." So I rushed around the village getting cans to put it in.' (Indeed it is locally held that Wilf was never to actually buy another drop.)

Wilf was also to supply a touch of romance involving a well-known local family. 'The ginger-haired young lady,' he maintained, 'one of the Helliwells, of Peakley Hill, later married one of the airmen ...'

The field has been in constant use in the years since the Harrow put down for its lengthy stay. Hardly surprisingly, then, nothing was found in a 2006 metal-detector sweep of the area, although the still extant water plant captured in the photograph of the aircraft on site furnished a good guide for the photo-match map reference supplied here.

Handley Page Harrow Mk.2 K6989, having forced-landed at Barlow (Photograph by courtesy of the *Derbyshire Times*)

2006, the site of Harrow K6989's precautionary landing

North American Harvard Mk.2B FT442, Shining Tor, near the Cat and Fiddle Inn, Buxton

SJ 99753 73746 530m
No.5 (Pilots) Advanced Flying Unit, RAF Ternhill (Market
Drayton, Shropshire), No. 21 Group, Flying Training
Command
30 November, 1944

Pilot: killed:
Sergeant Julius Sofranko, Czechoslovakian,
in the Royal Air Force

The Harvard trainer entered RAF service in January 1939, but the French Government too had taken deliveries, which meant that when France fell the *Luftwaffe* was able to press the French Harvards to their own use. Yet nationals of other overrun countries were also to train on Harvards, one being Sergeant Julius Sofranko, a Czechoslovakian airman who had made his way via Poland to the French *Armée de l'Air*, and so to the Royal Air Force, in order to fight on.

As a pilot Sergeant Sofranko was relatively experienced with over 300 hours total and 146 hours solo on type, and on 30 November, 1944, he was flying on a solo navigational cross-country. Two-and-a-half hours into the sortie, however, while on the return leg to his RAF Ternhill, Shropshire, base, he entered cloud and flew into the Shining Tor ridge. He was killed, and the aircraft destroyed.

Harvard FT442 on Shining Tor (Photograph by courtesy of Crown Copyright)

Because of the location of the crash site, just thirty-six miles from Ternhill, the court of inquiry was able to deduce that Sergeant Sofranko had commenced his descent to base on a pre-calculated and unamended estimated time of arrival, believing that he was clear of high ground. It had been Sergeant Sofranko's misfortune that in the course of the flight the wind had changed, increasing his headwind component, and so reducing his ground speed, as a result of which he was still over the hills when he blindly nosed down.

It was recorded that Sergeant Sofranko had been especially briefed not to persist in flight through cloud, and had signed as having read and understood the unit's 'Flying-Orders Book', which detailed the appropriate actions to be taken on encountering worsening weather. Just the same, Sergeant Sofranko's instructor was admonished for not having ensured that his pupil was cognisant with the correct radio procedures for obtaining assistance in such conditions. At the same time the radio mechanic was held to blame for certain discrepancies found in the frequency-setting crystals loaded into the set – each of the very restricted pre-tuned radio channels in the sets of the day being crystal controlled.

Mr Albert Heathcote, the shepherd who discovered the wreck

Mr Albert Heathcote, interviewed in 2005, was the first person to come across the wreck. Back in 1944 he was living with his parents at Saltersford Hall Farm, in the valley at Jenkin Chapel, and shepherding along the whole ridge. Seeing the crashed aircraft loom up through the mist as he was working along the slope, he craned to the badly shattered cockpit to see if he could help. But a glance both horrified him and showed him that there was no aid to be rendered. After that he could not remember arriving back home, although his parents set about raising the alarm. What he remembered with great clarity, however, is that while the wreckage remained there he gave it a wide berth.

The photograph taken when the recovery team reached the crash appears to show the aircraft on the level ground near the ridge path, although there seems to be no record of débris being found in that vicinity. As for the actual crater further downslope, which, in 2006 still harboured minutiae, this is held to have resulted from an amateurish attempt to salvage the valuable phosphor-bronze of the cylinder heads using explosives. Wreckage was still to be found in the gully below the site; indeed there was speculation that this Harvard 'tip' might also have been utilised to dispose of wreckage from the Norseman which crashed nearby in 1944.

The impact site of Harvard FT442, looking north-eastwards towards Errwood Reservoir

North American Harvard Mk.2B FX306, Foolow (north-east of Tideswell)

SK 18674 76837 291m
No.6 Flying Training School, RAF Ternhill (Market Drayton, Shropshire), No.23 Group, Flying Training Command
10 December, 1952

Pupil pilot: injured:
Pilot Officer Robert Windle

The Harvard entered RAF service in January 1939 and was retained as an advanced trainer until 1955. Although unsophisticated, it was a demanding machine – arguably the reason it proved such a good advanced trainer – and required its pilot to be cognisant of both its handling qualities and its technical foibles, as one pupil, Pilot Officer Windle, was to discover on 10 December, 1952.

The morning of the tenth was dull, but perfectly fit for flying, and Pilot Officer Windle was duly dispatched solo from RAF Station Ternhill. His brief was to carry out circuits and landings together with local map reading, the latter an exercise which, unlike a formal cross-country, did not necessarily call for detailed pre-flight navigational planning.

Once airborne, Pilot Officer Robert Windle elected to scout the local area to the north-east, evidently intending to leave the circuit-work until the end of the detail. However, after just over an hour without radio contact he was heard to call for navigational assistance, reporting that his engine was running unevenly. Ternhill Air Traffic Control were unable to establish two-way communication with him and directed another of the unit's aircraft to act as an airborne link, a measure that brought no results.

Even as this was going on, however, people at Tideswell, some forty-six miles to the north-east of Ternhill, were watching Pilot Officer Windle circle the town at a relatively low altitude in an evident attempt to determine his position visually. They then heard his engine cut, upon which they saw him head off eastwards in a straight glide: a glide which ended when he touched down in a pasture on the western outskirts of Foolow village, bumping over a series of sizeable hummocks before violently striking a drystone wall. Unhappily, both his seat and his harness attachment-points broke away on impact with the wall, so that he was thrown forwards and seriously injured.

The subsequent inquiry established that Pilot Officer Windle's engine had been perfectly serviceable, the rough running having been an indication of fuel starvation. Following which, because the warning had not been assimilated, and the fuel tanks had not been switched over, as the operating procedure demanded, the engine had simply stopped dead.

Further, while conceding that Pilot Officer Windle's radio jack-plug had probably been intermittent, the inquiry found that he had been flying at such a low altitude as to effectively cut himself off from both radar and the navigational assistance he had sought.

Pilot Officer Windle had 69 hours' solo experience but he had trained in uncluttered Canada, so it was understandable that he had become lost in trying to map read in poor visibility and over terrain so full of detail; he was, after all, still a pupil.

So presumably, with so much seeming to crowd in upon him – as indeed it had been – the basic desirability of touching down into wind must have fled from his mind. Accordingly, caught at relatively low altitude when his engine cut, he had not attempted to set up an emergency pattern, but had flown directly on until he was forced into a downwind – and therefore, a high-speed – landing.

Just the same, it was very bad luck that, due to the hummocky nature of the far end of the pasture, both seat and harness-attachment chose to break just as Pilot Officer Windle nosed into the wall. The injuries he received were severe enough to render him unfit for further RAF service and he duly relinquished his commission on 15 March, 1954. It would have been small comfort to him, then, that the accident led to a modification of the seat and the harness securing-points, and that Flying Training Command's contemporary apportionment of solo flight and dual supervision was questioned.

The crash site is on a pasture immediately beside a road, and in 2006 there was nothing to be seen of the incident, and only debris from the aircraft battery to be unearthed. The rocky hummocks which so unsettled the final part of Pilot Officer Windle's landing run had long been excavated away and the land refilled and returfed, restoring to its pastoral tranquillity this boundary of the archetypically English village beyond.

Nor was there anything to be found in Foolow to indicate what happened here. Or for that matter to record that a Shackleton aircraft later crashed even more disastrously on the village's other boundary.

Above left: The crash site of Harvard FX306 in 2006

Above: 93 The crash scene in 2006

Left: The salvage crew attending Harvard FX306, Foolow (Photograph by courtesy of Crown Copyright)

Douglas A-20G Havoc (Boston) 43-9958, Quarnford, A53, Buxton–Leek road

SK 03212 68074 448m
United States Eighth Army Air Force, 310th Ferry Squadron,
AAF169 (RAF Stansted), 27th Air Transport Group
3 January, 1945

Pilot: ferrying solo, killed:
First Lieutenant Eugene H. Howard, United States Army
Air Force

When UK-based A-20G Havocs required modifying, the work was carried out at the USAAF's
Base Air Depot at Burtonwood, near Liverpool. However, on 3 January, 1945, when a batch of
A-20Gs – a ground-strafing version of the type – was to be ferried to the Depot from RAF
Stansted, one of them, Havoc 43-9958, failed to arrive. It would transpire that the pilot, First
Lieutenant Eugene Howard, although he had 1,200 hours' flying time overall, had never before
flown the A-20.

The authorised route for the ferry, to be adhered to by all aircraft taking part, ran north-west
from RAF Stansted (Bishop's Stortford) to Leicester, where a left turn into a dog-leg centred on
Chester would steer them clear of high ground before their final northerly turn towards Liverpool.

The en-route weather showed frontal activity giving broken cloud, a low overcast masking
many hilltops, limited visibility, and rain, but equally significantly, a thirty-five knot wind from
the left at cruising altitude. 'Equally significantly', because, while all the other aircraft arrived
safely, First Lieutenant Howard's aircraft strayed right and struck high ground an hour after
take off, plunging into a field twenty-one miles east of track, at Quarnford, near Flash, beside
the A53, the Buxton to Leek road.

What caused First Lieutenant Howard to stray so far east of the authorised route was never
positively established but it seems likely that he failed to compensate for the strong wind from
his left. Always provided he flew north-west after the turn at Leicester, and not north-east: a by
no means unheard-of error even for a pilot flying a familiar machine.

But in either case, at his planned descent time First Lieutenant Howard could have had no
qualms about nosing down, on instruments, through the scattered overcast. Nor would there
have been a problem, had he only been over the Chester Plain, as he should have been – and as
he clearly believed he was – and not over the cloud-wreathed southern outliers of Axe Edge!

The accident committee had to rule that there had been an error of judgement on the pilot's
part in attempting to descend blind in order to re-establish visual ground contact. But they did
allow his total unfamiliarity with the Havoc to stand as a possible contributory factor.

By 2006 there was no surface evidence at the scene, only placid farm land beneath the imposing
ridge of Axe Edge. Just the same a metal-detector search turned up sufficient débris to positively
locate the site.

The crash site of Havoc A-
20G 43-9958, Axe Edge to
the north

Handley Page Heyfords

K4868, **SJ 96785 84713** 243m Homestead Farm, Disley, Cheshire
K6898, **SJ 96805 84619** 197m The Homestead, Disley, Cheshire
K4872, **SD 94939 08465** 226m Dingle Farm, Oldham
No.102 Squadron, RAF Finningley (near Doncaster), No.3 Group,
Bomber Command
12 December, 1936

K4868: Squadron Leader Charles W. Attwood and crew, uninjured
K6898: Pilot Officer Michael George Winsloe Clifford and crew, uninjured
K4872: Flight Lieutenant Charles Patrick Villiers, pilot, injured
          Observer, presently unidentified, uninjured
          Leading Aircraftman John Mackan, wireless operator, injured
          Leading Aircraftman Donald J.M. Keys, air gunner, injured

On Saturday 12 December, 1936, a markedly foggy day, two Handley Page Heyford bombers flying in company caused a stir when they unexpectedly began to circle in the vicinity of Disley, near Whaley Bridge, on the outskirts of Manchester, with yet more interest being generated when it was realised that they were probing the fog with the intention of actually setting down.

The first of the bombers, K4868, as it would transpire, the Heyford flown by Squadron Leader Charles Attwood, made its approach as the other, K6898, continued to circle. Squadron Leader Attwood chose a field of some length at The Homestead, on Jackson Edge, then the property of Mr R. Whitworth, touched down, and came to a halt, having landed safely. The other machine, flown, as the witnesses were to discover, by Pilot Officer Michael Clifford, then made an approach some two hundred yards off, only in the course of its landing run struck a telegraph pole and two fences before finishing up with its nose buried in Mr Whitworth's garden, its tail high in the air. Notwithstanding the upset, however, the crew emerged unscathed, even if with one of them, the leading-aircraftman wireless operator, shaken by having had a propeller blade slice through the thin metal wall of his station.

The unheralded arrival of these two monster aircraft, particularly in such poor weather, came as a surprise to the good people of Disley, but as both the local and the national newspapers would later inform them, the joint arrival told only part of a story. A story which had begun earlier that day when seven Handley Page Heyford bombers of No.102 (Ceylon) Squadron, having completed a detachment to RAF Aldergrove in Ulster (by 2006 Belfast International Airport), were detailed to return in formation to their home station of RAF Finningley, near Doncaster, in Yorkshire.

No.102 Squadron, a unit on the strength of a Bomber Command newly metamorph-osed from the bomber element of Air Defence of Great Britain (ADGB) Command, had itself only emerged from its sixteen years of post-First World War disbandment in October 1935, and had only been operating independently since March 1936. When the time came to leave Ulster the leader appointed was Squadron Leader Attwood. He would have been well aware that widespread fog and ice had led to chaotic conditions over much of the mainland, that only two days before bad weather had contributed to the disastrous crash of an airliner near Croydon, and that

Heyford K6898, its nose embedded in the garden of The Homestead (to the left; photograph by courtesy of the *Stockport Express;* vice Mr David W. Earl)

snow had now moved in to exacerbate the situation. This conjunction of fog and heavy snowstorms – a steep pressure gradient combating a slacker one – would also have suggested significant wind changes. As it was, probably not in the least mindful of the squadron motto which translated as 'Attempt and Achieve', Squadron Leader Attwood briefed his seven crews.

He planned to make a dog-leg of the flight, aiming for the shortest sea crossing during the anticipated good-weather phase of the route, some 115 miles with a landfall at Barrow, then steering directly for Finningley, 110 miles further on. A good plan, particularly in view of the weather, and one upon which each pilot and observer (navigator) would have conferred, each pair producing a flight plan for their own aircraft against the event that they became detached from the formation.

Regarding the latter, the Heyford had a good reputation as a stable machine for flying in formation, but to carry out such a flight while holding close station would have been unnecessarily stressful, therefore Squadron Leader Attwood probably settled upon a loose Vic disposition, with himself in the van.

Heyfords, held to be eminently suitable for formation flying (Photograph by courtesy of Handley Page)

By all accounts, the plan went well as far as the landfall. After that, however, the weather encountered seems to have been even worse than anticipated, and things began to go awry. What is clear is that only Pilot Officer Clifford found it possible, or politic, perhaps, to maintain station with the leader. But that the other pilots could not or chose not to do so would have been a matter of no great moment, for in their basic role as night bombers each crew was expected to be capable of operating independently.

So it was that, having found himself acting under his own auspices, Sergeant Pilot F. Biddulph followed his observer's directions, and, not without some difficulty, landed at Finningley only a little behind the planned estimated time. Interviewed in the eighties by author Ron Collier he was able to describe how, on arrival, he initially thought he was the last one to arrive and expected, therefore, some ribbing at the very least. Only to find that he was the first, and, for that day certainly, to be the only safe arrival. (Having landed safely, there was no requirement for Sergeant Biddulph to raise an incident report; consequently the registration of his aircraft remains to be determined.)

Flying Heyford K4864, Sergeant Pilot Williams had also distanced himself from the formation and flown on, but having let down in accordance with his observer's estimate, he had broken cloud to find that snow was now further reducing the fog-impaired visibility. At once, already aware that he was in severe icing conditions, he had decided upon making a precautionary landing, and seeing a suitable-looking field, had set up his approach. He had touched down successfully enough, but, like Pilot Officer Clifford at Disley, he too had encountered a telegraph pole in the course of his landing run. This had slewed him off into a ploughed field, badly damaging the aircraft but hurting none of his crew. A subsequent check on their position, however, had showed that while their track-keeping had been good, they had actually overflown Finningley by some 17 miles, having put down at Blyborough, in Lincolnshire.

Flying Officer John Gyll-Murray (in full Flying Officer John Edwin Campbell Gascoigne Flemyng Gyll-Murray), flying Heyford L5188, similarly made his way independently, but on letting down after the calculated lapse time and sighting the ground, found himself in the vicinity of York, the correct distance along track, but nearly thirty miles north of Finningley; a powerful indicator that a wind change had seriously upset his observer's calculations. Unfazed by this he pragmatically picked out a suitable field, let down, and made a successful landing; almost certainly then making a beeline for the nearest telephone.

At about the same time people on the ground at Moorside, to the north of Oldham, became aware that an aircraft – Heyford K4874, it would transpire, piloted by Flight Lieutenant Villiers – was circling in the clouds above them. The engine note went on for a good thirty minutes, during which time it became evident that the pilot was unable to find a break sufficient to show him the ground; it would also have indicated to the initiated that, having become uncertain of his position, Flight Lieutenant Villiers was not about to take the chance of descending blind. It is likely too, in view of the general weather pattern, that his aircraft was collecting a substantial amount of profile-spoiling ice on its lifting surfaces. The time came, therefore, when he gave the order to abandon, his three crew members taking to their parachutes in a disciplined fashion. The abandonment itself went well, but Leading Aircraftman John Mackan, the wireless operator, landed on a mill roof, and having divested himself of his parachute the better to slide further down, fell through a skylight and had to be hospitalised with a badly cut hand. Flight Lieutenant Villiers himself came down on the roof of a cottage and then fell off, breaking his leg. Another crew member, Leading Aircraftman Donald J.M. Keys, also had to be hospitalised with head injuries, but the fourth, presently unidentified, landed safely in the middle of a football field. Their abandoned Heyford, left to its own devices, lost height and crashed only yards from Dingle Farm, near Besom Hill Reservoir, impacting heavily and burning out. Press photographs of the burnt-out machine are graphic, but the fair prints have been disposed of and the extant copies are too blurred to usefully reproduce. Significantly, this aircraft, while only twelve miles off track, was forty miles short of Finningley when it crashed.

The crew of the final aircraft, K6900, were not as fortunate as any of the others. Piloted by Sergeant Victor Charles Otter, their aircraft too let down according to estimate, and emerged from the cloud rack, but into thick fog. Sergeant Otter at once levelled from his descent, and began to search out a landing site, only to fly into a steep hillside moments later.

Villagers a mile beyond Hebden Bridge, to the north-west of Halifax, who had heard the crash, hurried up the hill to lend assistance, but were hampered by the fog. When they eventually reached the scene it was to find that the aircraft had run on a hundred yards or so after striking but had then burst into flames and burnt out. Sergeant Otter was discovered to be alive, if injured, but the other three occupants had been killed: the observer, Sergeant D.G. Church; the fitter, Leading Aircraftman P.G Clements; and the wireless operator, Aircraftman C.V Bodenham. One of these, although which one is unspecified in the contemporary reports, had attempted to abandon, for his body, together with his partially streamed parachute, was found some way from the machine, suggesting that the aircraft, already heavy with ice, had been only marginally controllable and that an order to abandon might have been given. This aircraft too was reasonably on track, but some forty miles short of Finningley.

Of the dispersed aircraft, Heyfords K4868 and K5188 were flown back to base the next day. Nevertheless this was a debacle of the first order, and a setback to the Royal Air Force in the process, as it was, of building up its bomber force: indeed so great was the urgency of the build-up that six replacement aircraft were delivered to the squadron just three days later, on 12 December, 1936! It was a setback, however, from which lessons could be learned, and which spurred on the development of de-icing systems on large aircraft. Nor did it unduly affect the future of some, at least, of those pilots concerned. Certainly three of them survived the war, two achieving senior-officer status: Sergeant Biddulph rising to Squadron Leader, and Flight

Lieutenant Villiers to Wing Commander. Sergeant Otter, however, rose even higher, for he was commissioned in 1941 and had reached Squadron Leader by 1945 when he transferred to the technical branch. Progressing in that branch he reached Group Captain rank in 1956, and was then translated to air rank, to Air Commodore in 1962 and to Air Vice Marshal in 1967. Not too bad for a lowly Senior NCO pilot who, in 1936, could not even find his way from Ulster to Yorkshire.

In 2005 there was no visual evidence of the Disley setdown, and only Mr and Mrs Timothy and Miranda Johnson, owners of The Homestead – a vastly altered and strictly private property – were found who had any knowledge of the incident. Indeed it was Mrs Johnson who was able to advise that the photograph of the tail-high Heyford had for some years been displayed in one of the pubs in Disley.

There was rather more awareness of the Heyford descent near Oldham, however, for Mr Walter Taylor, of Button Hole, was able to point out the site where the aircraft had impacted and burnt out only yards from the erstwhile Dingle Farm, the full details of this Oldham crash being in *Peakland Air Crashes: The North*.

The general area of the setdowns by Heyfords K4868 and K6898 at Disley, viewed from Homesteads Farm in 2005 by the courtesy of Mrs Christine Grime

Klemm light aeroplane, Camp Hill Gliding Club, Great Hucklow

SK 17840 78833 407m (area of)
30 August, 1937

Pilot: Fraülein Eva Schmidt, uninjured

Following the post 1914–18 war ban on Germany building powered aircraft it was natural that air-minded Germans like Herr Wolf Hirth should turn to the development of gliding. In August 1937, as a pioneer in soaring, likewise in aerial launching and towing, he made an English tour to promote the two-seat version of his Miminosa glider, visiting, in the process, the Camp Hill Gliding Club at Great Hucklow where the British National Gliding Championships were being held. Travelling as members of his party were Fraüleins Eva Schmidt and Hanna Reitsch, each a celebrated aviatrix in her own right, with Fraülein Schmidt using a Klemm light aeroplane as transport, launcher and aerial tug. On 30 August 1937, however, the day before the group were due to leave again, Fraülein Schmidt, having flown off to refuel with the required petrol–benzole mixture, struck the remnants of a drystone-wall field division in the operating area, damaging the Klemm.

Camp Hill Gliding Club, Great Hucklow

This was not the last time a wall rump left when volunteers set out to open up the original farm fields was to cause an accident, for in 1943 a Miles Master would be more severely damaged after touchdown. Indeed, even in 2006 veteran club members still remembered the hazard represented by such remnants before they were finally cleared. Back in 1937, however, the Klemm was hangared while the

German crew, assisted by the club engineer, repaired the damage and successfully got their machine away on time.

The third pilot-member of the party, Fraülein Hanna Reitsch, very nearly made a return visit to Camp Hill in 1954. In the interim she had proved the efficacy of barrage balloon cables by deliberately flying into them, and had test flown machines as diverse as pioneer helicopters, the prototype V1 pulse-jet flying bomb, the rocket-powered Messerschmitt Me.163 and the jet-propelled Messerschmitt Me.262. She had been promoted to *Luftwaffe Flugkapitan* (captain) and awarded the Iron Cross and *Luftwaffe* Diamond Clasp. However, she had been, throughout, an enthusiastic supporter of Hitler, and this led to visa difficulties. Just the same, the holder of forty aviation records, she was subsequently welcomed on a tour of the United States, where a 2005 member of the Great Hucklow club met her, so closing the circle.

Hanna Reitsch

Lancaster, Townend Farm, Buxton (spurious)

SK 07502 73999 333m.

The source for this, almost certainly spurious, incident is an enthusiast's list of air crashes that correctly recorded some relatively obscure locations. In this instance, however, site visits and a diligent canvass of the area turned up no supporting evidence. Indeed, even the Groom family, in 2006 domiciled in Cirencester, but who owned Townend Farm from 1952, repudiated the report. It is included here, therefore, to obviate fruitless searches in the future, but also to cover all bets in keeping the report on record for posterity.

Lancaster site, Townend Farm (spurious)

Lysander V9577, Whaley Bridge (probably spurious)

Taken from the same enthusiast's list, nothing positive was forthcoming regarding this incident, either. Moreover, this particular Lysander is authoritatively recorded in the *Air Britain* series as having enjoyed an accident-free record throughout its span of service. Again, the record is included here for posterity.

Miles Magister Mk.1 L6908, Chapel-en-le-Frith High School grounds

SK 05313 30224 242m
No.16 Elementary Flying Training School, RAF Burnaston,
Derby, No.51 Group, Flying Training Command
27 August, 1941

Pilot: slightly injured:
Leading Aircraftman Muirhead, pupil pilot

On 27 August, 1941, pupil pilot Leading Aircraftman Muirhead, having logged twenty-three hours solo on the Magister, was dispatched from RAF Burnaston on a general-handling detail built around practising steep turns. It would seem, however, that he wandered somewhat, for some time later, lost and attempting a forced landing in a field at what was then Marsh Green Farm, Chapel-en-le-Frith, some thirty miles from Burnaston, he hit a tree and crashed, damaging his aircraft and slightly injuring himself.

In 2005 Mr George Barratt, formerly the incumbent of Marsh Green Farm, was able to point out this site, by then part of the grounds of the Chapel-en-le-Frith High School, and to show too, the route used to take away the wreckage by Queen Mary low-loader.

Above: Mr George Barratt, witness, then of Marsh Green Farm

The RAF accident report on this incident attributes the cause to the pupil pilot being lost and damaging his aeroplane in the course of forced landing. Unfortunately no details of pupil pilot Muirhead's subsequent career have come to light, although the indications are that he survived the war.

The tree line was still extant in 2006, but the terminal impact site had long since been landscaped to form a shrubbery between the railway embankment and the High School car park. The playing-fields area was also chosen for a setdown by another trainer in 1942: see the Lower Crossings narrative in this volume of the series.

The pilot approached parallel to where the cars above are aligned but struck the tree line and was swung off left, to impact just below the railway embankment

The terminal crash site of Magister L6909, beside the railway embankment, but at a level now swallowed beneath the landscaping of Chapel-en-le-Frith High School

Miles Magister Mk.1 N3811, Snitterton (west of Matlock)

SK 27830 60498 74m
No.16 Elementary Flying Training School, RAF Burnaston, Derby, No.51 Group, Flying Training Command
31 July, 1940

Pilot: solo, uninjured:
Leading Aircraftman K.P. Glassborow

On 31 July, 1940, Leading Aircraftman K.P. Glassborow, a pupil pilot with under fifty hours' flying experience, realised that he was lost during a solo general-handling detail and decided to make a precautionary landing. Several fields presented themselves to him but he had difficulty in making his choice for most were obstructed by 'anti-invasion' posts and ditches. Perhaps this unsettled him, because although the field he eventually chose was reasonably suited to the purpose, the downhill slope caused him to overrun and strike a low drystone wall. The damage the machine sustained meant that it had to be hauled away by road. LAC Glassborow, however, was unhurt.

Mr Harold Petts, witness, Snitterton

In June 2005 Mr Harold Petts, who was born in 1919 and farmed in the Snitterton area for much of his working life, was able to pinpoint where the setdown had occurred. 'I was working up at Masson Farm when the plane came down,' he explained, 'so I didn't see it arrive. But the pilot had been lost and evidently decided to land near a big house which was likely to have a telephone, only he ran into a drystone wall.' He reflected. 'When I saw the plane it was sitting in the first of Major Bagshaw's fields just beyond Snitterton Hall, and facing downhill. I don't know that we were allowed near it. But I remember that the chap who had Hall Farm at the time, a Mr Farmer, took the sentry a drink, and told us later, "The bloke had such a strange dialect that I couldn't make out a word he was saying." A day or two later, however, I saw them take the plane away, when the long low-loader had a lot of trouble getting past the sharp corner at the Bull Ring. Then my sister saw it entering Matlock, and having to be snaked along the road there to get through.'

He thought back. 'After the plane was taken away we heard nothing more about it, but of course you didn't in those days.' Then he smiled. 'My memory isn't bad, but it takes a while to get going. After all, I've been to bed a time or two since ...'

This incident, then, is one of the many relatively innocuous setdowns that occurred in the area when courses on elementary flying training were being forced through at a hitherto unprecedented rate. Not that it would have seemed innocuous to Leading Aircraftman

From the terminal area, looking back towards touchdown; Snitterton Hall is out of shot, to the left

Glassborow, for only after he found himself able to walk away from the machine would his fears of the initial outcome be allayed. And even then, it has to be remembered, he was a volunteer, as all aircrew candidates had to be, and therefore keen to succeed. Whereas now he had to explain his aircraft's presence in a field some twenty-three miles away from where he should have set it down. Notwithstanding which, such a mishap would almost certainly have been viewed with understanding. Unfortunately nothing is known of LAC Glassborow's future career.

As might be expected, the site showed no sign of the incident by 2006, but walkers frequently passed the spot, for two public footpaths led through the field.

Miles Master Mk.1 T8324, Upper Burbage Bridge (near Hathersage)

SK 25803 80805 320m
No.5 Elementary Flying Training School, RAF Ternhill, Market Drayton,
No.21 Group, Flying Training Command
26 March, 1941

Pupil pilot: killed:
Leading Aircraftman Edward John Marsland Atherton, RAF Volunteer Reserve

On 26 March, 1941, pupil pilot Leading Aircraftman Edward Atherton was dispatched from No.5 Elementary Flying Training School, RAF Ternhill, having been briefed to carry out a solo navigational exercise. At some stage he became uncertain of his position, and entering cloud, wandered off his planned, and approved, course into a hilly area, after which he struck the high moorland to the north-east of Hathersage. The aircraft was destroyed by fire and Leading Aircraftman Atherton killed.

In mid-2005 Mr Robert Stamper, of Hathersage, recalled, 'We had a succession of policemen billeted upon us to work with our regular PC, Ron Kirby, who lived with his wife in the police house. So when news came that this trainer had crashed, Rip – as we called him – told off the one we had at the time, either PC Gateskill or PC Fraser, to bike up and mount guard on it. But when the chap came back he was very upset. The plane having burnt out, it seems, a mortician from Sheffield had set his mallet-wielding assistant to straighten out the blackened body of the pilot. But what they regarded as an everyday process was altogether too much for our lodger. There was nothing he could do, however, but grit it out, and get on with standing guard duty.' Mr Stamper paused, and reflected. 'The wreckage was soon cleared, although I can't remember going up there myself. Possibly I was still too young to go wandering off that far.'

The crash site of Master T8324 in 2005, showing the water gauge

Mr Kenneth Wilson, of Greenwood Farm, on the other hand, not only remembered walking to visit the crash site as a lad but also discussing it with author Ron Collier many years later. 'The aircraft', he explained, 'had crashed between the railed-off 1927-vintage water gauge and the Edge, just yards into the moor, and may well have burned, but there were pieces of tubing, and the like, which I took for souvenirs and kept for ages, though they've long gone. But only about ten years ago, in the mid-nineties, I went back there when the heather was low, and there were still pieces sprinkling the ground.'

Mr Wilson, too, remembered the Hathersage police presence in the shape of the redoubtable PC Kirby. 'He'd carry home eggs from the farms in his helmet,' he smiled. 'And when some Germans had gone missing from Lodge Moor prisoner-of-war camp, he checked a barn, and seeing their feet protruding from the hay, had the farmer march them down to the police house with his shotgun. Then, after the army had collected them, he confiscated the gun because the farmer lacked the proper wartime licence.'

Mr Stamper, for his part, was able to provide a photograph vividly portraying wartime Hathersage, showing him among a group of Hathersage schoolchildren scrabbling about in one of the three bomb craters along the Sheffield Road. (Bombs held locally, as ever, to have been jettisoned by a fleeing German bomber which was then shot down into the sea.)

Schoolboy Robert Stamper (right-hand lad, front row) and friends, in one of the German bomb craters at SK 23500 814500 (Photograph by courtesy of Mr Robert Stamper)

Miles Master Mk.3 W8761, Camp Hill Farm, Great Hucklow

SK 17840 78833 407m (approximate terminal area)
No.16 (Polish) Service Flying Training School, RAF Newton, No.21 Group, Flying Training Command
21 March, 1943

Occupants: pupil and instructor, unhurt, Polish Air Force under RAF Command:
Flight Lieutenant Edward Suszynski
Sergeant Henryk Raczkowski

On 21 March, 1943, Flight Lieutenant Edward Suszynski, an instructor with the Polish Air Force under RAF Command, stationed at the Polish Elementary Flying School at RAF Newton, was authorised to carry out a formation exercise with his pupil, Sergeant Henryk Raczkowski. Instructor and pupil were to lead two solo aircraft, and duly took off in Master W8761 at 1545 hours. The exercise seems to have been uneventful until, after an hour or so, the trio ran into cloudy conditions with poor visibility below. At which stage the two formating aircraft became detached, and Flight Lieutenant Suszynski was unable to effect a rejoin.

In common with many of the Poles under RAF Command, Flight Lieutenant Suszynski had been a regular officer in the Polish Air Force. Indeed he had over eleven hundred hours' total flying with nearly six hundred on type; nevertheless, having realised that he had lost his formation, he then realised that he had also lost himself.

For some time he and his pupil searched downwards for a landmark. And an hour and a half after getting airborne they glimpsed not only a windsock, but a hangar belonging, it would transpire, to a hilltop gliding club. Loth to miss this chance of putting down, Flight Lieutenant Suszynski dived through the gap, and hurriedly lowering his undercarriage, set up an approach. However, it would seem that in his haste, he overshot, and towards the end of the landing run, and approaching the very edge of a plateau, struck the remnants of a drystone wall with one wing, so that the Master tipped onto its nose.

Neither occupant was hurt but the aircraft was too badly damaged to repair on site, and eventually had to be taken away by road.

The investigation found that the instructor had been guilty of an error of judgement in allowing his pupil to lead the formation having encountered poor visibility conditions: 'Only instructors allowed to lead in bad weather.' And yet, allowing the pupil to lead would have left the instructor free to concentrate on the navigation. It has to be assumed, therefore, that the pupil was known to have handled the controls rather too harshly at some stage, possibly when the formation was flying in echelon – that is, with the two followers strung out to one side. This would have meant that when the pupil nearest the leader lost contact both formating pupils would have been dropped. After which the cloud conditions made it virtually impossible to reform, especially as it is highly unlikely that inter-formation radio communication was in use.

The criticism levelled against Flight Lieutenant Suszynski notwithstanding, it would seem that, overall, the incident was accepted as a hazard attendant upon formation flying training, particularly as both solo pupils returned safely to base. Certainly the only recommendation made was by the unit's chief instructor who advised Flight Lieutenant Suszynski to take more care in teaching formation flying.

Flight Lieutenant Suszynski completed his stint on instructing eight months later and then moved onto twin-engined Operational Training Units. He converted to Blenheims and then to Mosquitoes before being posted to No.305 (Wielpolska) Squadron in May 1944. But on 11 July, 1944, he was reported missing in action – and subsequently presumed killed – in the course of a ground-attack operation in Northern France. By then, however, he had been awarded the Polish Silver Cross with Swords (the fifth grade of the *Virtuti Militari*, Poland's senior award for bravery), and the Cross for Valour. He left a widow, domiciled in Poznan, back in occupied Poland.

His erstwhile pupil, Sergeant Raczkowski, successfully gained his wings and was subsequently posted to various fighter-equipped squadrons. Initially he joined No.308 (Kraków) Squadron on Spitfires, then No.679 Squadron, operating Hurricanes on Army Co-operation duties, and finally No.302 (Poznanski) Squadron, again on Spitfires. He survived the war, having been awarded the Polish Air Force Medal, and left the Polish Air Force in 1947, three years after his promotion to Warrant Officer. Following the normal course of Poles who decided to remain in Britain, rather than return to their then-communist dominated homeland, he trained in the Polish Resettlement Corps before being finally demobilised in January 1949. After which, having married, he settled in Lancashire with Josephine, his English wife.

By 2006 Camp Hill Farm had long since been incorporated in the Hucklow Gliding Club, and the many drystone walls which marred the outer bounds of the landing site at the time – and which so upset the runout of the Master (and also a Klemm in 1937) – had long since been removed. Just the same, veteran Gliding Club members, pointing out the area where they had been, and therefore where the impact had probably occurred, advised that traces of them had been evident for many years after that.

Great Hucklow
Gliding Club

Miles Master Mk.3 W8455, King Sterndale (south-east of Buxton)

SK 09625 71497 247m
No.5 (Pilots) Advanced Flying Unit, RAF Ternhill (near Market Drayton), No.21 Group, Flying Training Command
12 October, 1942

Pilot: survived forced landing:
Sergeant F.J. Flower

In the early 1940s the Miles Master made an ideal stepping stone from the basic trainers to the more advanced fighter types, for although slower than the Hurricanes and Spitfires it shared many of the lively handling characteristics of the first-line duo. Yet with the heightened performance came the necessity for the pupil pilot to be equally up to the mark, the Master's cruising speed of 170 mph (148 knots) swallowing up the ground considerably more rapidly than did the 93 mph (81 knots) of the Tiger Moth or even the 123 mph (107 knots) of the Magister. Accordingly, when pupil pilot Sergeant Flower was dispatched on a general map-reading exercise from the Advanced Flying Training Unit at RAF Ternhill, near Market Drayton, Shropshire, he was briefed to remain within fifteen miles of the airfield.

Not, one might have thought, an altogether practical restriction given such a high-performance machine, which, even at a cruise, would eat up fifteen miles in under four minutes. Certainly it was a restriction that proved too much for Sergeant Flower, for at midday, two hours after getting airborne, finding himself hopelessly lost, and with his fuel tanks virtually dry, he set about making a forced landing at a spot just south-east of Buxton, and some forty miles adrift.

2005, Mr Joe Lomas, of King Sterndale

In 2005 Farmer Joe Lomas, of King Sterndale, whose land Sergeant Flower chose for his approach, and who had arrived on the scene shortly after the event, was able to piece together the actual touchdown. 'He came from the south-east,' he said, 'just cleared the gorge of Deep Dale, and landed uphill on our Footpath Field. It was a relatively smooth grass field – and there were no power cables then – but he obviously struck quite hard and bounced, for wherever he had touched the ground the propeller had churned out great grooves. Then the wingtips broke off, followed by the tail, and just before the plane stopped, the engine – one of the big radials – fell off.' He pondered. 'When dad and I got there the RAF still hadn't arrived, but a succession of villagers came to look. Although I never did see the pilot.'

Miss Freda Hamilton, of nearby Cowdale, however, was able to account for that. 'No, for our vicar, the Reverend Robert Main and his wife, were among the first on the scene and took him home to the Vicarage and fed him tea until the authorities came for him.'

It is to be hoped that Sergeant Flower enjoyed the tea, for he would have found the subsequent inquiry far less enjoyable. His commanding officer, while taking into account the bad visibility that had made flying conditions difficult, and noting that the pupil pilot had less than two hundred hours' total flying, and only five hours on Masters, recommended that the sergeant's flying log book be endorsed 'Carelessness and disobedience'. The Ternhill station commander, next highest up the chain of command, was even harsher, and clearly wishing to make the case that his subordinates had placed restrictions upon the flight – so clearing him – restated the fifteen miles limitation, fulminating, 'A stupid, careless, error of judgement'.

For all that, the forced landing itself had not been too badly done, the sergeant having clearly judged his approach to achieve his 85 mph (74 knots) landing speed, for he had put his wheels down a sensible distance up the field. Albeit that things had, quite literally, come to pieces rather after that, almost certainly because the rising ground – appearing flat from the air – had caused him to underestimate the degree of nose-up round out required. At least he had not tumbled backwards into Deep Dale, and in walking away from the wreck instead, had lived to fight another day. As one must hope he did, although his subsequent record is not known.

In early 2006 there was nothing to be seen at the site of the forced landing become crash-landing. Indeed, as Mr Lomas had explained a year earlier, 'The RAF dragged the wreckage up to the road and took it off on a low-loader. They had to take down a few walls, which they then rebuilt. But they didn't leave anything that I ever saw. Just the marks the propeller made, which were visible for years afterwards, although even those have long since been ploughed out.'

The touchdown area, looking upslope towards the Vicarage

Looking back over Deep Dale, with equally rising, but seemingly flat, fields beyond

Gloster Meteor TMk.8 WE904, Millthorpe (south-west of Dronfield)

SK 31722 76331 141m
No.211 Flying Training School, RAF Worksop, No.25
Group, Flying Training Command
12 May, 1955

Pilot: killed:
Pilot Officer Robert Anthony Tritton

The Meteor TMk.7 trainer entered RAF service in December 1948 and with its tandem seating and closely framed cockpit – and no ejector seat – served to introduce trainee pilots to jets until the mid-1950s, when the role was taken over by the Vampire. Another Meteor trainer also saw limited service, however, the unofficially-classified TMk.8, a modified F Mk.8 single-seater fighter which was used as an advanced trainer. No.211 Flying Training School at RAF Worksop was one those which had the type on its establishment and on 12 May, 1955, one of its trainees was detailed to fly Meteor TMk.8 WE904.

As an advanced pupil Pilot Officer Robert Tritton was briefed by his instructor to carry out a solo medium-level exercise in the course of which he would practise 'Homings and Controlled-Descents through Cloud', although, in this instance, merely simulating the cloud. The latter point being significant, for his instrument rating had been gained on piston-engined aircraft, and as he had not yet taken a formal instrument-rating test on jet trainers, his general briefing was that he should steer clear of actual cloud.

This recovery and let-down procedure, then the most common method of bringing an aircraft down through cloud, entailed it being passed instructions from a ground controller using direction-finding equipment, the pilot simply following instructions.

The aircraft, flying at operating altitude (typically either 20,000 feet or 10,000 feet), would first be homed to the overhead, then turned onto a safe heading away from the airfield, and descended to a specified height. Next, roughly halfway to this height, it would be turned inbound again, continuing its descent until it broke cloud and the pilot declared that he was in visual contact with the airfield.

The long-titled procedure was more succinctly known as a 'QGH', the tri-letter group being one of aviation's several survivors from the 'Q' brevity-code employed when most airborne communication was by wireless-telegraphy, and the ploddingly-protracted morse code. There were, however, two distinct types of QGH: a high-level, and a medium-level procedure, each differing somewhat, but most relevantly here in the height band within which the aircraft was operating when it was commenced. Pilot Officer Tritton had been briefed to practise the medium-level approach, starting at the 10,000 feet level.

After take-off Pilot Officer Tritton elected to clear from the airfield in a westerly climb. The next call to be expected from him would have been his declaration that he was at 10,000 feet and requesting a QGH. However, six minutes after departure he transmitted instead the confirmatory safety call, 'Oxygen checked', a necessary advisory with jet aircraft climbing so swiftly into more rarefied air, but only required when climbing through 20,000 feet to a higher level.

That Pilot Officer Tritton should make this call would hardly have been held a matter of import to those in the control tower, for nobody there would necessarily have known the precise terms of his briefing. Even the duty instructor, stationed alongside the air traffic controller for his term of office, would have assumed that the pupil's instructor had briefed him to carry out several practice QGH procedures, some high-level, some medium. However, just seven minutes after take-off, Pilot Officer Tritton's machine dived vertically into the ground and exploded, killing him instantly.

What had caused the unfortunate pupil pilot to crash had to be a matter of speculation, but despite his procedurally-correct oxygen safety call, his having passed out through lack of oxygen could not be totally ruled out.

The cause aside, however, witnesses saw the aircraft emerge from cloud in a near-vertical dive, but then recover somewhat, only to roll into a steeply banked turn and crash. This was testimony which aided the subsequent court of inquiry to find that Pilot Officer Tritton had run into cloud at high level, become disorientated, and lost control, thereafter entering a near-vertical dive from which, burdened by inexperience, he had been unable to recover.

Only then the inquiry rather harshly plumped for condemnation, for it recorded that in climbing above his briefed height the pupil had disobeyed instructions. And yet he was a pupil, and less severe appointees to the court might have taken the view that he had merely got the two types of QGH mixed in his mind, and had been mistakenly aiming for the high-level version. After all, he had faithfully transmitted his safety call, in effect, openly declaring that he was climbing through 20,000 feet: hardly the action of a pupil deliberately flouting his briefed instructions!

But the climate of blame extended beyond the pupil, for while concurring with the disobedience charge, higher authority directed that both Pilot Officer Tritton's flight commander and his flying instructor be reproved for their failure to properly supervise him.

More productively, perhaps, it was noted that, for a pupil at his stage of training, Pilot Officer Tritton's solo flying had exceeded his dual — that is, his supervised — flights by such a margin as to cast doubt on the acceptability of the currently allocated balance between the two. It was also observed that too little time had been devoted to instrument flying. Presumably these aspects of training, by which pupils were put at unnecessary risk through insufficient supervision and instruction, were promptly addressed.

In crashing, the aircraft had dived vertically into a barn adjacent to Brookside Farm, just north of the ford, in the village of Millthorpe, as the farm's incumbent at the time, Mr John Knight, attested. 'Although it's so long ago now,' he said soberly, 'it's as if it happened yesterday.' He paused, then mused reflectively, 'That poor young man!'

Mr Knight had heard the aircraft pass above him, 'Its engines sounding odd', but then almost at once approach again. 'It was a drizzly day,' he recalled, 'and I was just leading my toddler son, young John, into the barn – he must have been two or three then. In fact, I'd just reached up to push the door inwards when the aircraft arrived.'

Again he sobered, and with wonder yet in his tone, continued, 'Then there was no barn, just the door, and the stone surround! Behind me to the right, the house roof had mostly gone. Behind to the left, all the other barns were wrecked and roofless. And John and I were just left there, with not a mark on us.'

2005, and Mr John Knight, on a less sombre occasion, indicates the site of the barn. On 12 May, 1955, leading his toddler son by the hand, he reached for the barn door ...

Evidently, in that interim split-second as he reached for the door, the Meteor had plunged near-vertically through the barn roof, burying itself so deeply that the ensuing explosion had initially been contained at low level.

But as the blast had surged outwards above Mr Knight's head not a structure in the immediate vicinity had escaped! Even trees had suffered, some where the aircraft itself had sliced through, others having been struck by rotating components from the engines which had sprung upwards from the crater, one embedding itself in a trunk, another decapitating a crown before burying itself in a meadow 400 yards off, with a third missing other trees but scything its way through both walls of a second stone barn to fall just short of the main road.

Yet not an animal had been lost!

'As the roof of a cowshed was blown off,' Mr Knight smiled, recalling that scene of near-total destruction, 'the main supporting roof beam had fallen down across the brick-built separating compartments, but we found that each cow had simply lowered its back. Then a neighbour arrived and led all twelve away to his place for safe keeping. As for the pig pen, that had gone, and the three pregnant sows in it had panicked from the yard and up to that wood.' He pointed to a distant hilltop. 'Yet as they reached their normal terms each gave birth to a healthy litter.'

Compressor disc, buried in a tree (By courtesy of the *Derby Evening Telegraph*)

The cross adjacent to Brookside Farmhouse (on the left) marks the location of the erstwhile barn into which Meteor TMk.8 WE904 plunged

He parted his hands to represent the erstwhile barn door. 'On this side there was a calf. On the other, there was an old cinnamon mill standing on its box, with the door raised. Well, the calf was blown from its stall, across the barn, and into the box. But then the lid fell shut. Just the same, two days later, when we finally realised where it was, the calf was alive and well.'

He recalled too the RAF assessor ('They were all charming people'), on the spot within two hours, pressing him even amid the chaos for his estimate of the damage; and officialdom subsequently refusing to pay for rebuilding in stone, but only in the cheaper brick. Then there was the RAF salvage crew. 'They loaded the débris into this vehicle they called a "Queen Mary" and which completely filled the road! But people were picking up metal – aluminium, I suppose – for years afterwards.'

He recalled too, the visit by the trainee pilot's relatives ...

In 2006, only the trees bore scars, and those were much muted. For the ground gave no sign of what once happened on the spot. On the contrary, Brookside Farm had become very much a private residence; the barn site had become an adjoining private property; and the farm's onetime wilderness orchard had been tastefully and extensively landscaped into an idyllic, country-village garden.

The tragedy had not been forgotten, however, for a village group had positioned a memorial to the hapless Pilot Officer Tritton adjacent to the village well; although, for some reason, choosing to give most prominence to the date of their own involvement, fifty years on.

Memorial (SK 31741 76435)

Another former barn, pierced through (at 'X')
by a jet-engine compressor

Gloster Meteor Mk.8 WE916, Silkstone Road, Frecheville (Sheffield south-east)

SK 40477 83801 127m
No.211 Flying Training School, RAF Worksop, No.25 Group, Flying Training Command
26 May, 1955

Pilot: killed:
Pilot Officer John Alexander Cohen

Pilot Officer John Cohen, a pupil pilot at No.112 Flying Training School at RAF Worksop, had logged a total of something under 300 flying hours, dual and solo, including about 50 hours on Meteors, when he was authorised to carry out a night training sortie. In the course of his flying training he had been assessed as 'Average'– that is, perfectly satisfactory – and had already proved his ability to fly with reference to instruments alone, having acquired a White instrument rating card. This was a significant step up from the Basic instrument rating; indeed it was the working instrument rating for many first-line squadron fighter pilots of the day who never spent long enough in cloud to claim the Green or Master Green ratings. Just the same, Pilot Officer Cohen had only flown the Meteor for some five hours at night.

Having got airborne at 2300 hours he settled in with some circuit work, touching down and then getting airborne again without stopping. Next he climbed up to 20,000 feet, as briefed, to carry out a high-level controlled descent through cloud, a cloud-break procedure designed to keep him clear of all high ground during his descent while putting him into a position from which he could see the airfield, then visually join the circuit and land. The cloud conditions on this particular occasion, layered to 12,000 feet with a base of some 1,500 feet, meant that the procedure would be, for the most part, a real cloud-break procedure rather than a merely simulated one.

Pilot Officer Cohen climbed to height, and having been airborne for some fifteen minutes, called for the homing which began the procedure. Worksop's air traffic control descended him to 18,000 feet while bringing him to their overhead, then turned him onto the safe lane which ran slightly north of west (290° magnetic). Now heading away from Worksop, he was cleared to descend to 10,000 feet where he would make the left-hand inbound *descending* turn called for by the high-level procedure and designed to carry him back towards Worksop once again. Pilot Officer Cohen acknowledged this instruction and indicated that he was commencing his rapid-rate descent. As expected, getting on for two minutes later he advised that he was approaching 10,000 feet and turning left. This was acknowledged by the controller, so that the next call expected was Pilot Officer Cohen's confirmation that he had stopped his turn and was now descending on the easterly heading passed him (100° magnetic) as his initial course for Worksop. When no such confirmation was received the controller began calling Pilot Officer Cohen. Except that there was no reply, although the calls were continued until the news was received that the aircraft had crashed.

It was discovered that, moments after his last transmission, Pilot Officer Cohen's Meteor, still some thirty degrees off its assigned inbound heading, and still in a steep descent, had plunged into open farmland in a suburb of Sheffield and exploded fierily in a deep crater. Pilot Officer Cohen had not attempted to (manually) abandon his aircraft and had been killed on impact.

The investigation proffered the cause of the accident as loss of control during the descending left-hand turn, a quite demanding, and potentially disorientating manoeuvre when done at a rapid rate of descent, on instruments, at night, and almost certainly, in this instance, in cloud. However, as the holder of a White instrument rating, it should have been well within Pilot Officer Cohen's capabilities. Therefore all the senior officers in turn, the Worksop station commander, the Air Officer Commanding the Group, and the Air Officer Commanding in Chief, expressed the opinion that there was not evidence enough to determine the cause of the accident, and further, that no responsibility could be fixed. Not a satisfactory result, but the best that could be arrived at.

The aircraft had, it transpired, plunged into farmland at the end of Silkstone Road, Frecheville, startling many people who had stayed up late listening to the election results in which Anthony Eden had been returned. Others, woken by the sound of the crash, were thrown into alarm. One, a St John's Ambulance man, leaped from his bed, hurriedly wrapped a macintosh around himself, and ran from his house to help, to discover nothing but a smoking, twelve-foot deep crater from which the pilot's body would later be recovered.

Left: 2005, Mrs Ivy
Potts, witness

Far Left: 2005, looking
towards the crash site
from Silkstone Road

Impact point

In 2005 Mr James Hill points out the location

The impact crater (Photograph by courtesy of Crown Copyright)

Meteor WE916, the crash scene, short of the gully, facing the Glade and Jermyn areas (Photograph by courtesy of Crown Copyright)

The crash site in 2006, with matured vegetation obstructing a closer photo-match, particularly to the left

In 2006 many people approached in the area had never heard of the accident, but Mrs Ivy Potts, still of Silkstone Road, remembered the night vividly. 'It was gone eleven, and we were in bed,' she recalled, 'when we heard this screeching sound, like a bomb coming down. Then there came a terrible crash. We both ran downstairs, and from our front door we could see these flames in the fields at the bottom of the road.' She gestured down the road towards the corner. 'Of course, there were no houses then, the road finished at the junction with Silkstone Crescent, and there were no trees and bushes. My husband joined the people already running down there, but he found there was nothing to be done. Fortunately, working in the mines, he was used to gruesome sights, so what he saw didn't upset him unduly. But, of course, the poor young man was killed. And some days later his parents came to see where he had died: it was all very tragic.' And in another facet of the tragedy *The Times* recorded that Pilot Officer Cohen had recently signed as wicketkeeper and batsman for Glamorgan!

Mr James William Hill, also of Silkstone Road, who had spent four wartime years in Burma, separated from his fiancé and working on an earlier generation of fighter aircraft, on Spitfires and Hurricanes, was able to point out the site. 'I didn't see it for some time after the crash,' he observed, 'but the area's quite different now, for it was good pasture then, with none of this undergrowth.'

In mid-2006, with shrubs and brambles masking the ground, nothing was to be seen of the crash dive that had claimed the jet pilot's life, but a dog-walker's footpath still led within yards of where the crater had been.

Gloster Meteor Mk.8 VW267, Todwick, Sheffield

SK 48572 84100 97m
No.92 Squadron, RAF Linton-on-Ouse, Fighter Command
14 May, 1950

Pilot: solo, killed:
Squadron Leader Raymond Hiley Harries, Distinguished Service Order and Bar, Distinguished
Flying Cross and two bars

Mr Les Waller, Todwick

Corporal Les Gibson, of
Wales

On 14 May, 1950, Squadron Leader Raymond Hiley Harries took
off in Meteor VW267 to return to Linton-on-Ouse from Biggin Hill,
where he had been a guest of the officers' mess. In the course of the
flight he ran out of fuel, and was killed when his aircraft crashed at
Todwick ['todd-ick'], near Sheffield, after he had failed in his bid to
manually abandon. It became clear to the investigators summoned
to the scene that, once Squadron Leader Harries had left the cockpit,
his parachute canopy had become entangled with the tailplane.
Indeed, a Royal Observer Corps (ROC) post in Nottinghamshire
had reported a Meteor passing overhead in a shallow dive with its
pilot dangling in its wake. The unmanned – but banefully encumbered
– aircraft eventually dived into fields beside a copse at Todwick, locally
known as The Meadows, or alternatively The Oscars, and was seen,
in its last few moments of flight by, among others, Mr Les Waller, in
late-2005 a parish councillor.

'We were returning', Mr Waller explained, 'with a load of asbestos
which I'd begged for a local community project from the redundant
RAF radar station nearby. We heard this jet coming, and just as we
turned in towards the park so it dived out of the sky straight into a
field. It exploded in flames on impact and there were bits everywhere,
all across the field, some very gruesome. But close though we had
been, the police got to the scene before we did. They kept us well
back, and then the RAF arrived.'

Mr Len Gibson, in 2006, of nearby Wales, proved to have had an
even more intimate association with the crash. 'At the time,' he
recalled, 'I was a corporal with No.64 Maintenance Unit, RAF
Rufforth, and engaged in crash-recovery duties. On that Sunday
afternoon I was returning from a liaison visit to Air Ministry when I
was taken from the train and driven straight to the Todwick site. I
was told not to worry about accommodation, that my billet had been
fixed.' He smiled at his wife, Margaret. 'And he's still here, all these
years later,' she smiled back, then recounted her own experience of
the crash. 'I was making bread, and had just taken the loaf from the oven when the Meteor
crashed. And the "whoompf!" and the concussion made me throw the lot into the air! But it
was worse for my friends, John and Cynthia Thompson, who were courting at the time, and
were on the main Wales road when the aircraft flew overhead, for when they ran across the
fields towards it they came upon one of the pilot's legs.'

Mr Gibson nodded. 'Once at the site I found that the aircraft had impacted in quite a shallow
dive, finishing up with its nose semi-buried and both wings fragmented. There was no cockpit
canopy, the parachute was tangled around the tail, and it was clear from the state of the pilot's
body that he had been out of the cockpit at the time of the crash. It was a hideous scenario, even
though our medical officer reckoned he would have been, at best, in and out of consciousness.'

'Yet local people', Mrs Gibson put in, 'used to believe that the pilot had been trying to climb back aboard up the lines of the parachute.'

Mr Gibson was then able to supply a first-hand picture of the work of RAF salvage and recovery crews between 1946 and 1956. 'In this case', he explained, 'we used a Coles Crane to pull out the concertinaed wreckage, being very careful when we got to the cockpit, for that was where we were most likely to find clues. Here, it was evident that the pilot had been on a "jolly", for jammed down beside the seat we found golf clubs and balls, and golf shoes, all damaged. Although we customarily looked for and reported anything that seemed out of place. In fact, our task was wide-ranging, for we didn't only categorise crashed machines but also carried out a variety of repairs, although big jobs would be taken to the maintenance unit at St Athan. Our official brief was to make no statements to the press at all, but unofficially the line was, "Tell them anything; just get rid of them." Regarding clearing the sites, if aircraft parts had buried themselves over twenty feet deep we could get permission to leave them, otherwise our responsibility was to clear up every bit of metal, taking particular care if the land was to be grazed upon. It was the team leader's responsibility to liaise with landowners and obtain a clearance certificate to show that their land had been fairly restored. He'd do all the paperwork, arranging compensation and the like.'

And the conveniently arranged billet? 'Strange as it's seemed since,' Mr Gifford confessed, 'the whole week I was in the house I didn't even notice their daughter ... not until I'd left ...' At which his wife gave a quiet chuckle.

The crash, as a non-operational accident, had an especial irony in that Squadron Leader Harries, a pilot with some 1,700 hours' experience, had begun his flying career in the Battle of Britain and then survived four years of operational flying, downing a total of 24 enemy aircraft and gaining for himself the Distinguished Service Order and bar, the Distinguished Flying Cross and two bars, and the *Croix de Guerre* from both the French and the Belgians.

In view of Squadron Leader Harries' illustrious record it was doubly unfortunate that the court of inquiry had no option but to be uncomplimentary, unequivocally finding that the primary cause of the crash had been a 'lack of firm pre-flight briefing by [the] pilot'. For Squadron Leader Harries had embarked upon a thirty-five minute flight with fuel enough for just forty minutes, and, not having assimilated that the destination homer was unserviceable, had then steered a heading which took him significantly left of the track for Church Fenton: the crash site was fifteen miles off that track. He had, of course, expected to be flying at high altitude, except that the oxygen bottles had not been topped up before departure. Then again, he had known before take-off that a critical channel on his radio was unserviceable. Just the same, having been airborne for 39 minutes, at which time he was flying at just 6,000 feet, a height at which a jet engine would simply guzzle its paraffin fuel supply, he did manage to advise Church Fenton that he was baling out due to lack of fuel. In fact, the picture that emerges of this tragic flight lends credence to the story, apparently current among the members of the crash team at the time, that the officers' mess at Biggin had proved to be rather more than just a little too hospitable. The kindest the Air Officer Commanding in Chief could allow was to record that the accident had been caused by 'Pilot's error of judgement'.

As might be expected on a working farm, by 2006 the site showed no trace of the tragic finish to this ill-conceived flight. Just the same, Mr Bert Weller, of nearby Hardwick Farm, found débris on the site in 2003.

Mr Richard Waller, at the impact point, where his father found debris in 2003

Gloster Meteor Mk.8 WB108, Treeton Colliery, Rotherham

SK 43746 88039 74m impact point
SK 43602 87820 68m pit reservoir terminal point
No.211 Flying Training School, RAF Worksop, No.25 Group, Flying Training Command
21 December, 1954

Pilot: pupil pilot, solo, killed:
Pilot Officer Douglas Gibson Edwards

At 1130 hours on 21 December, 1954, Pilot Officer Douglas Edwards got airborne from RAF Worksop on a solo general-handling flight. Just twenty-three minutes later, however, his aircraft was destroyed and Pilot Officer Edwards was killed when he lost control and crashed onto a colliery spoil tip at Treeton, Rotherham.

Until his fatal flight Pilot Officer Edwards had been making satisfactory progress on his course. During his basic training he had flown nearly 300 hours on single-engined aircraft and had been assessed as proficient. Subsequently, having passed on to the advanced-training stage, he had flown 22 hours on the twin-jet Meteor, eight of them solo, and had gained a White instrument rating, the latter indicating that his instrument flying was everything it should have been. Deciding what caused him to crash, therefore, had to be, to a certain degree, speculative, but the investigation concluded that a loss of radio contact with the ground had played a major part, together with a possible misreading of his altimeter.

Having cleared to the east of Worksop, it seems evident that Pilot Officer Edwards encountered cloud conditions which precluded him from carrying out any useful upper-air work. Accordingly he decided to commence a free let down but, judiciously, called for a homing before descending in order to ensure that he did not wander too far astray. In all, he was given four check-headings, or 'steers', until the indications were that he was back over Worksop. After he acknowledged this fourth steer, however, radio contact was lost, and nothing further was heard of him until the news came in that his aircraft had crashed.

It was later established that, having passed the Worksop overhead, Pilot Officer Edwards had embarked upon his free descent but that his chosen heading had taken him into the Rotherham area where industrial haze – in those days a perennial condition – had vastly reduced the visibility. Realising that he had little visual reference, and in a measured endeavour to determine his position without further assistance, he had lowered one-third flap (and thereby the Meteor's nose) and extended his airbrakes, a combination of 'power-against-brake' that would have been condemned by previous generations of piston-engined pilots, but which, on a jet-engined aircraft, both enhanced his view from the cockpit and allowed him to fly relatively slowly while giving him the swiftest possible power response. Only it seems likely that he had misread his altimeter, for witnesses saw him appear through the murk in a descending right-hand turn, hurriedly level his wings and raise the nose to check his descent, but still only just clear the crest of Spa Hill. After which they saw the aircraft sink markedly to strike the spoil tip beyond, cartwheel, and then explode, 'with some violence', as the official RAF crash report had it: clearly the hasty nose-up control input had caused the Meteor to stall.

The wreckage spill was widespread, with at least one engine hurtling downhill to land in the colliery reservoir, some hundreds of yards closer to the colliery buildings. Just the same, nobody on the ground was hurt, and although there were extensive fires beyond the impact point, these were mainly confined to the area where fuel had sprayed. As reported in the *Sheffield Telegraph*, some 150 surface workers gathered in an attempt to rescue the pilot but found the flames too fierce, so that only when the fire was doused by the pit's fire brigade could his body be removed from the aircraft.

In 2005 Mrs Dorothy Stevenson, of Treeton, recalled that day. 'My husband', she explained, 'was a surface worker at the Treeton Pit. As it happened, I was on the Catliffe Road when I heard the engine note and saw this aeroplane appear. Then it disappeared below my line of

2005, Mrs Dorothy Stevenson, witness, on Treeton spoil heap

sight and exploded in, as I found out later, what my husband and I called Tip Field. All I could think of was, "Who is at work above ground today?"'

Mrs Pat Nuthall, also of Treeton, was somewhat better placed to see the final stage of the fatal plunge. As she explained, 'We'd usually congregate in the street while waiting for Roly Payne and his fruit and veg van, but as it was snowy and bitterly cold I'd decided to watch for him from my bedroom window.' She paused. 'I suppose it was the impact that made me look up, nevertheless I retain this impression of seeing the plane instants before it hit. It struck the crest of the hill, and there was this great cloud of billowing black smoke, and fierce flames. My only thought was that there must be someone in it. And that was horrible. For it was clear that nobody could have survived.'

In 1967 engine sections were recovered from the pit reservoir, and in 1976 more débris was unearthed when a slurry pit was excavated, parts which were housed for some years in the colliery. By 2005, however, the pit was little more than a memory, with housing burgeoning where its buildings had once stood. The spoil heap itself had mellowed with the years and pathways threaded up to cross its crest, purposely flattened in the wake of the 1966 Aberfan slag-heap disaster, one footpath lifting from the former reservoir beds, since become Cannonthorpe Rise.

Back in 1954, the finding had been that the crash was caused by an error of judgement on the part of the pilot, but that this had been due to his inexperience on the type. However, it had also been apparent that Pilot Officer Edwards had not expected to find himself so close to the ground; accordingly the board recommended replacing the easy-to-misread variant of the Mk.14 altimeter currently used on Meteors, a flight-safety measure subsequently adopted.

Impact point

Above left: Mrs Pat Nuthall, of Treeton

Above: Mrs Nuthall's skyline view of the crash

Left: 2006, the crash site, from Cannonthorpe Rise

It was only to be expected, perhaps, that fables would attach themselves to a crash which happened so close to a populated area. But it is unfortunate, perhaps, that these held sway in 2005 when a consensus was held to name the fast-maturing amenity which the spoil heap had become. Among contenders were what seemed to be the eminently fitting 'Colliers Crest', suggested by crash-witness Mrs Nuthall – 'built by generations of miners, so commemorating miners'. The title chosen, however, was 'The Edwards Meteor Way', with the local news-sheet enthusing, 'The brave pilot crashed into the tip after circling the village a number of times to avoid hitting homes and causing civilian casualties.' Unfortunate, because while cold-shouldering the very real bravery of untold generations of Treeton miners, such a fallacious gloss hardly does service to the cause of flight safety, the cause in furtherance of which the hapless Pilot Officer Edwards actually gave his life.

The Treeton crash site may not present itself as a natural venue for even suburban-tied walkers in the Peakland fringes, but it is one which, with the once-perennial smoke-based haze a thing of the past, affords both a superb overview of the area's rich tradition of industry and a pleasing panorama embracing the built-up areas, the parks, and the distant upland moors.

Treeton colliery and the pit reservoir, 1941
(Photograph by courtesy of Mr Hedley Frost)

2006, a photo-match of the above scene, with
Cannonthorpe Rise replacing the pit reservoir

Noorduyn Norseman UC-64A, 43-35439, Shining Tor (west of Buxton)

SJ 99831 73393 490m
United States Ninth Army Air Force, Allied
Expeditionary Force, 10th Air Depot Group,
10th Air Depot Repair Squadron, Burtonwood
29 September, 1944

Pilot: slightly injured:
Second Lieutenant Arnold Fredrickson, United
States Army Air Force

Having first flown in 1935, the ten-seater Noorduyn Norseman UC-64A was a veteran type by 1944, but being rugged and adaptable, it was widely used by the United States Army Air Force as a light transport.

This was the role in which Norseman No.43-35439 was being employed when, on 29 September, 1944, USAAF ferry pilot Second Lieutenant Arnold Fredrickson lifted it off from RAF Winthrop, near Newark, in Nottinghamshire. He had merely dropped in to pick up the kit of a Polish flying officer and was now to return to RAF Burtonwood, just east of Liverpool, at that time the United States Army Air Force's No.1 Base Air Depot. Having encountered, as he later reported, 'just five minutes' cloud' on his forty-five-minute inbound flight he seems to have paid scant attention to the weather report made available to cover the return flight.

Had he done so, it would have shown him that, regardless of the virtually clear skies he had so recently transited, he must now expect a thirty-knot headwind, total cloud cover low over the hills, and scattered showers beneath that to cut the visibility still further. Yet in the face of this he submitted a return flight plan for a visual-contact flight! Evidently with under five hundred hours of flying time he was also lacking an appreciation of the rapid weather changes to be met with over such temperate-zone high ground as the Peakland area.

Notwithstanding this, and unlike so many other airmen of his era, Second Lieutenant Fredrickson did, at least, elect to climb to a safe altitude to carry out the flight. And when he found himself bucking, as his accident report reflects, 'fog and a terrific headwind', he recognised that conditions had changed drastically, and duly amended his estimates.

The flight to Newark had taken forty-five minutes, so he now reasoned that adding an hour to the time from then on would see him clear of the high ground. Accordingly, when his recalculated estimate was up, and confident that he was now over the Cheshire Plain, a low-lying area hardly anywhere rising to more than 400 feet above sea level, he commenced his descent. Almost at once he entered cloud, so that by 2,300 feet he was settled onto his instruments. As his altimeter needle passed through 1,800 feet, however, he glimpsed hills ahead, and hastily powering up and reverting to his instruments, he adopted a climbing attitude – but almost immediately struck the ground.

On impact the aircraft turned over and caught fire. But Second Lieutenant Fredrickson, suffering from little more than superficial cuts, bumps, and bruises, resolutely kicked himself clear of the cockpit and distanced himself from the conflagration. Thereafter, shakily making his way from the scene, he initially found succour at a local farm, after which he was taken to the Cat and Fiddle Inn to await pick-up by ambulance. And in due course the wreckage was recovered by the RAF's No.75 Maintenance Unit, then located at RAF Wilmslow.

In the face of the total write-off of the aircraft the view taken by the American Accident Committee is intriguingly benign, particularly when compared with the harsh findings of so many RAF courts of inquiry. For despite the fact that a comprehensive, and evidently very accurate, actual-weather report had been made available, the recorded opinion of the Committee was that 'the accident is solely a result of weather'. A finding which Second Lieutenant Fredrickson must surely have reckoned as the second time Fortune had favoured him that day.

The site of Second Lieutenant Fredrickson's crash, held to be where the footpath crosses a culvert, showed no sign of the incident in 2005, and even metal-detector searches failed to reveal the slightest trace of aircraft débris.

The crash site of Noorduyn Norseman UC-64A 43-35439, with Shining Tor upslope to the left, along the footpath

Airspeed Oxford Mk.1 HN429, Axe Edge (south of Buxton)

SK 03156 69217 544m
No.11 (Pilots) Advanced Flying Unit, RAF Calveley (north-west of Crewe), No.21 Group, Flying Training Command
3 November, 1944

Crew: all injured:
Flying Officer C.V. Mayhead, RAF Volunteer Reserve, staff instructor, pilot
Flying Officer A.C. Mullen, Royal Canadian Air Force, pupil pilot
Flying Officer J.S. Bean, Royal Canadian Air Force, pupil pilot

The twin-engined Airspeed Oxford served as a multi-engined trainer throughout the Second World War and was used by every Commonwealth air force, a series of modifications enabling it to be utilised for almost all categories of aircrew training. When Oxford Mk.1, HN429, crashed into Axe Edge near Buxton, in Derbyshire, however, it was in its role of advanced pilot-trainer. The machine was totally destroyed, and all three airmen aboard were injured.

At the time, Flying Officer Mayhead, a staff instructor of No.11 (Pilots) Advanced Flying Unit, located at RAF Calveley, just north-west of Crewe, was tutoring two pupil pilots on Standard Beam Approach techniques.

The Standard Beam Approach System (SBA), effectively the forerunner of all modern instrument landing systems, was designed to enable a pilot to descend in cloud to 100 feet above the ground, at which height he had a reasonable chance of seeing the runway, and then landing. However, the SBA demanded a lot more from crews than modern systems, and in its earliest form it required constant monitoring of audio headphone-signals.

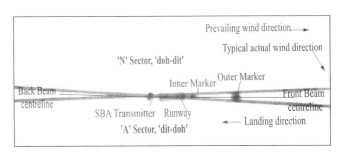

The Standard Beam Approach System (SBA)

When approaching the runway to land, a pilot flying to the left of the centre line would hear the continuously repeated 'dit-doh' of the morse-code letter 'A'; if to the right of the centre line, the continuously repeated 'doh-dit' of the morse-code letter 'N'; and when actually on the centre line –'on the beam'– he would hear the steady note formed by the merger of the two.

In order to determine his distance-to-run to touchdown, he would have to recognise two other signals. The first was that of the Outer Marker, three miles out (in those days). On hearing this, and having already descended to 600 feet above touchdown (unbelievably low to those flying since), he would commence his final descent. The next range signal would be that of the Inner Marker, just 150 yards from touchdown.

It should be noted that although instruments already existed which would give visual indications of the aircraft's position with respect to the beam and the marker beacons, not all aircraft would have had them. Further, in order to talk to ground control, or even to use the intercom, the pilot might have to temporarily switch away from – and so lose – all these vital SBA signals in his headset.

The initial step in the procedure, however, was to home to overhead the main airfield beacon at a height of around 1,100 feet: specific heights and distances varied from airfield to airfield, depending upon the nearby terrain. Once overhead the pilot would turn onto the beam and fly away from the airfield in order to distance himself for the approach. His first range marker, flying outbound, was the Inner Marker beacon (to reiterate, 150 yards out from touchdown), and some forty-five seconds after that, the Outer Marker Beacon (three miles out). At this point he would carry out a teardrop-shaped 'procedural turn' which would bring him back onto the beam, but facing towards the runway. During this turn, and knowing that he was within five miles or so of the airfield, he would descend to 600 feet. Next, he would prepare the aircraft for landing so that the moment he heard the Outer Marker beacon he could throttle back and commence his final descent at a measured rate of some 400 feet a minute. This meant that on hearing the Inner Marker he would be at just 100 feet and 150 yards from the runway. At this stage he would look up, and if he saw the runway he would land. Alternatively, if he could not see the runway, then he would apply full power, climb away to a safe height, and have another little think.

Straightforward enough, in the classroom, and even at pre-flight briefing. But when concentrating on instrument-flying in cloud, perhaps at night and in bumpy weather; when assessing the drift, and then altering heading accordingly to stay on the centre line; when taking instruction, making radio reports, and carrying out cockpit checks; with the very beam-signal in the earphones subject to a variety of local distortions, it could be very confusing, even if the pilot was aided by an otherwise-uninvolved navigator.

Evidently, on the final practice-approach in question, the operating pupil pilot of Oxford HN429 found things altogether too confusing. It is clear that he had successfully tracked to overhead Calveley, but that from then on, heading outbound along the front beam, preparatory to turning inbound on his actual landing approach, something distracted him.

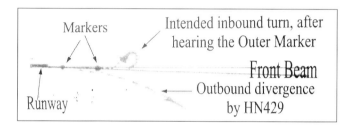

The outbound procedure on SBA: dots show the inbound turn HN429 intended to make; dashes, the divergent course actually flown

Whatever caused the distraction on this occasion – but one thinks of a too hasty adjustment inadvertently de-synchronising the heading reference – the operating pupil pilot, hearing 'off-beam' signals in his headset, and attempting to re-establish on the centreline, turned the wrong way. But this took him outside the narrow vertical beam of the markers which would have told him his range from the airfield. And at 163 mph (142 knots) he was diverging further from the centre line every second. So it was that, although he maintained 1,650 feet on his altimeter – and quite likely just as instructor Flying Officer Mayhead decided it was time to take a hand – the aircraft flew into the summit of the 1,800 feet high Axe Edge.

The point of impact showed that the aircraft had strayed sixteen miles off the centre line, and so into terrain far beyond the safety-altitude zone afforded by overflying the Outer Marker. Fortunately, although the aircraft was totally destroyed, there was no fire, and all three crew survived, albeit suffering injuries.

The court of inquiry found that the operating pilot had failed to adapt quickly enough to the technique required for tracking the beam outbound. It found too that, flying in cloud, he had underestimated the wind effect helping to drift him off the beam. Additionally, that by switching from radio to intercom he had missed the vital markers. However the accident was recognised as one inherent in beam training, although as an immediate measure it was recommended that operating heights for RAF Calveley be reconsidered in view of the proximity of high ground.

In early 2006 a modest amount of surface débris was still to be found just below the ridge on the western slopes, with undercarriage members predominant.

Left: The crash site of Airspeed Oxford HN429 in 2006, looking north-easterly, up towards the Axe Edge impact point

Airspeed Oxford Mk.1 EB717, Burbage Edge, east of Derbyshire Bridge (south-west of Buxton)

SK 02559 71720 495m
No.11 (Pilots) Advanced Flying Unit, RAF Calveley (north-west of Crewe), No.21 Group, Flying
Training Command
2 May, 1943

Pupil pilot: solo, killed:
Sergeant John Henry Langley Wilson

The Oxford, though robust and dependable, was never to engender the same regard among
those who flew it as the Anson, generally agreed to be altogether more docile and easier to
handle. But the very care needed to fly the Oxford helped make it the admirable trainer it was.
Just the same, while it is axiomatic that all aircraft are capable of biting, then the Oxford, unless
the pilot was continually attentive, was to the fore of those most likely to. As a trainee pilot
from No.11 (Pilots) Advanced Flying Unit, operating from RAF Calveley, near Crewe, was to
discover on 2 May, 1943.
    Sergeant John Wilson was relatively experienced for the day, with 280 hours total flying and
102 hours on Oxfords, both unexpectedly high totals for a pupil. Just the same, in terms of
general air-awareness his experience level was low, and when, in the course of a night cross-
country from RAF Calveley, the weather deteriorated below that forecast, he became, at best,
uncertain of his position.
    In the pre-dawn light he found himself over a blacked-out but singularly-shaped town. Having
descended in order to pick out features that would enable him to determine which town this
was, he set up a wide circle and would have been flying, one eye on the ground over the town
side of his cockpit, and one on the map, as he tried to correlate the two.
    The town was, in fact, Buxton, and cradled among high hills. But with Sergeant Wilson's
concentration fixed downwards, towards the inside of his turn, it is likely that his attention
wandered from his height keeping so that his altitude decayed. It further seems that, when he
passed to the south-west of Buxton on what was fated to become the last of his orientating
orbits, he strayed into what he must have hoped would be only momentarily-veiling cloud.
Except that before his turn could bring him into the clear once more he had flown into the high
ground of Burbage Edge, his aircraft striking heavily and disintegrating as it breasted through a
drystone wall. There was no significant fire, but Sergeant Wilson did not survive the impact.
    The court of inquiry, finding Buxton to be far removed from Sergeant Wilson's assigned
routings, realised that some gross error of navigation had occurred. Possibly the wrong heading
had been set on the compass at one of the turning points. Alternatively the other prime directional
instrument, the directional-gyroscope indicator, might not have been checked and reset as
frequently as good practice demanded, so that it was likely to have drifted, taking Sergeant
Wilson progressively further from his intended heading.
    That a fledgling aviator, no matter how advanced in training, might get lost was, of course,
only to be expected, and in that event to circle over some prominent feature in order to obtain
a fix was perfectly proper as a first step towards relocation. But there is a fine judgemental
balance to be observed between confidently persisting in trying to sort things out unaided, and
making a timely decision to seek assistance. Clearly the inquiry felt that Sergeant Wilson, finding
himself both lost and faced by weather conditions that had deteriorated below those he had
been briefed to expect, should have exercised more judgement and called upon any one of the
radio-based 'get-you-home' facilities available to him.
    At the crash site, high on Burbage Edge, and with the Cat and Fiddle Inn prominent on the
western skyline, the only visible evidence of the accident in early 2006 was the stretch of drystone
wall demolished by the plunging Oxford. However, although reasonably thorough metal-detector
searches revealed nothing, physical delving with a bared arm into the reed-fringed, deceptively
deep, and sludge-floored pond (then ice-capped!) just downslope from the wall, yielded not

only fragments of aircraft metal, but also sizeable sheets of the plywood with which the Oxford was skinned. (It should be recorded that the author did not recognize them as such, believing, at that time, that Oxfords, like all proper aeroplanes to which he had entrusted himself, were made of metal.)

Debris, metal and plywood, from the pool

Airspeed Oxford Mk.1 EB717: looking eastwards, showing the rush-fringed pool. The demolished section of wall extends to the right, out of the picture.

Airspeed Oxford Mk.1 DF485, Castleton, near Hope

SK 15773 83191 170m
No.42 Operational Training Unit, RAF Ashbourne, No.70 Group, Army Co-operation Command
19 February, 1943

Occupants: uninjured:
Flying Officer W.M. Bray, Royal Canadian Air Force, pilot
Two aircrew trainees and one passenger, all unidentified

In the course of converting onto multi-engined aircraft in preparation for a posting to the heavy aircraft of either Bomber or Coastal Commands, Flying Officer Bray, an American serving with the Royal Canadian Air Force, was dispatched on a cross-country exercise. Clearly this was to be a routine sortie for, as became evident to some – although not to Authority – along with his trainee crew Flying Officer Bray took aboard an unauthorised, joyriding airman.

Taking off from RAF Ashbourne and flying at an indicated 1,200 feet, Flying Officer Bray dutifully followed the courses fed him by his navigator until, after two hours in the air, they began to run into rough weather. Being a typical February day this would have been par for the course, but the navigator, head down and concentrating on his plot, began to feel queasy, and as the turbulence persisted and the misery of debilitating airsickness took over, so he had to cry off, and cease work altogether.

A half an hour or so later, Flying Officer Bray, finding that he was not that certain of his position, called upon his wireless operator to get him a course to steer for Ashbourne, only – very likely because of their low altitude – the wireless operator was unable to make contact.

Reverting to the original flight plan, as standard procedure dictated, Flying Officer Bray would have taken up an approximate heading for base. But the turbulence radically increased, and after a particularly severe wing drop, Flying Officer Bray lost control, the machine beginning to spiral.

He managed to make a partial recovery, but only at an estimated two hundred feet above the ground. Without a doubt very shaken, but finding a field directly in front of him, he dropped his flaps, and leaving his wheels up – again in accordance with contemporary standard procedure – hastily put the Oxford down, even then clipping a tree before settling.

Farmer Irvin Robinson had seen from the start that the machine was in difficulties, and as he was to affirm later, had run towards it with a mind full of misgivings. For only four days earlier a Wellington bomber had crashed catastrophically across a brook just a few fields away, exploding and killing all its crew. Now, he recalled asking himself, was it about to happen again? Four days ago the township of Hope had witnessed tragedy. Was it now to be Castleton's turn? For his farm's track formed the boundary between the two communities.

Fortunately, on this occasion, the machine touched down, skidded on its belly, and sedately ground its way to a halt. There was no explosion, and no fire! And even as he crossed into the field, so Mr Robinson saw men beginning to emerge.

'What happened?' he asked the pilot, when he reached the aircraft. Whatever the evidently shocked pilot answered, Mr Robinson would thenceforth hold that it was 'sparking-plug trouble' that had brought the machine down. But at the time something else was occupying his mind. Puzzled, he looked from the pilot, to another man, and then to a third, this last rather more sickly-green than ashen. He then craned to peer around the fuselage. 'But I could have sworn I counted four of you get out.'

The grins this brought, as he would recall later, were still somewhat shaky. 'We had a chap who was along for the ride,' the pilot explained, pointing to a figure hurrying towards the Castleton Road, 'so we've packed him off before anyone asks questions.'

The aircraft was to remain under guard for several days but in the interim an RAF officer came to discuss its recovery, the decision having been made that, although damaged, the Oxford was still repairable. He eyed the field doubtfully. 'Don't let our chaps take their vehicles onto here,' he advised, 'they'll mess up the surface for you. And, knowing them, bog themselves down into the bargain.'

The officers forming the court of inquiry into the crash-cum-forced-landing were less censorious. They simply recorded the facts, or something near the facts. For the spiral becomes a 'spin'– their quotes – and the distinctly un-aviator-like term 'air pocket' is advanced as causing the upset. The failure to make wireless contact is noted, but it seems that the whole incident was pragmatically regarded as one to be expected in flying training, the Air Officer Commanding concurring with the recommendation that no further action need be taken.

Certainly there was nothing heinous to censure. Nothing, for example, like the carrying of an unauthorised person aboard one of His Majesty's aircraft.

By 2006 there was no trace of the incident to be seen, only pastures with their horizon fringed with high, and not-too-distant hills. But as Mr Irvin Robinson's son and daughter-in-law, Eric and Noreen, were able to point out, the actual field had changed significantly in the interim, for after the war a filtering plant was constructed where the aircraft made its initial touchdown, although even that had long become redundant.

The remaining section of the field that presented itself to Oxford Mk.1 DF485

Mr and Mrs Eric Robinson, of Marston Farm

Airspeed Oxford Mk.1 V3210, Chapel-en-le-Frith area

No more exact location established by mid-2006: see text
RAF College Cranwell, No.21 Group, Flying Training Command
2 September, 1941

Pilot: pupil, solo, injured:
Leading Aircraftman B.C. Forsdick

On 2 September, 1941, pupil pilot Leading Aircraftman B.C. Forsdick, stationed at the RAF College at Cranwell, near Sleaford, Lincolnshire, was detailed to carry out a solo cross-country flight in Oxford V3210. Leading Aircraftman Forsdick had a little under one hundred hours' total experience, and so would have been relatively advanced in his training. But just after midday, having encountered cloudy conditions, with fog masking the terrain, and with only ten hours' practice in instrument flying, he struck high ground, and although there was no fire, was injured.

No details of the route set him are known, but it seems likely that he had gone badly astray, for the investigation criticised him for not having had his courses checked before departure. Further, the unit's navigation instructor was criticised for having failed to carried out such a check. Indeed it appears that the incident revealed a weak spot in the training organisation, for the Air Officer Commanding immediately had instructions issued to all flying schools requiring the pupils' courses to be checked before any solo cross-country flight.

Leading Aircraftman Forsdick was also criticised for having entered cloud, his commanding officer stressing that he had been specifically ordered not to do so. But such a criticism cannot be taken too seriously, for as all authorising – and investigating and reporting – officers would have known, in the United Kingdom unexpected weather changes are virtually the norm. Further, it is only too easy to attempt to penetrate a patch of cloud, only to find that it is far larger than expected. And in this case, evidently, a lot more solid than it may have appeared.

Regrettably, this is a Peakland site that, by mid-2006, remained untraced, although, arguably, the only one. The summary of the RAF crash report, the handwritten Form 1180, has the crash occurring at *Consburn Moor*, Chapel-en-le-Frith. However, Form 1180s are notoriously lax when it comes to site location. Sometimes, even when distance and bearings from known locations are given, evidence on the ground proves them to be significantly astray. In part, this was because names of locations would often have been jotted into notebooks after being ascertained from local witnesses. And there are many instances where regional accents led to misunderstanding when locals and airmen – whether the latter were investigators, sentries, or survivors – came into contact. In one instance, for example, 'Moorwood Manor' appeared as 'Maud Manor'. And it seems as if something similar may have happened with Oxford V3210, for although the handwriting is relatively clear, no such place as Consburn – possibly Cowsburn – Moor exists.

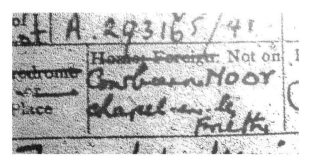

The location given on the RAF crash report summary

The initial supposition was that the Cowburn Tunnel area was indicated, although the surrounding moorland is not generally known locally as Cowburn. Just the same, from early in 2005 all the relevant farms in that zone of Chapel-en-le-Frith were canvassed for recollections. But although life-long residents revealed an intimate knowledge of other crash sites in the area, and despite appeals in the local press, none knew of this one. The same applied to the Combs area. Finally, the supposed faint similarity of the name 'Ollerenshaw' (shaw, moor) Farm, initiated a search of the farms on Eccles Pike, but again with negative results regarding the crash in question.

Researching the two light-aircraft crashes in Chapel itself seemed to offer hope when the first informant spoke of one aircraft crashing 'near where the police station is now' – Lower Crossings – but thought that the one crashing below the railway embankment had been 'much bigger'. Then again, crash reports, with pilots' names, exist for the Magister and the Oxford, but none for the Lower Crossings aircraft. Yet the informant for the latter categorically held that he recognised the pilot as a member of a local family, and having checked with other long-term residents, named him. Further, flat marshy farmland beside a railway embankment hardly accords with the 'flew into a hill' of the RAF report for Oxford V3210.

Reluctantly then, this is a very real, and impeccably documented, crash which, presently, can only be recorded for posterity in the hope that future research will reveal exactly whereabouts it occurred.

Airspeed Oxford V3626, Fawside Edge, Longnor

SK 06759 65163 360m
No.12 Flying Training School, No.21 Group, Flying Training Command, RAF Grantham (post-1944, renamed RAF Spitalgate)
16 November, 1941

Pilot: solo, killed:
Leading Aircraftman Raymond Henry Wattie Dix, RAFVR, pupil pilot

On 16 November, 1941, pupil pilot Leading Aircraftman Raymond Dix was dispatched from RAF Grantham – to become RAF Spitalgate after March 1944 – on a general-handling sortie which was to include local flying and circuits. During his detail he wandered sixty miles from his base and became lost in bad weather over high ground. After which, in the course of trying to establish his position, he flew into Fawside Edge, Derbyshire, killing himself and destroying his aircraft.

In 2005 Mrs Nellie Slack, of Fawside Edge, remembered the crash well. 'I was cooking the Sunday dinner,' she recalled, 'when we heard this great bang. We all ran out to see what it was, although it was so foggy you couldn't see a hand in front of your face. Mind you, we didn't know whether to run fast or slow, not knowing whether it was a good aeroplane, or one of *theirs*: you heard these stories, and we'd had the bombs by that time …'

Mrs Nellie Slack and Mr Walter Limer display a souvenir

No rings or pendants were made of the perspex!

Mr Walter Limer, who would later serve in the Royal Artillery, also remembered the day. 'I was thirteen,' he said. 'We were working down the hill when we heard this aircraft. Then its engines powered up, but almost at once there was this mighty crash. So we ran up, to find he'd just missed clearing the brow. It was totally wrecked, but it didn't burn. Only the Longnor police were already there, the sergeant and his constable, and they wouldn't let us come close.'

Mrs Slack's sons, Tony, and Edward – the latter to discover the celebrated Wilmslow peat-bog man!– were able to show where they used to find wreckage: 'And we've still got a bit at the house,' Edward advised. 'In fact, recently it was used for a school project.' With Tony adding, 'The neighbours chopped their fire wood with the Oxford's fire-axe for years, despite its bent handle ...'

Following the crash ten or twelve airman, it would seem, arrived as a recovery party and were billeted in the cow-barn at the adjacent Edgeside Farm while they removed, buried, and burnt the wreckage. 'They stayed for two weeks,' Mrs Nellie remembered. 'All of them very nice young men.' She smiled winsomely. 'I was just eighteen at the time ...'

By 2006 most surface evidence was gone, leaving just the odd scrap of molten and corroded metal. Nor did a rather cursory detector search reveal anything more.

The impact point

The gutter in which debris collected

Airspeed Oxford Mk.1 LX745, The Tors, northern slope of Shining Tor

SJ 99813 74626 500m impact point
SJ 99818 74648 489m embedded fuel tank
No.11 (Pilots) Advanced Flying Unit, RAF Calveley (north-west of Crewe), No.21 group, Flying Training Command
12 March, 1944

Crew: all three injured, died of exposure after the crash:
Flying Officer Charles Stuart Grant Wood, pilot, instructor
Pilot Officer Gerald Campbell Liggett, pilot under training
Flight Sergeant Joseph George Hall, navigator/wireless operator

On 12 March, 1944, staff instructor Flying Officer Charles Wood was tasked to fly a short night cross-country from RAF Calveley, north-west of Crewe, during which much of the communication (including weather updates) and the major part of the navigation (all fixes, bearings, and homings) was to be carried out through the medium of W/T; that is, by wireless-telegraphy, employing morse code, as opposed to voice.

To the pupil pilot destined for a multi-engined role, but so far having experienced only single-crew operation, the exercise would convincingly demonstrate the advantage to be gained from having crew members to assist him; on this occasion a wireless operator. It would also usefully exercise Flight Sergeant Joseph Hall, one of the unit's staff navigator/wireless-operators who, as was often the way with dual-role aircrew categories, had patently spent most of his post-qualifying time in his primary role; in his case, as a navigator.

In the event, things did not go to plan, for the aircraft failed to return to RAF Calveley, nor did the subsequent overdue-action investigations bring any news of it. Indeed not until a considerable time later would it be found, in the vicinity of the Cat and Fiddle Inn, above Buxton, shattered on the northern slopes of the high moorland edge of Shining Tor, with the bodies of its crew huddled together alongside the major portion of the wreckage.

The investigating officers, working from Flying Officer Wood's planned route, were able to establish that the crash site put LX745 well south of track. From which they were able to deduce that a promulgated wind change, occurring after he had taken off, had not been compensated for. It was evident that the pupil pilot, having encountered cloud, and not appreciating that the wind had changed, had turned on his planned estimate for the final leg, and after a certain interval, believing himself to be well on the way to base, had been allowed to commence his descent. As it transpired, however, LX745 was still twenty-eight miles from Calveley, and still over high ground.

Various recommendations were made, especially regarding instrument-flying training, the junior-officer investigators being chastised by the Air Officer Commanding for suggesting that instrument flying, or lack of it, had had no bearing in this accident: although the senior officer's ire might be wondered at, considering that the aircraft had been in a stable and perfectly-controlled descent, if undeniably out of position, when it struck.

The prime criticism, however, was of the demonstrably poor standard maintained by the unit's dual-category aircrew – whether navigator/wireless operators or wireless operator/air gunners – with procedures being instituted to have all of them periodically demonstrate their continued efficiency as wireless operators. An understandable requirement, for while fulfilling the navigator's or gunner's role it was only too easy to lose the finesse demanded by the wireless equipment, and easier still to lose the ability to read morse-code communications, even at the relatively low rate at which aircraft (as opposed to maritime) W/T traffic was conducted.

In the instance of the fatal flight the ground wireless-telegraphy logs would have revealed just what, if any, weather and navigational assistance the pilots had been supplied with once they were airborne. But clearly neither pupil nor instructor was passed the significantly revised winds. Equally clearly, no fixes or bearings were supplied from which to revise that final, and as it transpired, fatally-displaced turn.

Because of their terms of reference, the investigators also had to observe that Flying Officer Wood had not made use of 'Darky', an emergency 'get-you-down' facility. This was a system in which operators at a ground-based high frequency R/T (voice) station would hear a pilot call and know by virtue of the short range of the standard aircraft TR9 set of the day that he was in their area. They would then pass him the pre-calculated track-and-distance to the nearest airfield. At the same time the adjoining HF station in that direction would be warned by telephone to listen out for his aircraft's engines and guide him onwards, from post to post, until he was over the airfield.

But although the 'Darky' network was especially alerted when it was realised that LX745 was overdue (notwithstanding that by that time the crew had already crashed), this merely supports the contention that neither pilot ever considered himself either lost, or for that matter, in any form of trouble. After all, if the crew considered that they were reasonably on track, and running to time, they would have had no need – indeed it would have been highly irresponsible of them – to have bothered 'Darky' or any other emergency facility.

The crash site lies just yards off the much-frequented ridge path running between Pym Chair and Shining Tor. Even so a considerable amount of wreckage remained in mid-2006. There was a central pool, and just feet away, a fuel tank deeply embedded in the earth.

As a further, and yet more sobering reflection on this tragic incident, the crew members, injured though they were, might well have made their way to safety. Except that, being either shocked, or intent on obeying the air-search precept that it is always best to stay with the

aircraft – a wreck being easier to see than a person – they remained where they were, and not being found in time, died of exposure.

This fatally ironic turn of events is not recorded on the RAF's summary crash report but it was verified in 2005 by Mr Albert Heathcote, who was the shepherd of the Pym Chair–Shining Tor Ridge when the aircraft crashed.

Airspeed Oxford Mk.1 L4601, Shutlingsloe, Wildboarclough

SJ 97639 69347 431m
No.17 Service Flying Training School, RAF Cranwell (Sleaford, Lincolnshire), No.21 Group, Flying Training Command
4 April, 1945

Occupants: two passengers and one pilot killed; the aircraft captain and a passenger injured:
Flying Officer K.H. Shawyer, pilot, instructor, injured
Flight Lieutenant Horace Garth Featonby, pilot under training, killed
Corporal A.J. Burd, passenger, injured
Leading Aircraftman Frederick Roscoe, passenger, killed
Aircraftman First Class George Fishwick, passenger, killed

On 4 April, 1945, just a month before the end of the Second World War in Europe, Flying Officer Shawyer, a staff instructor on Airspeed Oxfords at No.17 Service Flying Training School, was detailed to supervise a pilot under training on a daytime navigational cross-country exercise. Three off-duty airmen, taking advantage of the spare seats, went along for the ride.

Just forty-five minutes after getting airborne from Cranwell, however, Flying Officer Shawyer found himself faced with lowering cloud. Aware of the nature of the terrain ahead, he had several alternatives. He could abort and turn for base; he could direct his pupil to climb to a safe height and continue on the planned exercise; he could deviate around the cloudy area and then carry on; or he could maintain ground contact and continue the sortie below cloud.

Reluctant, perhaps, to upset his pupil's navigational timing by a climb, and undoubtedly conscious of the fact that his three passengers, most recently used to seeing nothing but the Lincolnshire fens, would have been craning from window to window and over the pilots' backs, feasting upon the hill scenery of Buxton and Wildboarclough, Flying Officer Shawyer decided to maintain ground contact and have the flight continue.

Only it is in the nature of cloud that even wisps of vapour seem to unaccountably expand into vast tracts once they are penetrated. And during the course of such a penetration Oxford L4601 was flown into the southern shoulder of Shutlingsloe. There was no fire, but the impact killed three of those on board. Flight Lieutenant Horace Featonby, the trainee pilot, died, as did passengers Leading Aircraftman Frederick Roscoe and Aircraftman First Class George Fishwick. The aircraft captain, Flying Officer Shawyer, and the passenger Corporal Burd, were injured.

The inquiry held that Flying Officer Shawyer should have climbed to a safe height on encountering cloud and not tried to fly below it. This view was strongly supported by both the Air Officer Commanding and the AOC-in-Chief, and a summary of evidence – the normal precursor to a court martial – was duly ordered to be held once the instructor was deemed well enough to appear. Patently, that three non-aircrew airmen should have been involved made the occurrence even more worthy of investigation. What the outcome of the summary was, however, and whether or not it led to a court martial, is not known.

Nevertheless, it does seem hard that Flying Officer Shawyer was to be even mildly criticised for not having had his passengers strapped in. For when the crash occurred the flight was in neither the take-off nor the landing phase, nor even, despite being at relatively low level, in turbulent conditions. But no doubt that was a case he would have argued at the appropriate time.

In 2005 Mr Phillip Sharpley, who was brought up at the Crag Inn and whose family also farmed Shutlingsloe Farm, on Lord Derby's Estate, remembered that he had been absent at another farm when the Oxford crashed. 'In fact', he said, 'my fourteen-year old brother, Frank, was alone at home when the police turned up. It seemed they couldn't get a vehicle up to the crash site but needed a trailer to carry down the casualties. We had my 1937 Fordson Tractor – I only got rid of it a year or two ago – and Frank said he could drive that up, with a trailer. Getting it up there, however, required going some distance on the public road but without hesitation they urged him to get under way. He did so, and duly brought back three bodies. At which the police told him they'd now prosecute him for driving on the public road! Though they were probably joking.' Mr Sharpley sobered. 'The plane had stopped just short of our boundary wall, having come down on Higher Nabs Farm. At that time both Higher and Lower Nabs Farms were run by the War Agricultural Committee using their own labour, but Mr John Flint, of the Old Mill House, Lord Derby's Estate Agent, was experienced in first aid, and he and his daughter, Betty, assisted the injured at the site. Betty later moved to Guernsey, but the survivors communicated with her for many years afterwards.'

In 2006 the shoulder slopes of Shutlingsloe were still estate-owned moorland but evidence of the crash was found in the shape of a single corroded fragment discerned close to a boulder which could be taken to mark the location of the impact point.

Right: The crash site of Oxford L4601, looking towards Crag Hall, Wildboarclough

Airspeed Oxford Mk.1 DF408, Dawson Farm, Bosley, near Macclesfield

SJ 93163 67270 378m impact site
SJ 93167 67318 376m terminal site
No.1531 Beam Approach Training Flight, RAF Cranage (south-west of Macclesfield), No.5 Group, Flying Training Command
15 January, 1943

Crew: two, one injured:
Flying Officer G.C. Smith, Royal Canadian Air Force, instructor, injured
Pupil pilot, unidentified

On 15 January, 1943, Flying Officer Smith, of the Royal Canadian Air Force, a staff instructor on the Beam Approach Training Flight at RAF Cranage, was detailed to carry out an instructional sortie of beam approaches. He had been airborne for just twenty minutes when, at 1230 hours, his aircraft, flying outside the safe range of the facility, and in cloud, struck a hillside. There was no fire, and although the aircraft was destroyed and Flying Officer Smith suffered a slight injury to his foot, the pupil pilot was unhurt and both men were able to make their way to Dollards Farm, Sutton, where they found succour.

The Beam-Approach system of the day, as described earlier in this volume, was based upon a radio beam projected down the extended centre line of the runway with a range marker at three miles, and another at 150 yards from the runway. But to use the system, it will be recalled, it was necessary to home to overhead the main airfield beacon, then to maintain 1,100 feet while flying outbound on the beam in order to distance the aircraft preparatory to turning inbound and descending to land. Flying outbound from the airfield would initially allow the pilot to hear the Inner Marker beacon, and some forty-five seconds later, the Outer Marker beacon. At which point, knowing that he was three miles from the airfield, he would make a stylised teardrop-shaped turn which would bring him back onto the beam facing towards the airfield at not more than five miles range: well clear of any high ground.

All very well in theory, and in later years, with improved instrumentation, such a procedure became very straightforward. But in 1943 the system was more rudimentary. For a start, although instruments existed which would help the pilot keep on the beam, not all aircraft had them fitted. Lacking such assistance, therefore, the pilot had to rely upon aural signals in his headset. Then, in cross-wind conditions, he had to apply himself to 'bracketing' the beam; that is, he had to adopt various headings until he had correctly assessed the drift and was able to maintain the centre-line signal.

At the same time there were radio calls to be made to ground control, which, in certain cases, required the pilot to temporarily tune away from the beam signal. Then again, on dual sorties, he might need to seek guidance, or receive information from his instructor on intercom, again taking him – or at least his concentration – from the audio signal. Nor would any marker-beacon audio signals invariably share the beam frequency; indeed markers often only triggered off lights.

As for the marker-beacon signals themselves, these were transmitted as relatively narrow cones, pointing vertically upwards, so that should the pilot have strayed from the exact centre line – if he had been slow to detect and then allow for a wind change, for example – he could well pass outside the cone of a marker, and so miss it altogether. The drill was to keep a check of the elapsed time while setting up the approach, ideally using a cockpit clock. So that, having passed over the Inner Marker outbound the pilot would expect the Outer Marker to come up within something like forty-five seconds. If it failed to come up, however, then he should have been on his guard, for to fly any great distance beyond the Outer Marker in an outbound direction was to move outside the safety-height for the approach. And long before that, he should have realised his error, made a politic inbound turn, and started off the approach again.

The inquiry into this accident duly established that the pupil pilot had failed to carry out such a timing check. Further, that when no Outer-Marker signal was heard outbound – almost certainly because he had already drifted south, off the beam – he had been allowed to carry on 'for at least four minutes', flying so far beyond the safe sector that the machine had eventually crashed into a spine of hills a full twelve miles from the airfield, and at some 1,300 feet above sea level; that is, as would be expected, some 1,100 feet above the elevation of Cranage.

The court of inquiry also found that the pupil pilot had made 'an error of judgement in that he failed to hear the signal, coupled with a bad error of judgement in failing to appreciate' the lapse of time, a finding upheld by all higher authorities. It was further observed – but only as a supplementary cause!– that much was due to 'the pre-occupation of the pilot instructor when faced with conditions he had not previously encountered'. The pilot instructor being Flying Officer Smith, who, after all, was wholly responsible for the conduct and safety of the flight.

In mid-2005 Mrs Evelyn Naden, then of Cheddleton, but who was brought up on Golden Hill Farm, Bosley, had vivid memories of the crash.

'It was a very misty day when the RAF plane crashed,' she recalled, 'hitting near the top of the Sutton Moor ridge, in Dawson Farm's Black Hill Field; in fact, had it been only a matter of feet higher it would have been all right. However, that field's marshy – indeed there's a never-failing spring just below where the plane touched down – so it skidded left and slid on through the drystone wall onto Upton Fold Farm's land. One of the two men hurt his foot, but both were able to follow the wall through the mist, first up, and then down, until they struck the track and made their way yet further down to Dollards Farm. As it happened, in following the wall they only just missed the radar station – it was sited rather lower down than the 1947 GPO tower – for the RAF had phones there, and airmen who were billeted at Dollards and Golden Hill farms.

'Later, visiting the crash site with my brother, we found that the aeroplane was on its belly but still quite whole, so that the sentries let us sit in the cockpit. Eventually, though, the RAF chopped it into pieces and my father dragged it down to Upton Fold Farm, then carted it off. Of course, it was only a farm track then, but the route was the same: uphill from Upton Fold Farm – and now, around the GPO tower – beside Lingerds Farm, then downhill, past the entrance to Dollards Farm, and finally to the road, the A54, where the RAF had one of their long low-loaders, opposite Golden Hill Farm.'

2005, Mrs Evelyn Naden, her back to Upton Fold Farm, indicating the terminal site from the point at which Oxford DF408 slid through the wall

In 2006 there was no surface evidence of the crash at the site, only pasture, the marshy ground above the never-failing spring, and to the west, the low-lying Cheshire Plain, which would have presented not the slightest obstacle to DF804, had it only been turned back towards Cranage at the proper time.

Airspeed Oxford Mk.1 LX673, Dingers Hollow Farm, north of Wildboarclough

SJ 98076 70876 387m impact point
SJ 98142 70919 352m débris pool
No.21 (Pilots) Advanced Flying Unit, RAF Wheaton Aston (near Stafford), No.21 Group, Flying Training Command
11 January, 1946

Crew: both killed:
Flying Officer David Fairless Oliver, RAF Volunteer Reserve, staff pilot
Flight Sergeant Eric Bulcock, RAFVR, pupil pilot

Although the Second World War had finished six months earlier, training courses continued at RAF Wheaton Aston, converting pilots to multi-engined aircraft, and where necessary, re-introducing them to temperate-zone flying conditions. On 11 January, 1946, one of the Advanced Flying Unit's staff instructors, Flying Officer David Oliver, took off with his pupil, Flight Sergeant Eric Bulcock, to practise carrying out Standard Beam Approaches in the local area. In the course of this particular training session, however, a mistake was made – so that the pupil was allowed to come 'too low on the back beam', as the RAF accident report summarised – and the aircraft was flown into a gully above Dingers Hollow Farm, just north of Wildboarclough, killing both pilots.

Enough aspects of the Standard Beam Approach (SBA) procedure have been described in this book to show that it was only too easy for even an experienced pilot to become confused regarding his whereabouts on the pattern. This was especially the case when a pilot was making what was known as a 'back-beam' approach, for it was a characteristic of the SBA radiation pattern that beams were transmitted in both directions.

There was the front beam, extending thirty miles downwind with respect to the prevailing wind. But there was also a mirror-image beam, known as the 'back beam', extending to thirty miles in the opposite direction, upwind, in terms of the prevailing wind. And when the actual wind's direction dictated, this back beam could be used for a landing approach.

The major complication in such an approach was that the back beam had no marker beacons to tell the pilot his range from the runway. This meant that a relatively complicated timing procedure was called for in order to determine how long to head away from the airfield before turning back and beginning the final descent to land. The relevance to Oxford LX673 being– to reiterate – that the accident report specifically recorded that the pupil pilot had got too low on the back beam, and that the instructor had not corrected him in time.

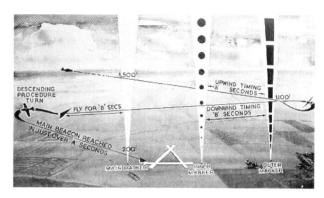

Back-Beam SBA Approach (*RAF Flying Manual*, AP129)

Determining when to turn back required an initial pattern to be flown on the front beam during which the lapse times from beacon to beacon would be noted, both inbound and outbound. And only with these times established would the actual procedure be flown on the beaconless back beam, utilising the noted timings as the basis for the distance to fly outbound, and the point at which to commence the final descent to land inbound.

Nor should the task of collating, assimilating, and applying a few timings be disparaged. For throughout the procedure the pilot would be concentrating on flying with reference to instruments alone, and as the RAF's 1941 *Air Navigation* manual warned, 'mathematical ability is one of the first faculties … to suffer in flight'.

The main finding of the investigation, however, held to determine the reason for this accident, while almost certainly accounting for the cause, does raise interpretative problems. For it is difficult to reconcile this crash site with either the front or the back beams of any of the region's Training Command airfields. On the other hand any back beam from the northerly runway at RAF Ashbourne would have run directly overhead the site, although it seems doubtful whether, if such a facility ever existed, it would still have been operational in 1946. But putting aside the question of which beam the aircraft was attempting to fly – for that would have been known to the inquiry, after all – the reason for the timing being so grossly inaccurate was never established. Only it was this faulty timing that resulted in the aircraft being flown outbound to a distance markedly beyond any protected zone, and therefore, at a height far below its safe altitude.

There were two witnesses to the tragedy: Mr John Finney, of High Ash Farm, and Mr W. Hoggarth, of Dry Knowle Farm. They heard a low-flying aircraft droning through the thick mist and heavy rain, and formed the impression that it was lost. Then the twin-engined trainer emerged from the mist. They saw it strike the top of the hill, and one of its wings detach, after which it reared nose up, only to fall backwards down the slope and into the gully, breaking up as it went. The two would-be rescuers made all speed to the wreckage, but found both occupants dead.

Viewing the surrounding high ground from the initial impact site it becomes dramatically evident just how low the aircraft was being flown. But by 2006 no evidence of the impact remained, not even a scar. However, not that many years before, a search by enthusiasts in the gully below the impact point produced not only flight instruments but components from a parachute harness. In 2006, on the other hand, even a metal-detector search revealed only corroded scraps of débris. Yet even these were sufficient to identify the aircraft as an Oxford, and so reconfirm it as Oxford LX673, which an unkind set of circumstances caused to impact on the rim of the gully, so close above the buildings of Dingers Hollow Farm.

Impact point

Left: Oxford Mk.1 LX673; the gully below the impact site above Dingers Hollow Farm

Above: 2006 debris (re-interred), including lengths of the singular metal ribbon used to electrically bond (that is, earth) the wooden-framed Oxford

McDonnell Douglas Phantom RF-4C 64-1018, Rose Wood, Unthank, near Chesterfield

SK 31062 75722 187m
SK 25630 75250 pilot landed
SK 25720 75310 navigator landed
United States Air Force in Europe, 3rd Air Force, 10th Tactical
Reconnaissance Wing, 1st Tactical Reconnaissance Squadron,
RAF Alconbury, Huntingdon
6 May, 1970

Crew: ejected; smashed thigh, and minor injuries:
Major Donald Eugene Tokar, USAF, pilot, smashed thigh
Major Peter Martin Dunn, USAF, navigator

The McDonnell Douglas Phantom RF-4C was the unarmed photographic reconnaissance version of the Phantom F-4C fighter, but although the Phantom's sheer nippiness had got it out of many scrapes, notably in Vietnam where, it is held, none were shot down by other aircraft, successful evasion by the unarmed version called for the adoption of extreme tactics, and these, in turn, sometimes led the aircraft to be placed in equally extreme attitudes.

It was necessary, of course, for such manoeuvres to be practised, and this was the purpose of the sortie upon which Major Donald Tokar and Major Peter Dunn, his navigator, embarked on 6 May, 1970. The exercise was to be carried out in combination with another Phantom, one attacking, the other evading, but only after burning off enough fuel weight in mild zoom-and-roll aerobatics to enable the steeper and faster manoeuvres to be flown in safety. For being non-operational flying, safety was paramount, so that loss-of-control recovery techniques (even to the extent of streaming the drag parachute in flight!) had been particularly stressed at the pre-flight briefing. All of which was just as well, for forty-four minutes into the sortie Major Tokar, in seeking to recover from a steep dive ('low-nose, high speed maneuver'), found that his controls were not answering.

Mr Ken Adlington, of Curbar

The subsequent investigation would focus upon the position of the moveable-tailplane assembly, but at the time it was sufficient for Majors Tokar and Dunn – each having around three thousand hours of flying experience – to know that the situation was beyond recovery. Accordingly Major Tokar issued the order and both ejected safely, landing in the Curbar Edge area. Major Dunn came down lightly, albeit suffering abrasions when he was dragged by his parachute, but Major Tokar, landing among rocks, smashed his thigh.

Farmer Ken Adlington, latterly of Curbar, lived in Warren Lodge, just below Curbar Edge, at the time. 'As I drove home,' he recalled in August 2005, 'I saw the parachutes. One of these – the navigator's – was hanging over the Edge. Having raised the alarm, I climbed up with Brian Whittaker, Police Constable Charlesworth, and a few more locals, to find that the other American had fallen among the rocks and broken his leg.' He smiled. 'Once we'd got the navigator off the cliff he began telling us how grateful he was for his English ejection seat, and that as they'd been coming down the pilot had pointed at Barbrook Reservoir and then to the rocks, and called across, "Well, that's it. We're either going to drown or get smashed on the rocks." Anyway, we got them both down to more level ground where Dr Dalrymple Smith and the ambulance crews tended them until, about half an hour later, an RAF helicopter arrived and lifted them both away.'

Just a week after the crash Major Dunn, the uninjured navigator, wrote a general letter of appreciation to the local newspaper thanking all the Curbar villagers for their assistance, making particular note of one act of kindness. 'A wonderful gentleman named Mr Village', he wrote, 'even made a quick trip home and came back with a bottle of brandy – I've never had a more enjoyable tot.' And three months later, with Major Tokar still on crutches after two months in traction, the pair entertained villagers from Curbar, and also from Millthorpe, at their Lakenheath base.

For the day of the crash remained a vivid memory, too, to those at Unthank Lane Farm, Millthorpe, where the abandoned Phantom had come down just inside the adjoining Rose Wood, diving almost vertically into the ground and creating a wide, deep crater, as Mr Ian Biggin, the son of the owner, recalled in 2005. 'I was working up at John Lowe's farm,' he said, 'when I heard this aircraft diving, and then saw it plummet into the wood. A massive mushroom cloud went up, with débris flying everywhere, and then, for a long time after everything else had settled, streams of film began descending, much wider than 35mm cine film, and much of it alight. But even before anything much had settled another Phantom appeared, roaring past, virtually scraping the woods, evidently trying to see what had happened.'

Major Tokar being stretchered from the rocks (courtesy of the *Sheffield Morning Telegraph*)

Reunion at Lakenheath, July 1970. Left to right: Councillor Ken Adlington, Major Tokar, Police Constable Charlesworth, Andrew Adlington, (in the Martin Baker ejection seat) Major Dunn, Brian Whittaker, and Dr Dalrymple Smith (courtesy of *The Derbyshire Times*)

'Ah! didn't it?' Ian's father, Neville, confirmed with some feeling. 'I was in the barn, and following so close after the explosion I thought it was the crashed one bouncing my way, so I dived into the hay.'

'Extreme low flying was something we got used to while the Americans were on site,' said Neville's other son, Stewart. 'We'd never seen anything like it. In fact, they set up a caravan just beyond the road corner and when a bigwig came in his helicopter some days later another Phantom very nearly crashed into it. In fact, we heard them on the radio ordering him to 'Get his arse out of here', or suchlike. But minutes later he came screaming down the wood again – multiple airshows every day, it was!'

Mr Neville Biggin in 2005: 'Uncle Sam, sir, about my forty yards of wall ...'

'The whole thing was incredible from the start,' Neville agreed. 'Lakenheath, their main base, is about a hundred miles away, yet after the crash some Americans were here within an hour. In great high wheeled vehicles! And eventually they'd coach in sixty or seventy black airmen every day, putting bits in plastic bags.' He paused. 'There was a hole in the barn roof, and another in the house, near the weather vane, and the undercarriage was by the hedge in the field to the side. Then there was a great tree, blown up by the roots, just outside, and clods of earth everywhere – one fell on a wheelbarrow which our chap had only left moments before, enough to overfill both it and him. So it was clear there'd have to be some compensation. Then I remembered that a tumbled forty-yard stretch of wall ran from just near the crater, and thought I might get a new one out of them.' Again he paused, and this time grinned ruefully. 'But of course, that particular Phantom squadron's job was aerial reconnaissance, and all they did was send me a photograph of the area, taken before the crash, showing the wall already flat!'

Son Ian, with a wide reputation as an auto-engineer in addition to his farming duties, displayed a box full of fragments, including the aircraft's radar altimeter. This is a 'second generation' height-reading device which, by bouncing signals off the earth, gives the aircraft a true indication of its height above the terrain directly beneath it. A device, that is, that could have saved a great number of the aircraft covered in this Peakland series. 'But scraps are always coming to light,' Ian said. 'I've also got the cockpit clock, stopped at the moment of impact.'

Above: The aircraft's radar altimeter. The pressure altimeter is merely a barometer calibrated to indicate height above any set datum. The radar altimeter, in contrast, shows the true height above the terrain directly below.

Left: Mr Ian Biggin

Mr Stewart Biggin shows where débris came through the roof

Ian's brother, Stewart, pointed out where a great chunk of débris had come through the barn roof, explaining then: 'But over in the wood where the plane itself landed, it had always been marshy, and although they brought in a massive great digger, in the end, they just gave up trying to get up the rest, and backfilled the hole.'

Well before 2006 the backfilled crater site, situated just beyond the junction of a popular footpath and a bridleway inside Rose Wood, had long since become covered with brambles. But odd scraps of surface débris could still be found among the dead leaves; pieces discarded, no doubt, by careless crash-site seekers.

A slightly more protracted search discovered copious fragmented airframe parts just beneath the surface, many in an advanced state of corrosion quite unlike that normally found with débris from earlier, particularly Second-World-War, crash sites. The built-in redundancy of the times, perhaps? Although a more striking sign of changed times would be to compare the relative experience of the Phantom aircrew involved, with the lack of it among aircrew of earlier years, the Phantom pilot, with 3,000 hours, having fourteen years of Service flying behind him, rather than the four or five years and the 700 or so hours of the majority of his World-War-Two forebears.

The impact site of Phantom 64-1018

Debris in an advanced state of corrosion

Curbar Edge, above Warren Lodge, where the crew landed

Percival Proctor Mk.3 HM324, Middle Hill, Wormhill Moor, Hargatewall

SK 10822 77052 353m
Metropolitan Communications Squadron, RAF Northolt, No.47
Group, Transport Command
5 March, 1945

Occupants: pilot and two passengers, all killed:
Pilot Officer Raouil Eugene Clements Serruys,
Royal Belgian Air Force
Two passengers: presently unidentified

Percival Proctor Mk.3 HM324, on the establishment of the Metropolitan Communications Squadron located at RAF Northolt, near London, was a dependable communications machine which would carry up to four passengers and cruised at 140 mph (122 knots).

On 5 March, 1945, Pilot Officer Raouil Serruys, of the Royal Belgian Air Force, was detailed to fly two passengers on a daytime flight that took him north-west into the Buxton area. The Midlands weather was poor, with low cloud and even lower visibility beneath it, and at some stage in his flight Pilot Officer Serruys became lost and flew into the crest of Middle Hill, Wormhill Moor, at an elevation of 1,100 feet above sea level. The aircraft, heading in a north-westerly direction, struck the ground and shed a trail of wreckage until it crashed through a drystone wall, demolishing it, and coming to a stop just yards into the field beyond.

The weather was so bad that the machine was not located until the next day when it was found that at least one of the occupants had survived the impact, for he had managed to crawl downhill into the field below the crash site, only to perish overnight.

The court of inquiry was forced to speculate in trying to determine whether Pilot Officer Serruys had descended in order to pinpoint himself, having got lost, or whether, having become short of fuel, he had been trying to make a precautionary landing. The latter was held to be the most likely, though, for while the aircraft's fuel tanks were broken in the crash it was established that they had been virtually empty.

Much concern focused upon what was held to be Pilot Officer Serruys' lack of experience, this notwithstanding that he had of the order of five hundred hours' total flying, a reasonable enough level of experience for that era. There was, of course, some censure in that he had not returned to base on encountering bad weather, or alternatively put down in good time at some other airfield, but then the view was expressed that a pilot 'with little experience' should never have been dispatched on the flight at all: a direct slap in the face for whoever authorised the flight!

In all, no firm conclusion could be reached, but to descend below a safe altitude in order to pinpoint oneself was such a commonplace practice – the great majority of pilots coming to no harm – that all the higher formations concurred with the rather indeterminate finding of the inquiry.

Interviewed in mid-2005, Mr Teddy Mosely, of Knotlow Farm, Wormhill, had no difficulty in recalling the wrecked Proctor. 'I was on the adjoining hill with my father the day after the crash,' he said. 'The plane stood out well, being orange-coloured, and it had crashed through the drystone wall to finish up by the rough area on the summit.' He reflected. 'I didn't go there at the time, for it wasn't our land

Mr Teddy Mosely, of Wormhill, who was able to identify the site

then, and besides, they weren't allowing anyone near. But we took over the fields in 1947.'

Mr Mosely vouched for the fact that for many years after he took over the land they would plough up pieces of aluminium, 'You'd see it when you walked the land afterwards. But I can't remember when any last surfaced.'

A metal-detector search in early 2006 discovered just two scraps of débris, but those aside, the pasture showed no sign of the tragedy enacted amid its grasses on that fog-shrouded day in 1945, while even

Looking back along the approach of Proctor HM324, past the rebuilt wall

the rebuilt section of the drystone wall had so weathered as to be indistinguishable from the rest. And poignantly, the field down which the stricken survivor crawled towards the farm he might have seen beckoning in the hollow, unlike the thronged higher pastures, was empty, even of a single grazing sheep.

Pierre Robin R1180TD G-CRAN, Staden Industrial Estate, Buxton

SK 07044 72118 333m
Private aircraft, Tatenhill, Needwood
15 June, 1996

Occupants: four, all killed:
Mr Joe Smith, pilot
Miss Mary Jane Smith, aged 11
Miss Joanne Smith, aged 12
Miss Elizabeth Skupien, aged 11

On 15 June, 1996, entrepreneur Mr Joe Smith took off from Tatenhill Airfield, near Needwood, in Robin G-CRAN on a pleasure trip to mark his daughter Mary Jane's eleventh birthday. His other passengers were Mary Jane's sister, Joanne, and a friend of the two girls, Elizabeth Skupien. On reaching the Buxton area, however, the aircraft was stalled, and crashed, killing all on board.

The flight had started off well, Mr Smith having planned an imaginative route, taking in several of the district's features most likely to interest the children. In accordance with this, having got airborne from Tatenhill at 0930 hours, he had headed north for the adventure playground at Alton Towers, holding the height throughout at 500 to 1,000 feet in order to provide the girls with a good view as they took their photographs. Next he turned the machine for Riber Castle, the folly above Matlock, after which he headed out towards Monyash and the ancient stone circle at Arbor Low, where he made a right-hand orbit. Clearing that area, he then turned towards Buxton, first circling the village of King Sterndale before altering course towards Slade Farm, Staden, to the south of Buxton,

The crash of Robin G-CRAN
(Photograph courtesy of the *Buxton Advertiser*)

where there were family friends whom his daughters had been visiting only the evening before.

In late 2005, Mr John Brittain, of Slade Farm, described how he was serving a customer in the farm shop when the Robin came into sight. 'I was intent on what I was doing,' he remembered, 'and even when it waggled its wings I didn't associate it with the birthday flight. Indeed, when it had passed over and there came a loud bang I wasn't really serious when I said to my customer, "I wonder if that aeroplane's crashed?" Nor was she, for she said "I shouldn't think so", and we carried on with the transaction.'

His grandson, Phillip Brittain-Cartlidge, however, had been left with no such ease of mind. 'I knew whose plane it was at once, of course,' he recalled, 'and I waved to them as they passed. Mr Smith was waggling his wings, going slowly, and so low that I could see he had his flaps down. In fact, later I would wonder if the flaps being down meant that he was already in trouble. But then he turned away towards Slade House and the ridge. And suddenly the engine misfired!' He paused. 'I saw the nose dip down and the plane begin to descend even lower. But then it passed out of my line of sight towards the ridge. And I began to run.'

Mr John Brittain and Mr Phillip Brittain-Cartlidge, indicating the crash site

Other witnesses from the nearby industrial estate told the coroner's court that when the engine had misfired the pilot had turned to line up with one of the service roads and seemed all set to make a forced landing; that at an estimated one hundred feet above the ground, when the engine had picked up once again, they had seen the nose lift sharply. And finally they described how the nose-high aircraft, apparently balked by the wooded ridge, seemed to them to stagger, then fall off into a tight, steeply nose-down spiral to the left and impact heavily with the ground.

Aerial view of Slade Farm

Youthful Phillip Brittain-Cartlidge reached the aircraft in a matter of moments, as he related. 'When I got there two men from City Electrical Factors, which the plane had overflown, were already there. There was no fire, but the perspex canopy had gone, leaving the cockpit open to view, and it was only too obvious that nothing could be done.' Again he paused. 'It was only later that the full trauma of it began to come home to me.'

Phillip's mother, Mrs Elizabeth Brittain-Cartlidge, touched on the trauma too. 'For quite a time we wondered if we'd distracted them by waving. We even wondered if having his flaps down had been wrong! And what made it so much worse was that the girls had been with us only the night before. In fact, I drove them home, and just before Mary Jane left my car she whispered that she had something to tell me. It was late, though, and her mother was calling, so I put her off. "Tell me tomorrow, dear," I told her.'

Equally distressed was their own daughter, Susanne, for Mr Kevin O'Neill of neighbouring Slade Hill House, arriving home just minutes after the crash, was told of it by the sadly distraught girl. 'I'd hardly taken in what Susanne told me,' he said, 'when a man from the *Advertiser* arrived, and wanted to know where the crash site was.'

There had been no fire, but one of the ironies was that the tragedy occurred during the 1996 firemen's strike, so that four RAF support vehicles and an army Green Goddess fire engine arrived in answer to the emergency call. 'Regrettably there was not a lot to be done at the scene,' the secretary of the striking Derbyshire Fire Brigade Union was quoted as saying.

The official inquiry ascertained that Mr Smith had held a Private Pilot's Licence, and that he had flown a healthy 865 hours, albeit only four on the Robin, and over a span of years. As was normal for the type of flight he had undertaken, he had not maintained radio contact with any control tower; poignantly, therefore, the route he had taken was pieced together not only from radar sightings, but from the photographs the girls had taken during the ill-fated tour.

The investigators carried out an exhaustive examination of the Lycoming 0-360 engine, a well-tried and dependable power source, yet although they discovered an anomaly in the fitting of one component, they were quite unable to reproduce the symptoms reported by witnesses prior to the crash. It had to be found, therefore, that the aircraft had, after all, been asked to climb with great suddenness from an extremely low altitude, that it had most likely been stalled in consequence, and had then fallen off, effectively, into an incipient spin, nosing steeply into the ground before any recovery action could have been effective.

And there was another inescapable fact to be considered. Low flying affords superb views, and carried out at a low enough level, is exhilarating in the extreme. Only it has its own hazards, because of which aviation law lays down strict safety rules. These include the requirement to fly at a height which will ensure that a machine can land clear of any residential or industrial area should an engine fail; they also dictate a minimum height of 1,500 feet above the highest (nearby) fixed object. To reiterate, low flying is exhilarating in the extreme. But it is perilous to an even greater degree should the slightest thing go wrong.

In early 2006, the crash site, long since scoured away for the foundations of new industrial buildings, showed no trace of the tragedy, but in an endearing touch, the side garden of nearby Slade Farm had been planted with daffodils which, in springtime, blossomed to form the initial letters of each girl's name: *Rough winds*, indeed, *do shake the darling buds....*

Robin G-CRAN; the impact site in mid 2006

Supermarine Seafires FMk.17 SX314 and SP325, Tagsclough Hill, Wildboarclough

SJ 99010 67434 437m SX314 beside wall
SJ 99063 67387 439m SP325
SJ 99202 67385 439m wing débris in gully
No.1831 Royal Naval Volunteer Reserve Squadron, HMS Blackcap, RN Air Station Stretton (south-east of Warrington)
16 July, 1949

Pilots: two, killed:
Lieutenant Hugh Eccles, Royal Naval Volunteer Reserve (SX314)
Lieutenant Frank James Dyke, Royal Naval Volunteer Reserve (SP325)

On 16 July, 1949, two Royal Naval Volunteer Reserve pilots were killed during a formation exercise when they flew into high ground at Tagsclough Hill, a mile south-east of Wildboarclough. Flying Seafire Mk.17s, they had been briefed to carry out a formation sortie in a specified area to the south of RNAS Stretton, flying at a minimum height of 2,500 feet. The authorised sortie length was forty minutes; accordingly, towards the end of that time, the leader, Lieutenant Eccles – call sign 103, spoken as 'One Oh Three' – called for a homing and controlled descent.

The call was received by their flight commander, manning the tower at Stretton. It was a formalised and therefore anticipated request, and although there would have been no indication of the formation's range from base, a heading to steer was passed, together with a clearance to descend to 1,500 feet. Exactly what heading was passed is no longer on record, but the coroner would be told that the pair had drifted twenty miles eastwards from their authorised area.

In any event the expected direct acknowledgement of the heading was not forthcoming. Instead, Lieutenant Eccles radioed back, 'This is 103 –'. Only then his carrier wave was abruptly cut off. After which nothing more was heard, despite repeated blind calls.

The response, although truncated, is significant to anyone familiar with R/T procedure. For had Lieutenant Eccles received the generally northerly homing course he anticipated, say 350 degrees, the procedural acknowledgement would have been a terse 'Three Five Zero, One-Oh-Three: cleared to fifteen hundred feet'. Whereas the discursive phraseology, 'This is 103 –', suggests that something had puzzled him; that he needed time to assess the bearing which, from the crash site, would have been of the order of 295 degrees, only a little north of west. The fact that the rest of his response was terminated by the impact has to be purely coincidental. Certainly there was no suggestion that the truncated response had been one of alarm.

At the time of this exchange, recorded as 1245 hours, Farmer John Robert Lane, of Bennettshitch Farm, busily engaged in gathering a pair of horses from a field, was startled when two aircraft in tight formation suddenly appeared from the mist and flew undeviatingly past him, 'At about two yards above the ground', as he would tell the coroner, 'and five feet from where I was standing ...' Transfixed, he saw the machines hit a wall, then flames break out from the one on the right, before both disappeared back into the mist. The horses, he recorded blandly, took fright.

In 2005 Mr Lane's grandson, Mr Thomas Victor Ferns, of Longnor, recalled that traumatic day. 'My grandfather would always say the two planes had been racing, one being slightly ahead of the other [a graphic description of echelon formation]. As it happened, he'd only just left the field they crashed in, and had dropped down towards the farm to collect the horses. I was nearer the farm with a friend, Peter Dodd from Gradbach, and although we heard the planes coming, very close, and very low, we couldn't see them for the mist and rain. And then we heard this great bang. Immediately we dropped everything, and ran towards it, meeting my grandfather and the horses almost at once. We continued up the moor, and found where the wall had been smashed away, and beyond that, wreckage for a good half a mile, even into the next holding. As for the pilots ... We found one body, and then another, by the far boundary wall. But there was nothing we could do. It was horrible. With flames everywhere, and the smell of burnt rubber ... I just panicked.'

In fact, far from panicking, the youthful Victor made exactly the right decision. 'We didn't have a phone at Bennettshitch at that time. So we ran on, over the moor – how fit we must have been then!– to the Rose and Crown at Allgreave, where they called the authorities.'

Supermarine Seafires, flying in echelon-starboard formation

Mr Thomas Victor Fern in 2005, with the New Testament from Mrs Eccles

Mr John Bowler, of Torgate Farm, and his father, were also early arrivals, having been given a lift to the moor by the local grocer. 'When we got there,' he recounted in late 2004, 'it was to find a great length of wall down, and wreckage wherever you looked. The engines and propellers had broken away beyond the main wreckage and ploughed long furrows across the ground.'

There was, of course, a Royal Naval court of inquiry, but no records from this appear to have survived. It is known, however, that the naval court impounded the radio-record of Stretton's air traffic control tower, an act which incensed the coroner. 'The public', he fulminated, 'ought to know the last words of these airmen which were recorded. The court of inquiry had no right …'

Because no records have been traced, it is not known what the Royal Naval inquiry found to be cause of the accident. But it can be deduced that the leader, holding a considerably lower altitude than his authorised minimum height of 2,500 feet, and operating in poor visibility, inadvertently drifted eastwards from the 200 feet or so elevation of Stretton to the 1,500 feet above-sea-level moors of Wildboarclough. It would follow that as the pair impacted at an elevation of 1,433 feet, but with their altimeters still set – in accordance with contemporary practice – to register the height above Stretton, Lieutenant Eccles would have expected there to be over a thousand feet of clear air below him. So that with him concentrating on his instrument flying, and with his number two fully intent on holding station, neither realised that they were merely skimming the ground as they flashed past farmer John Lane. Indeed it seems likely that realisation would never have come to Lieutenant Eccles and that even Lieutenant Dyke would only have had time to wonder at his leader's sudden disintegration before he too knew nothing but oblivion.

In the aftermath, Mrs Eccles, the mother of Lieutenant Eccles, movingly expressed her thanks for the aid young Victor Ferns had tried to render her son, sending him a New Testament that was still a much prized memento in 2005.

The letter from Mrs Eccles, thanking Mr Fern for his efforts

I am the mother of one of the young men who were killed on July 16th 1949.
You did your best to get help quickly, by running a great distance & I have always been grateful to you, though I do not know you.
Will you please accept this little gift as a memento of my gratitude. It did not cost a great deal, but it is the finest book there is. Both the young men who were killed that day, though both happy & gay, knew the value of its teaching & so I hope you will value it also.
A.L. Eccles

In 2006 visual evidence of the double tragedy was still to be found at the scene. Indeed there were three associated sites.

The damaged section of wall which finally stopped SX314 still stood, while a small collection of débris had been placed in mid-field, where SP325 came to rest, just 130 metres to the south-east. Then there was a mainplane component in a gully some 140 metres east of the latter site which, being quite weighty, seemed to stand a reasonable chance of being left in situ for some time to come. Regarding SP325, only a minimal amount remained, while of SX314 there was no trace at all. It is known, however, that enthusiasts did find débris adjacent to the wall, so evidently they saw fit to remove it.

The crash site is a drab location on all but the sunniest day, most often quite joyless, and in 2006 still trackless, with much hummock-grass to labour over from any recognised pathway; a site, moreover, from which even the skyline scenery seems uneasily diminished.

Termination site of SX314. Debris was found here but none seems to have been left at the site.

Mainplane component in a gully

Contemporary photograph of the scene (courtesy of Crown Copyright)

2006, from the SP325 impact point

Avro Shackleton MR Mk.3 (prototype) WR970, Foolow (north-east of Tideswell)

SK 19331 76643 275m
A.V. Roe and Co. Ltd., Stockport
7 December, 1956

Occupants: all killed:
Squadron Leader Jack Bertram Wales, OBE, DFC (A.V. Roe test pilot)
George Alan Blake, flight engineer
Charles O'Neill, technical observer
Roy Greenhaigh, technical observer

The Second World War proved both the efficacy of, and the necessity for, an efficient maritime reconnaissance (the MR of the designation) patrol aircraft. As a result the Avro Shackleton was developed to replace the Lancaster. The squadrons began receiving the type in April 1951, and while the maritime versions were withdrawn from service in the early 1970s, variants still flew with the RAF until well into the 1990s.

Although deemed pleasant to fly from the start, the type was constantly being updated, the modifications invariably increasing both weight and dimensions. So it was that in September 1955, when the tricycle-undercarriaged Mark 3 version was first flown, considerable testing was called for. Indeed it was not until a full year after it first flew that the Mark 3 prototype, WR970, was handed to The Aeroplane and Armament Experimental Establishment (A&AEE) at Boscombe Down for additional testing. Then, on 28 November, 1956, it was returned to Avro's Woodford plant, near Stockport, for further stall-warning development tests. And it was in the course of these that it crashed at Foolow, in Derbyshire, narrowly missing the village, but killing all on board.

Crashing within the bounds of the village, as it did, meant that there were many witnesses; in particular an ex-RAF flight engineer who was to recall that as the aircraft broke cloud it was spiralling, and doing no more than 60 knots. From this he deduced that it had been locked into some form of deep stall.

Another witness was the then-farmworking teenager Mr Les Bond, years later to return to become the landlord of the village's Bull's Head pub. In 1956, looking up from his mucking out, and shocked at seeing the machine flying so low and in such obvious difficulties, he had screamed out, 'Get up, you bugger! You're going to crash!'

Then, as he explained, when the worst happened, he had run to the scene. 'On the way I overtook Frank Harrison …' He paused, and suddenly smiled. 'He was carrying a little fire extinguisher, although what good he thought that would do.' Then, abruptly, he sobered. 'But he did find a use for it. For when he caught up with me I'd come to one of the crew.' He paused again. 'There was nothing left of his clothing, and although Frank played the extinguisher on him we were far too late. All we could do was cover him up.' Again he reflected. 'There was so little to be done that after a while I just went back to my mucking out.'

But he remembered too, later that evening, sitting at home listening to the wireless, and wondering at the inaccuracies which abounded in the reports, scarcely able to credit that the august BBC could get so many things so wrong.

The official inquiry was able to substantiate much of what the witnesses – if not the BBC – had reported. The testing, it seems, had reached the stage of examining the stalling characteristics of the aircraft with bomb bays open and radar scanner extended: the attack configuration, as it was known. It appears that, in the course of this, a level turn was commenced and the speed reduced towards the stall. Except that, as on a previous occasion at Boscombe Down, and as witnessed now by the crew of a coincidentally passing Lincoln bomber, the aircraft rolled markedly, then fell away into a spin which, in this case, took it down into thick cloud.

Shackleton WR970 on a happier occasion (courtesy of Ian Allan Publishers, photographer Leslie Hammond)

What none of the witnesses could have known, but what subsequent examination of the engines showed had happened, was that during its passage through the cloud the Shackleton had actually been totally upset, spinning belly up for some time before righting itself just before it emerged from cloud to end its fatal fall.

One witness, however, Mr John Hancock, might have been able to put the investigators on the track of this rather earlier. 'I was at Shepherd's Park Farm,' he recounted, 'just to the north of the village, when

Witnesses, Mr Les Bond and Mr John Hancock, photographed in late 2005

I heard this noise of aero engines hunting up and down – trying to break the stall, as I thought later. Then the aircraft appeared out of the clouds at about a thousand feet, between me and the village. I've always fancied that the first thing to appear was the tailplane. But then the whole machine fell from the cloud with one wing hard down, and that was the way it hit the ground.' As it transpired, however, Mr Hancock was not interviewed by the investigators. He went on, 'I rushed over in my car; to find that, although the heat was intense, the aircraft wasn't all burning, for some of the crew members had been thrown clear: I remember one was wearing an Irving flying jacket. But there was nothing to be done for any of them.'

There was no visual evidence of the crash to be seen in 2006. And a

Above: The impact wreckage of Shackleton WR970 (Photograph by courtesy of the *Derby Evening Telegraph*)

Right: The site in 2006, looking towards Foolow

temporary plaque that had once been erected on the war-memorial site in the centre of this archetypically English village had long since disappeared. Nor was there any indication that a drystone wall on the far boundary of Foolow had stopped short the careering run of a forced-landing Harvard trainer in 1952.

But at the Shackleton crash site, below the cropped-turf surface of the drystone-walled enclosures, fragments still remained, with most centred on the pasture where WR970 first struck, as half-inverted still, it spiralled itself, together with its hapless crew, into the unforgiving and unyielding earth.

Douglas C-47 Skytrain 41-38608, Dawson Farm, Bosley, Macclesfield

SJ 92674 66630 232m
United States Ninth Army Air Force, No.363 Tactical Air Command, 333rd Photographic Reconnaissance Squadron, Le Culot (Belgium) 22 December, 1944

Occupants: three passengers, four crew; only the aircraft's captain survived:
Major Theodore A. Rogers, aircraft captain, survived
First Lieutenant J.E. Barnby, co-pilot
Technical Sergeant W.E. Davis, crew
Technical Sergeant C.P. Ingram, crew
Lieutenant-Colonel R.L. Cardozo, passenger
Lieutenant-Colonel H.R. Payne, passenger
Major David C.R. Steele, passenger, survived only briefly

The Douglas C-47 was the modified version of the Douglas DC-3 civil transport aircraft known to the RAF as the Dakota which, with its wide cargo door and strengthened flooring, particularly lent itself to the passenger-cum-freight (PCF) role. The role, indeed, in which C-47 41-38608 was configured on 22 December, 1944, when Major Theodore Rogers and his crew were dispatched from American Air Force designated airfield AAF590 (RAF Burtonwood), near Liverpool, with three senior-officer passengers and a freight load which included a jeep.

The weather was cloudy, with nine-tenths – almost solid – cover, a base of just 800 feet, and a visibility, even in the clear air below the base, reduced to 1,100 yards by mist and industrial haze. Not unreasonable conditions, however, and crew and passengers duly got airborne at 1415 hours. Except that, after flying for twenty-seven miles, their machine struck a tree at an elevation of just 800 feet above sea level, crashed into a lower pasture and then burnt out, with only the handling pilot, Major Rogers, surviving.

The American accident investigators submitted that Major Rogers had exercised bad judgment in even attempting to maintain contact by flying below the ceiling. At the same time they recorded that he had flown a total of 1,200 hours, with 88 hours on C-47s, but that his record showed a serious lack of experience in instrument flying. A point which became of particular significance when it was established that the initial impact was with a tree. The investigators would have appreciated that contemporary practice was to set the altimeter to read zero before take off, and to leave it at that setting throughout the flight. Just before impact, therefore, with Burtonwood being a mere 76 feet above sea level, Major Rogers' altimeter would have been telling him that he was almost one thousand feet high, by modern standards unthinkably low in such weather conditions, but not abnormally so for those days. What his altimeter would not have told him, however, was that he had moved over markedly rising terrain, and that he was now barely skimming the ground.

Yet what mystifies still is why the aircraft crashed where it did. The given initial destination – before crossing to Belgium – was American Air Force airfield No.519. But this was RAF Station Grove, near Wantage, in Oxfordshire, the track for which was some 160°T – effectively southerly – to be reached having overflown the flat, low-lying Cheshire Plain. But having gone such a short distance, the C-47 crashed fifteen miles off the direct line for Grove, the machine having been flown almost forty-five degrees off track.

It is conceivable that the pilot, with little enough instrument experience, had mis-set either his compass or the gyroscopically-controlled directional indicator (basically a slave compass), and so followed a false heading. On the other hand, the track for another frequently-used American station, AAF 555, or RAF Shepherd's Grove, north-east of Bury St Edmonds, Suffolk, was 115°T– effectively easterly – and this track passes virtually overhead the crash site, but also over appreciably higher terrain. It is at least possible, then, that at the planning stage, the track for Shepherd's Grove was laid in, instead of that for Grove.

In 2005 the incumbent of Golden Hill Farm, Mr Alfred Bullock, was able to point out the crash site across the valley, beyond the A54 road. 'I was thirteen when the plane crashed,' he recalled. 'It came down in Swanslake Field, on Dawson Farm, which George Naden had at the time. So while his son, Kenneth, drove round to Stye Farm, where there was a phone, George and his other son, Maurice, ran to see what they could do. The plane was an inferno, but they managed to get two men out, and although one died shortly afterwards, the other survived. When I got there I found débris all over the place, with the main wreckage in a shallow crater. But as the fire had died down by then I could see a burnt body inside, trapped beneath a jeep.'

And there Mr Bullock had touched upon one of the drawbacks of the passenger-cum-freight configuration of the day, when cargo was loaded aft of passengers, potentially hazarding them should the lashings break in the event of a crash or even a too-abrupt halt.

Mr Alfred Bullock, of Golden Hill Farm, witness

In more enlightened times, in Dakotas and other types – RAF Argosies in the 1960s come to mind – with no under-floor hold, freight would always be loaded forward of passengers.

The efforts made by Mr Naden and his thirteen-year-old son, Maurice, to extricate survivors from the burning aircraft gives a dimension to this air accident which is very seldom matched in this Peakland series, for the higher echelons learnt of the manner in which the pair had hazarded themselves. Accordingly, letters of appreciation were written to each of them by the Chief Constable of Cheshire, by various major- and brigadier-generals of the American Ninth Air Force, by the Air Council, and by Mr Herbert Morrison, MP. The acme was the award to both father and son of the King's Commendation for Brave Conduct, signed, on His Majesty's behalf, by the Prime Minister and Lord of the Treasury of the day, Mr Winston S. Churchill, entitling them to wear the silver laurel spray symbolising the gallantry award.

By the KING'S Order the name of
Francis Maurice Naden,
Schoolboy, Bosley, Cheshire,
was published in the London Gazette on
8 May, 1945,
as commended for brave conduct.
I am charged to record His Majesty's
high appreciation of the service rendered.

Winston S. Churchill

Prime Minister and First Lord
of the Treasury

Maurice Naden, aged 18, wearing (beneath an unidentified badge) the silver spray of laurel leaves which denotes the award of a King's Commendation for Brave Conduct (All documents by courtesy of Mrs Evelyn Naden)

Mrs Betty Steele and Joyce, her daughter, visiting the American Cemetery at Cambridge in 1963 (courtesy of Mrs Evelyn Naden)

Mrs Betty Steele, Major Steele's widow, was equally appreciative of their efforts and later corresponded with the family, a source of support she clearly found comforting. So much so that, in 1963, in what turned out to be the final exchange of letters, Mrs Steele regretted the fact that only a short while before, when she had finally visited the Bosley crash site with her then grown-up daughter, Joyce, the Nadens had been on a National Farmers' Union visit to the burgeoning Heathrow Airport, where they were struck, above all, by the sight of a Dakota!

Harking back to the 1943 crash, and stressing again how much she had owed in the interim to the Nadens' letters, Mrs Steele came back to what had clearly become a perennial grievance for the dependents of those involved: that the American government had been so grudging in giving them information. For years, for example, Mrs Steele had known little more than that her husband had lived for three hours after the Nadens had extricated him

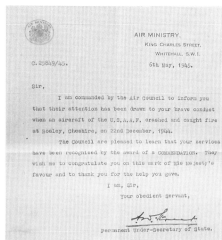

One of several letters of appreciation from the American Ninth Air Force reflecting the unhesitating gallantry father and son displayed in exposing themselves to 'great personal hazard' despite the imminent danger of explosion (Both letters by courtesy of Mrs Evelyn Naden)

Recognition by the Air Council of the award of a King's Commendation for Brave Conduct

from the wreck, and that the pilot had survived. And when she eventually came into contact with the pilot's wife it was to discover that she too had been told just as little. As for the pilot himself, the fact that his crew and his passengers had died had been deliberately kept from him for some time for fear of the psychological effect the revelation might have. Even so, he had required hospital care – 'counselling', it would later be termed – for many years after his return home.

It was from the pilot's wife too, that Mrs Steele had learnt that the weather had been so foggy on the day of the crash that passengers and crew had deliberated on whether or not to set off on their return to their Le Culot base. 'In the end they flipped a coin and decided to go back to the continent,' Mrs Steele recounted, commenting then: 'They'd have been better to have prayed, and gotten their answer in the right way.'

For Mrs Steele, it had been a case of being left alone to bring up her young daughter, and shelving the plans the family had made to move to, and see out the rest of the war in, Switzerland! Instead, she had been obliged to return to college to finish qualifying in order to resume her career as a child-care social worker. And illumining the 1963 scene she concluded her letter with her address, rather sceptically commenting on America's newly-introduced 'zip' code (postcode), 'which will make the mail go quicker – so they say.'

One of the unsung, and normally unidentified participants at crash sites, a member of the American salvage party. Airman Bill Floyd was struck by the young Mabel Naden, Maurice's sister, and sent her this greetings card and photograph, to which (alas!) the maiden, undesirous, it could be, of swelling the ranks of 'GI Brides', declined to respond.

By the time the Johnson family took over Dawson Farm in 1948, the Nadens had already left. Just the same, Mr Tom Johnson and his brother, Alec, still the incumbents in 2005, felt that they themselves had grown up with the crash site. 'The plane crashed', explained Tom, 'in what we now call Bottom Pasture. It came from the direction of Primrose Bank Farm and took the top off an oak tree, the stump of which stayed on the skyline for many years, but has long gone. Much later still people from Macc [the local abbreviation for Macclesfield] would come digging up bits of metal and taking them away.' Mr Johnson indicated the farm drive. 'It now runs straight through the wood to the main road. But it used to bend, and run along the gully where the salvage crew tipped much of the wreckage. Only the people from Macc took that, too.'

2005, Mr Tom Johnson, of Dawson Farm, at the main impact point

As Mr Johnson indicated, enthusiasts had so assiduously busied themselves in removing débris from the site that by 2006 nothing remained on the surface to show where the tragedy occurred, or where such selfless heroism was displayed.

Supermarine Spitfire Mk.2A P7560, Thirkelow Farm, near Harpur Hill, Buxton

SK 04975 68961 430m
No.131 Squadron, RAF Atcham (Shrewsbury), No.9 Group, Fighter Command.
22 November, 1941

Pilot: safely abandoned by parachute:
Flight Sergeant Briggs, Royal Australian Air Force

Judging by the perfection of the elliptically-based wing-shape of the Mark Two seen in plan-view photographs, it would seem that 'clean-cut' can be applied to any facet of the celebrated Vickers-Armstrongs Supermarine Spitfire bar its manufacturer's cumbersome title. And in truth, the latter requires some unravelling.

The 'Supermarine' came into being in 1916 when a forerunner company was taken over and the 'Supermarine Aviation Works Ltd' formed, a title that was retained as a separate entity when Vickers acquired it in 1928. It again survived when Vickers merged with Armstrongs to become 'Vickers-Armstrongs Ltd' in 1938. Indeed it only lost its identity in 1960 when the parent company became part of the British Aircraft Company (BAC). So, although generally known simply as the Supermarine Spitfire, the famous fighter, like any decent thoroughbred, has a string of pedigree forebears in its lineage. Not that the title itself, 'Spitfire', was a foregone conclusion. For it is held that R.J. Mitchell, the machine's celebrated designer, when told of the name first mooted by the managing director of Vickers, snapped, 'Just the bloody silly sort of name they would choose.'

It is not known whether the failing Mitchell lived long enough to be reconciled to the name that was to be forever linked with his, but he must surely have preferred it to the leading contender, 'Shrew'. Although had the casting vote been given to Flight Sergeant Briggs of the Royal Australian Air Force, in the briefly traumatic period as he parachuted down through a November sky in 1941, the outcome might have been rather different.

The function of No.131 Fighter Squadron within No.9 Group was to protect north-western England and Northern Ireland, but although the squadron would engage in convoy protection over the Irish Sea, and provide air defence over Scapa Flow, it was often moved south to carry out offensive sweeps over France. The duty in question for new squadron member Flight Sergeant Briggs, however, was to carry out a practice sweep – basically a navigational exercise – in order to build up his operational experience. The sortie began well enough, but as he moved over an area of high ground he found cloud closing about him. Appreciative of the fact that he had very little experience in flying in cloud on instruments, he called for instructions, asking whether he should abort the exercise or carry on. It would be deduced later that his radio had, in fact, become unserviceable, but hearing nothing he decided to carry on with the exercise. Only within minutes a hill loomed before his canopy forcing him to realise just how perilous his situation had become, yet hastily throttling up and pulling back on the stick took him into even thicker cloud which so disorientated him that he lost control.

Descending, with everything swiftly winding up around him, and well aware from his glimpsed sighting just how close he was to high ground, he must have known that he had scant time to spend in attempting to regain control. So, using a degree of judgement hardly to be expected of his skimpy 140 hours of flying experience, he promptly pushed back his hood and baled out, when the fact that he landed within only a few hundred yards of his aircraft showed just how wise a decision this had been.

The abandoned aircraft, the full-power crescendo of its engine warning of its approach, plunged into the yard of Thirkelow Farm and caught fire, one wing slicing through the roof of a substantial stone barn in which three boys, playing in the yard only seconds before, had hastily taken shelter.

The 2006 incumbent of Thirkelow Farm, Mr John Swain, an ex-career policeman who retired to run horses on the land, recalled that one of the boys was a son of the Wain family who then owned the farm, the other two being Michael 'Mick' Berrisford and Michael Staden, himself a subsequent incumbent. From their accounts it appears that the pilot, having landed in one of the farm's fields, near the road, bundled up his parachute and hurried down the track to the farm. However, his reaction on discovering how narrowly a tragedy had been averted is not recorded.

The field into which Flight Sergeant Harris parachuted. The T-junction of track and road is to the right, Thirkelow Farm off to the left.

The RAF investigation partly attributed the loss of the aircraft to the wireless problem. But clearly the main cause was the inexperience which had caused Flight Sergeant Briggs to lose control. Accordingly the commanding officer of the squadron simply penned 'lack of airmanship in deciding to continue on course when R/T had failed', and no further action was taken. After which it is presumed that both he and Flight Sergeant Briggs went back to the job in hand.

The wreck was quickly cleared, although Mr Swain still found it a source of wonder that the salvage crew managed to get a 'Diamond Tee'– a very large recovery vehicle, it seems – down the track, for, as he said, until he widened it he could not imagine it having accommodated anything larger than a horse and cart.

Thirkelow Farm, and the barn in which three lads took shelter. The Spitfire impacted where Mr John Swain, the 2006 incumbent, is standing, one wing slicing through the roof slates just above the door.

Clearly some débris was overlooked, for when Mr Swain first took up residence some aluminium members, aircraft-derived, still lingered in a corner of the damaged barn. Then, many years later, while lowering the surface of the yard itself, he discovered the blue, verdigris-like corrosion so indicative of an aircraft crash site. The roof of the damaged barn, however, which for many years had shown the mismatch where the original grey-stone tiles had been replaced with blue slates, he later re-roofed, incorporating the tiles into the farm proper, after which no trace of the Spitfire crash remained.

Flying Goggles:
Top, author's personal issue from the 1950s
Bottom, mid-1940's pattern, Thirkelow
As they bear no RAF 22/C Stores Reference Number and no Government Arrow, the authenticity of the pair from the 1940s was initially doubted. But then it was found that those personally issued in 1956 similarly lack references.

What Mr Swain still possessed, however, was a set of cobweb-covered pilot's goggles found in the barn, an item of flying clothing which he had no reason to doubt had been there since being cast aside on that day of manifestly mixed fortune in November 1941.

Short Stirling Mk.1 W7467, Corner Farm, North Anston, Sheffield

SK 51459 84424 94m initial impact point, on railway
SK 51272 84235 91m terminal impact point
No.149 Squadron, RAF Mildenhall (south-east of Ely), No.3 Group,
Bomber Command
16 January, 1942

Crew: eight; seven parachuted and survived, captain successfully forced landed (Other than the pilot, the crew categories, not being known, are assigned on the assumption that the Air Britain source listed them according to the traditional crew hierarchy)
Acting Flying Officer W.G. Barnes, pilot
Sergeant Baker, observer (navigator)
Sergeant Townsend, bomb aimer
Sergeant C.W. Dellow, flight engineer
Sergeant Heron, wireless operator/air gunner
Sergeant Crook, wireless operator/air gunner
Sergeant F.T.P. Gallagher, air gunner
Sergeant Collins, air gunner

On 15 January, 1942, No.149 Squadron, stationed at RAF Mildenhall, was tasked to dispatch its Stirlings to raid Hamburg. Among the aircraft taking part was Stirling W7467, under the command of Acting Flying Officer W.G Barnes, who was logged as getting airborne at 1823 hours. His crew successfully reached and bombed their target, but while still over Hamburg, and in the process of turning away, amid the flak, searchlights, incipient mayhem and confusion, they suffered a common-or-garden engine failure, which must surely have required them to exercise the qualities encapsulated in their squadron motto of 'Fortis nocte' ('strong by night'), given that any of them even knew of the motto, the serving RAF never having been unduly attuned to Service history.

To employ the phrase 'nothing daunted' seems problematical, for such a stroke of untoward misfortune must have rocked any crew, notwithstanding which the aircraft was turned onto a heading for home. The crew might well have hoped for clear weather conditions as they neared their Suffolk base, but the night was not yet to go their way, for, finding themselves in conditions of very reduced visibility, they droned the time away, fruitlessly trying to locate themselves, until eventually the fuel state became critical.

At 0208 hours Acting Flying Officer Barnes advised control that he had made the decision to abandon the aircraft, and with the order given in good time, all seven members of his crew made successful parachute descents. It is not known why Acting Flying Officer Barnes himself did not follow suit, although one wonders if a natural reluctance to leave a still controllable aircraft was not complemented by a concern that once he left his seat the Stirling, although trimmed to compensate for its asymmetric state with him in situ, might then heel over, generating aerodynamic forces that would prevent him from exiting. As it was, he seems to have elected to bring the bomber in for a forced landing.

How he went about this must remain a puzzle, for not only was the blackout in force but a seasonal low-level fog was exacerbated by the then inveterate industrial haze drifting eastwards from Sheffield. Whether Acting Flying Officer Barnes saw it or not, the field that presented itself to his descending machine, it transpired, was at Corner Farm, North Anston, a full hundred miles from Mildenhall. True, he clipped a railway embankment, skipped a field, then finally touched down for good, careering on across other fields and a brook before coming to a halt. But, against all the odds, he survived, although suffering injuries, the nature of which are not specified on the RAF crash report summary but which, according to local accounts, seem to have been only slight. For when daylight came, it is said, he was found in his seat, fast asleep.

The aircraft, however, was very badly damaged and in the next few days was removed by Queen Mary trailers accessing the site from the A57.

In early 2006, Mrs Grace Waller, of Hardwick Farm, Todwick, had no need to cast her mind back to recount her experience of the incident, it was still so fresh. 'We were living at Corner Farm, North Anston, at the time,' she said. 'I was fifteen, and was sleeping with one of my sisters when we heard this terrific noise. If there had been an air-raid siren Dad would have made us go to the barn: it only had a relatively-light pantile roof, whereas to have the stone house come down on us would have been a different proposition. But the siren hadn't sounded. And once the roaring sound had passed, there was silence. The whole family crowded to the landing window, but there was nothing to be seen outside. It was dark, of

2006, Mrs Grace Waller, back at Corner Farm

course, but also it was foggy. And in those days they were real fogs, for we were downwind of Sheffield with all its factory chimneys, so that folk said you could only see Sheffield when it rained.' She paused. 'Once it was light, and we heard about the plane, Dad decided we'd go and see it before morning milking. We found that it had come from an eastwardly direction, somehow managing to miss the high part of the village by descending with the slope of the ground. Evidently it had come over Corner Farm, skimmed our front field, just touched the railway – there was a definite mark on the embankment – then actually come down on its belly in our back field. It had left great skid marks – we followed them through the fog. Then it had gone down the slope to Anston Brook, somehow negotiated the far bank of that, but in doing so had been spun to one side, so that it finished up facing towards South Anston.'

She smiled, indicating the site. 'Of course there were no trees then, and even the Brook was different. But back then the first person to find the plane was one of Turner's men who had taken his plough team into the field; only as he worked towards the railway so this great aeroplane took shape in the mist. In fact, he found the pilot had either stayed in his cockpit, or gone back to it, and was asleep. For my part I remember the great belts of bullets they had to feed the guns. We'd come from the direction of the farm, of course, and so we got quite close because the bobby from South Anston was stopping people coming from the road – the A57 – and was surprised and annoyed when he eventually saw us. He shouted for us to go away. "But it's my field," my father yelled back. Just the same we weren't allowed to get too close. And soon the Home Guard came, and eventually, the RAF. In the end they brought long trailers into the field, dismantled it – it was very big – and took it away. And that's really all we ever found out about it. We heard that the crew had baled out near the coast, but we never really knew.'

The RAF crash report summary does not actually mention the crew, or specifically detail the way in which Acting Flying Officer Barnes set about landing the aircraft in the pitch dark. But then these were pragmatic times, and the bare minimum sufficed. After all, a bomber had done its job before being wrecked, and once its captain had recovered, its crew was fit for future operations. But in all conscience, Acting Flying Officer Barnes can have had no idea what sort of terrain he was descending into. Ironically, the area beyond the crash site, towards Todwick, was so flat that parts of it had been earmarked for Sheffield Airport, a scheme successfully fought off as far back as 1933. Yet his aircraft's belly must have been unbelievably close to ground as he descended over the highest part of North Anston. What does occur is that Mildenhall is only 33 feet above sea level. Which means that as the ground came up his altimeter would still have been reading 300 feet. It is almost certain then, that this was not a deliberate forced landing as such, but a totally unexpected touchdown which interrupted a gentle descent in which blind faith alone led Acting Flying Officer Barnes to hope that he would eventually see enough to allow him to round out. But certainly not yet, not with another three hundred feet to go! However, false though Lady Luck may have played him over the target, she certainly atoned for her capriciousness when she set him safely down at North Anston.

Railway embankment impact point

Terminal area, the approach, and the high ground beyond Corner Farm

Mrs Grace Waller indicates the terminal site

The terrain beyond the impact point, an area proposed for an aerodrome in the 1930s

Republic P-47D Thunderbolts 42-7872 and 42-7898, Cats Tor (area of the Cat and Fiddle Inn)

SJ 99506 75402 480m
United States Eighth Army Air Force, 8th Fighter Command,
2906th Observation Group, Training HQ & HQ Squadron,
AAF342 (RAF Atcham), south-east of Shrewsbury
30 September, 1943

Occupants: two pilots, killed:
Captain Malta L. Stepp Jr., United States Army Air Force
Staff Sergeant Lynn R. Morrison, USAAF

Successful as the P-47 had proved itself as both a high-level escort fighter and a low-level fighter-bomber, steady attrition on the operational squadrons led to a constant need for new pilots as replacements. It was imperative, however, that when such pilots arrived in the United Kingdom they were introduced to the conditions – and particularly the weather conditions – they would daily encounter in the European theatre of war. Despite this, many of the in-place USAAF pilots, although by now veterans of several missions over the Channel, were still relatively new to such conditions themselves.

For this reason, therefore, Staff Sergeant Lynn Morrison, a recent arrival with under 500 hours' total flying and only 15 hours on P-47s, must have considered himself fortunate when Captain Malta Stepp Jr. was assigned as his mentor in formation flying. For Captain Stepp, having served as an American volunteer with No.121 (Eagle) Squadron, RAF, had only transferred to the USAAF 4th Fighter Group in September 1942 when the Eagle squadrons were disbanded, and had, therefore, a good two years of experience of European conditions.

The pair took off from RAF Atcham, near Shrewsbury, and headed north-eastwards, Captain Stepp having elected to carry out the exercise in that sector of their local area. The weather was not that promising, with a general cloud base of just 1,500 feet. Just the same, the visibility below the base was given as unlimited so that the terrain-delineated, below-cloud arena would afford adequate room for lateral, if not for vertical, manoeuvres.

The sortie then, would have involved Staff Sergeant Morrison flying in the various positions expected of a number two, easing smartly from one to the other as his leader called the changes – or rather hand-signalled them, for it was as well to learn from the start that any radio call could betray one's position to the enemy.

So Staff Sergeant Morrison might well have started off tucked behind Captain Stepp's right wing in the starboard-echelon position, slipping back, after a while, into the close line-astern position – when he would hold the leader's nose just above his canopy – varying that by sliding across to the left wing, into close port-echelon. It would have been stimulating in the extreme, but demanding too, requiring unceasing concentration on the tyro pilot's part, for with undulating ground below, and the constant variations of heading Captain Stepp would have made, from slight alterations to full-circle turns, the going would have been neither smooth nor stable.

There would, of course, have been a few moments of relaxation now and again when Captain Stepp signalled his follower to open out in order to look inside the cockpit to check that all was well with engine, instruments, and fuel. Moments when Staff Sergeant Morrison might savour the countryside around which they were flitting, and receive updates from his leader regarding their current location in the event that he lost station and found himself alone.

But clearly Staff Sergeant Morrison had learnt his business well, for all his lack of experience, for the pair never did split up. And when, just twenty minutes after take-off, he was led directly into the face of Cats Tor he was in a precise echelon-port position, impacting just feet upslope from his leader, dying almost certainly without having even glimpsed the cloud-mantled ground; his last impression, perhaps, vague wonder that his leader should have so suddenly checked, then so disconcertingly flicked back past his right wingtip.

The time of the crash was established by a farmer who heard the double impact, but when the rescue services arrived at the scene there was nothing to be done for either of the two airmen.

The accident investigators were unable to fathom what had driven Captain Stepp to fly through cloud at low level in the vicinity of ground peaking at nearly 1,800 feet above sea level, striking indeed at a full three hundred feet below that. Indeed, despite all their deliberations a rational reason never did suggest itself.

At best they could only speculate that something might have been wrong with Captain Stepp's communications radio, basing even this on the fact that no request for a fix had been received. But only twenty minutes into the sortie, and flying in visual contact, with nothing to do but keep track of his position, why would Captain Stepp have had need of a fix? Further, had he been in the least doubtful of his position, or the serviceability of his radio, he had only to hand-sign his number two to take the lead and make the call for both of them.

Mr Albert Heathcote, speaking in 2005, remembered his frequent transits of the crash site in the course of his shepherding duties on Shining Tor. 'We lived down in the valley,' he explained, 'at Saltersford Hall Farm, and although I was only a lad at the time, I had a beat that covered the whole ridge. My younger brother, Ben, though, he was still at school, and along with the other lads would have been able to spend much more time gathering souvenirs.'

Revisiting the crash site in 2006 it was evident that any of several slight depressions in the hillside might be taken for the two impact points; indeed only when a metal detector was brought into play was it possible to decide which were the correct hollows. The metal detector, however, swiftly removed any doubt, and also showed that the number two had, indeed, been holding a precise echelon-port position.

Mr Albert Heathcote, in 1943 a youthful shepherd, and sheepdog Jim

Not that there was much to be found, when the site had been picked over so often. But the sweep did reveal débris enough to confirm the types involved. It included evidence, moreover, of just one reason for the P-47's reputation as a formidable hard-hitter: an American half-inch calibre cartridge, exploded by the fire on impact, but by its sheer bulk proclaiming the advantage it had over the lighter weight 0.303-inch calibre ammunition in general use by the British.

Other wreckage was to be found tumbled further down into the valley, but it was in these two depressions, high on the slope, yet only feet below the popular ridge path, that the careers of two pilots, one already experienced, and the other demonstrably very promising, came to their untimely ends.

Above: Thunderbolt operating instructions for flap and undercarriage (courtesy of Mr Martin Glover, P-47 41-6628 Thorncliffe; see *Peakland Air Crashes: The South*)

Above: Republic P-47D Thunderbolts 42-7872 and 42-7898, Cats Tor, from Staff Sergeant Morrison's impact point, looking towards his leader's who, impacting instants earlier, struck slightly downslope (Shining Tor off to the south) Insert top right: American half-inch calibre cartridge unearthed
Lower insert: American half-inch calibre cartridge, compared with a British 0.303-inch round

Republic F-84F Thunderstreak 52-6692, Lodge Moor Hospital, Sheffield

SK 28745 86183 290m
United States Air Force in Europe (USAFE), 20th Tactical
Fighter Bomber Wing, RAF Station Wethersfield,
Braintree, Essex
9 December, 1955

Pilot: solo, successfully ejected, slight leg injury:
First Lieutenant Roy G. Evans, USAF
Casualties on the ground: hospital patient Mrs Elsie Murdoch, died of injuries:
seven other patients suffered from minor injuries and shock

During the afternoon of 9 December, 1955, First Lieutenant Roy G. Evans, of the United States Air Force in Europe, attached to RAF Wethersfield, took off from the American Air Force base at RAF Sculthorpe, near Fakenham, Norfolk, on a solo instrument-flying sortie. After some time, however, and while he was flying in cloud at a medium to low altitude, the engine of his F-84 Thunderstreak failed, or in jet terminology, 'flamed out'. He at once began a series of attempts to get the engine going again, attempts, that is, to 'relight', all to no avail. At the same time, while gliding lower still, he transmitted a message to base.

The circumstances in which he found himself – in a single-seater aircraft with engine failure – dictated the immediate transmission of an 'Urgency' emergency message, to be updated equally swiftly to a 'Mayday' distress call the moment it became evident that the engine was not going to restart. It seems, however, that the correct procedure went from Lieutenant Evans' head, for he only informally declared his emergency condition in the broadcast call he made. But this was essentially immaterial, for in the event he received no answer, almost certainly because he was over a hundred miles distant and at that time descending through three thousand feet. Colonel Harold Bailer, of Base Operations, Burtonwood, tasked a little later that day with issuing an official statement, told the press, 'The trouble started over Derbyshire, but while we could just faintly hear Lieutenant Evans, he could not hear us. "I have a flameout – leaving the aircraft"; that was the last we heard of him.' Adding, somewhat unaccountably, 'We couldn't quite get what he was trying to say.' (Bringing to mind the semi-jocular cockpit brief to student or passenger: 'If I say "Eject" don't say "What?" or you'll be talking to yourself.')

Lieutenant Evans' position was hardly enviable: at relatively low level, in cloud, deprived of radio assistance – or companionable acknowledgement of his plight, at least – and flying what was now an extremely inefficient glider, he decided to abandon. Accordingly, the altimeter needle having passed three thousand feet, and having retrimmed the aircraft for relatively level flight, as he would have done, he fired off his ejection seat. The ejection was successful and the brief parachute descent uneventful, but Lieutenant Evans suffered a slight leg injury on coming to earth at what he was to learn was a spot to the east of Hathersage. Phone calls followed, after which, in view of his injury, he was not recovered directly to his home station but taken instead to the American Air Force base at Burtonwood, just forty-five miles distant, where he was to be hospitalised for a number of days.

It is not known whether he was made aware of the consequences of his abandonment that night, or if he was kept in ignorance in order to avoid exacerbating the shock of his ordeal. Unfortunately, the ease of mind he would have been left with was not to last long. For although Lieutenant Evans had ejected over open country, he had been in cloud, and unbeknownst to him, the sprawl of Sheffield had been filling the horizon immediately ahead. So it was that the aircraft, weighing by that time some 25,000 pounds, cruising at some 550 mph, and now become a flying missile, overflew some four miles of inviting open moorland before coming to earth on the very western extremity of the city. Except that at that western extremity was the major facility of Lodge Moor Hospital, built where the moors finished, and at an elevation of 950 feet above sea level.

There was no lack of witnesses when the aircraft impacted. 'It was five o'clock in the afternoon', Mr Charles Leech, of Redmires Road, told the newspapers, 'when it roared over the first hospital building and crashed into the second. I was in my house opposite the main gates and heard the plane coming, then crash. I saw flames, and ran across the road to help. The plane was in two parts, blazing furiously, and ammunition was going off.'

Similarly, Mr Selwyn Williams, of Lodge Moor Road, told reporters that, having phoned 999, he jumped in his car and drove around to where the aircraft lay. 'Its tail was leaning against the wall, and a number of people with blackened faces were running about...' In fact, the rear section of the airframe had come to rest by the hospital mortuary, while the burning engine was only yards from the ambulance station where a thousand gallons of petrol was stored.

Porters were among others who bravely fought the flames before the fire service arrived, and, although ill-equipped for the task, even penetrated the wreckage to the cockpit, well aware of, but selflessly setting aside, the risk from exploding ammunition, intent as they were on seeking to extricate the pilot they expected to find trapped within.

'Don't make me out a hero,' protested porter Mr George Littlewood, when later singled out for commendation. 'We all did no more than our duty in the circumstances.'

The tailplane and rear fuselage portion of the F-84, amid the wrecked Ward North One (Photograph courtesy of Mr Derek Cooke via Mrs Diane Couldwell)

And the burning wreck aside, circumstances were horrendous. For it was seen that although the aircraft had missed striking the lofty hospital water tower, and had overflown many of the twelve single-storied cubicle blocks, it had then struck the roof of Ward North Two, demolished the interlinking glass corridor, smashed through a sanitary block into Ward North One, then, breaking in two, had burst into flames in the quadrangle beyond.

In its progress through the building, moreover, it had caused not only material devastation, but left seven hospital patients with injuries which later needed treatment. Of the cubicles the aircraft actually tore through, the first had only moments before been vacated by a nurse, Mrs Margaret Schoefield, and a patient who had left to get a cup of tea. Tragically, the second and adjoining one contained the hapless Mrs Elsie Murdock, of Sheffield, mother of a family, rapidly recovering from gastroenteritis and expecting to be released after two more days. Nurse Schoefield, steadfastly collecting herself, clambered back into the now ruinous cubicle, only to find that her patient had received mortal injuries to her head. Yet amid all the turmoil and confusion, with detonating ammunition zipping through the air, and flames threatening a secondary explosion at any moment, Nurse Schoefield remained with Mrs Murdock, comforting her until she died, and only then leaving the danger area to tend to the living, patients and staff alike, almost all of whom she found to be in states of shock and in need of her assistance.

Shocked though the staff understandably were, it is evident that they behaved in exemplary fashion, for by the time the hastily summoned fire service had extinguished both the fires, order had been re-imposed, patients having been re-allocated to undamaged wards with all dispatch. Nor were the patients unappreciative, youthful Nurse Shirley Taylor being deservedly eulogised as 'the little nurse of North Two'.

The Lodge Moor Hospital Board paid their own tributes, meeting just days later to bestow formal thanks upon those members of staff whose conduct had been brought to their notice. In the aftermath, too, the local member of parliament was to approach then-Prime Minister Anthony Eden regarding the additional hazard presented by the aircraft having carried live ammunition, taxing him to demand that USAF and RAF aircraft were not to be armed as a matter of course, but only when engaged in active live-firing exercises, and that the latter should, as far as possible, only take place over the sea.

An American board of inquiry was set up immediately after the accident – it would generate a report comprising 480 pages with 15 photographs – and for the next few days the *Sheffield Independent* duly recorded the names of the succession of high-ranking officers and their entourages who processed through the hospital, observing some days later that on that particular day there 'were two colonels – one bringing his wife along too – from Burtonwood.'

Two official statements were made by USAFE in the days after the crash. The initial one admitted baldly, speaking of Lieutenant Evans, 'We have no idea what caused him to eject himself. We think he ejected at 2,500 feet. He has very minor injuries'. But subsequently, having observed of the F-84 Thunderstreak, 'It is a one-man aircraft and only well-qualified pilots are allowed to take them up,' the spokesman went on to tell the press, 'The aircraft crashed after it apparently ran out of fuel.'

Lodge Moor Hospital had been built in 1887 and for many years had served as an isolation hospital, although by the time of the accident it had developed into a major General Hospital offering a wide variety of medical specialities. It was to close as a hospital in the early 1990s and although some hospital buildings were still extant in 2006, notably the imposing 1903 hospital tower rearing high over both the facility and the moors, most of the grounds, and certainly the site of what used to be Wards North One and Two, were then covered by equally imposing private houses. No trace, therefore, remained of the crash which resulted in such an unfortunate fatality.

Above: The 1903 hospital water tower

Above right: The water tower from the impact area, 2006

Right: 2005, and Mrs Diane Couldwell, former Acting Matron, indicates where she saw the fires burning: 'There were no houses intervening then.'

Garage, mortuary adjoining

Water tower

Ward North One

Ward North Two

The plan of Lodge Moor Hospital in 1955, showing no more than a tenth part of the complex, and the path of the F-84 (Plan by courtesy of former Matron Diane Couldwell)

Mrs Diane Couldwell, of Redmires Road, however, was able to point out where the blazing wreckage had finished up. Beginning work at the hospital as a part-time staff nurse, Mrs Couldwell had long held the post of Acting Matron when the establishment was forced to close. Recalling the day of the crash, Mrs Couldwell remembered, 'I was off duty, but when I heard the noise, I looked out of my front window and between the hospital houses by the roadside – there were no houses beyond them then – and I could see the flames from the plane rising up.'

It would have been no consolation to the bereaved family of the fatally injured patient, or to anyone else involved on that dire day, to observe that had the aircraft struck any sooner in the hospital complex, or any further eastwards in the city, then casualties would almost certainly have been far higher. But tragic as the fatality at the hospital was, one must spare a thought for Lieutenant Evans, for how wretched he must have felt, no matter when he heard the news! For having soared with elation over his own escape, he must have plumbed the depths on hearing what had happened. How traumatic it must have been to reflect that, given but the slightest break in the clouds before he ejected, merely a nudge of the controls would have brought the nose around to face the open moorland!

De Havilland DH82A Tiger Moth, Concord Park, Shiregreen, Sheffield

SK 37543 92235 130m
RAF Training Command
Late 1942–1944
Solo pilot: unidentified, unhurt

In October 2005 Mr Patrick Flynn, who spent from late 1942 to 1944 as a gardener's mate in Concord Park, remembered standing guard on a Tiger Moth while the pupil pilot, who had got lost and run short of fuel, went to find a telephone. Eventually an RAF support crew arrived, but in driving their truck directly across the park and proceeding to refuel the trainer with petrol from jerry cans – leading, no doubt, to a certain amount of spillage – they incurred the displeasure of Mr Flynn's boss, the head gardener. Indeed the impression given is that only after placating him was the aircraft allowed to be flown off to its home station.

The setdown area in Concord Park

The open area, still generous in 2006, had been shortened in the 1990s by the construction of a golf driving range. A setdown, rather than a crash, but of interest, perhaps, to walkers sampling Concord Park.

De Havilland DH82A Tiger Moth, Rushup Farm, Sparrowpit

SK 09351 81188 346m
Elementary Flying Training School, RAF Sealand (Chester),
Flying Training Command *c*.1941

In about 1941 a Sealand-based Tiger Moth, lost in mist, put down in a large field at Rushup Farm, Sparrowpit. The pupil pilot spent a cosseted night at the farm, and next morning a sergeant flying instructor arrived to recover pupil and machine, performing aerobatics for the then-incumbent farmer, Mr Alan Virtue and his wife, before setting course for base. Another precautionary setdown, rather than a crash, but one which recalls the reminder given in the contemporary *RAF Elementary Flying Manual* concerning forced landings: 'Pay for hospitality. Country folk are often poor as well as generous.'

The setdown site at Sparrowpit

In 2006 the field in question had long been divided across by a fence.

De Havilland Vampire T.11 XE866, Crow Chin, Stanage Edge

SK 22437 85694 427m
No.4 Flying Training School, RAF Worksop, No.23 Group,
Flying Training Command
8 August, 1957

Pilots: both killed:
Flying Officer Phillip Redvers Jones, instructor
Flying Officer Derek John Brett, pupil pilot

The de Havilland Vampire dual-seat trainer T.11 ('Tee Eleven'), first flown in 1950, and with over 600 being subsequently produced, was to remain in RAF service until 1966. From its inception it proved a particularly valuable acquisition, not least because for the first time pupils at the Advanced Flying Training Schools were afforded the benefit of having an instructor sitting alongside to demonstrate, observe, and monitor, their progress. For monitoring in flying training, it might be argued, had become more necessary at that time than ever before,

The Mark 14 Pressure Altimeter

Tens-of-thousands of feet needle: very easily missed, especially behind other needles, and in a poorly lit cockpit

Barometric sub-scale: very easy to dial an incorrect pressure setting

By 1959, just two years later, the RAF Flying Manual, the AP129, would actually warn of the unsuitability for jet operations of both the miniscule tens-of-thousands of feet needle and the hard-to-read barometric sub-scale of the Mk.14 altimeter.

because the new jets could climb, and descend, at rates hitherto unknown. So, in the Vampire T.11, the RAF had a trainer that would take only twelve minutes to reach 30,000 feet from take-off, and at 250 knots and with airbrakes out could descend again in a deceptively short time.

With 'deceptive' being used advisedly, because in comparison with piston-engined trainers, flight in a jet trainer was so smooth, and the rate of change of altitude so high, that height slipped by almost imperceptibly in ascent and, often more critically, in descent. Unfortunately this generic problem of jet-flight was to be exacerbated in the new trainer, for it was fitted with the standard RAF altimeter of the day, the Mark 14, and this had a built-in deceptiveness of its own.

The trouble lay with the presentation. For a long pointer indicated hundreds of feet; an intermediate pointer, thousands; and a truly miniscule pointer tens of thousands of feet. Yet at jet rates of climb and descent all three wound around with great rapidity, with the last being even easier to misread than the other two. Certainly the author will not be the only one to have pattered out a whole session of medium-level aerobatics (at Central Flying School, with a steely CFS instructor alongside), only to discover – both of them!– that for forty-five minutes they been a whole 10,000 feet higher than they had thought: 28,000 feet instead of 18,000 feet!

When practising instrument flying it was customary for the student to wear a hood which prevented him from seeing anything but his instruments, the instructor being responsible for maintaining a lookout. But with this mark of altimeter it was so commonplace for a student under the hood to be sitting at 10,000 feet, while believing himself to be just a thousand feet above the ground, that a fiendish breed of instructor evolved. As the student gingerly prepared to ease down towards the final approach, such a one would take control, roll the aircraft onto its back – and pull through into a near-vertical dive.

And that it was just as commonplace to be 10,000 feet *lower* than was thought was shown by the same breed of instructor who, as yet another student prepared to lower the nose and smartly descend at high rate from what he mistakenly thought was 10,000 feet, would take over control and whip off the student's instrument-flying visor, to reveal to him the tree-, wave-, hill- or rooftops flashing past the canopy.

So it really was that easy to misread the Mk.14 altimeter. But although modification followed modification, none satisfactorily solved the problem. Which meant that each of the aforementioned factors was still relevant when, on 8 August, 1957, Worksop instructor, Flying Officer Phillip Jones, got airborne with his pupil, Flying Officer Derek Brett, in Vampire T.11 XE866.

The programme Flying Officer Jones had set was a climb to 40,000 feet, followed by a session introducing the effects of high-speed flight on the Vampire, effects that would have been examined in the course of carrying out certain evolutions at Mach numbers of the order of 0.75M – that is, 0.75 of the speed of sound. Finally a 'compressibility run' would have been carried out, an exercise which involved the aircraft being dived at full power to achieve, and initially hold, 0.85 Mach, transferring, as the height wore off, to the maximum-permitted indicated airspeed, which was then held in its turn until all the high-speed effects had been duly noted. The main concerns throughout the run would have been preventing the nose coming up, and maintaining a hawk-eyed lookout for other aircraft, twin occupations which vied to take the attention from the height being so rapidly reeled off!

Then, with the high-speed phase of the exercise completed, it would have been a case of levelling off, rechecking the gyroscopically-controlled instruments, and preparing for the let down and recovery to base.

Only following all that bustling about, and especially after the deliberately-protracted, full-powered dive, it was absolutely crucial that the height read off the altimeter was checked – and double checked. The height, that is, read off the *Mk.14* altimeter. For the next exercise was to be the Controlled Descent Through Cloud, or, utilising a long-clinging term from the morse-derived 'Q' brevity code, the 'QGH'. This involved air traffic control descending the aircraft so that when it broke cloud the pilot could see the airfield and rejoin for a visual landing. A painless exercise for the pilot, all the navigation and timing being done by the ground controller, the pilot simply following instructions.

To reiterate from an earlier passage (p77) as a refresher, the aircraft would initially be homed to the overhead. After that it would be turned onto a safe heading and descended at high rate away from the airfield. Then, at a given height it would be turned back towards the airfield and descended further. But over the course of time two distinct descent profiles had been developed which differed significantly when it came to the inbound turn. The high-altitude procedure called for an uninterrupted rapid descent, the pilot advising as the turning height was reached, but not levelling off. The descent from medium altitude, on the other hand – the descent Flying Officer Jones was engaged in, having dived off so much of his height –, required the pilot to level out at the turn height and slow down, continuing the descent only when heading towards the airfield.

The height of the inbound turn when flying the Worksop procedure was 6,000 feet, accordingly Flying Officer Jones duly reported that altitude. Only within moments of his check-call Vampire XE866 flew into the ground at high speed, careered along flat moorland, then catastrophically struck the vertical face of Crow Chin on Stanage Edge, exploding as it did so. Neither occupant survived.

The members of the board of inquiry ('board', now, in 1951, no longer 'court'!), while precisely costing out the accident – crew and aircraft – at £73,801, admitted that they had been hard put to reach any useful conclusion regarding cause; that what they had eventually decided upon had, of necessity, to be in the nature of educated speculation. Accordingly they submitted two possible causes, allowing that even these might well have been operating in combination.

Their first submission was that Flying Officer Jones had mistaken the type of controlled descent he was engaged in; that instead of levelling out when required to turn, he had continued the descent unabated, flying into the ground in a port bank only half way around the inbound turn. Their second submission was that the altimeter had been misread.

As indicated earlier, the board's reasoning in the latter case would have been that in the course of the high-speed dive, while intent on stopping the nose from rising during the transition from Mach number to airspeed, and while concentrating on the high-speed effects, the crew had levelled out 10,000 feet too low, not noticed their error, and proceeded with the controlled-descent profile, in cloud, at heights 10,000 feet too low throughout.

No.4 Flying Training School's commanding officer, having weighed both possibilities, plumped for the second as being the most likely to have been the root cause of the accident. Which was, regretfully, only to be expected. For it really was that easy – and that common – to misread the Mk.14 family of altimeters.

The area of the crash site, Crow Chin, a prominent feature on Stanage Edge, has always been well frequented by climbers. So, although newspaper photographs of the time (the copies being too badly scratched to include here) show parts of the widely-scattered wreckage draped across the rocks, it would now be unusual to find any evidence of the tragedy. Certainly, sweeping the plain of Moscar Moor with metal detectors, from the point of first impact, produced nothing in a 2005 search, while the crevices of Crow Chin itself had long been meticulously plundered.

Yet against all the odds débris was found by the writer in 2004, when a component discovered wedged in the rocks was later identified by the de Havilland Mosquito Trust, at Hatfield, as a retaining bracket for the under-fuselage doors of a Vampire. Which meant, then, from Vampire T.11, XE866, the fragment's fractured state testifying to the violence with which XE866 impacted into the boulders of Crow Chin at the end of its slide on that fateful August morning back in 1957.

Far Left: de Havilland Vampire T.11 XE866, Crow Chin, terminal impact site

Left: A retaining bracket for the under-fuselage doors of Vampire XE866, found in a rock crevice in 2004. The plywood construction and the presence of wood screws led the author to believe it to be part of a rucksack, not having realised when he flew Vampires that they could have been made of anything other than solid metal.

De Havilland Vampire FB Mk.5 WA400, Strines Moor

SK 21842 89801 346m
No.102 Refresher Flying School, RAF Finningley (south-east
of Doncaster), No.25 Group, Flying Training Command
25 July, 1951

Pilot: grazed knee:
Flying Officer Lawrence Leslie Beckford

The Vampire entered RAF service in 1946 but until 1950 no
dedicated trainer existed, the Mk.5 Fighter-Bomber variant
being used for the task. Only there were shortcomings with
the single-seat Vampire as a trainer, not least that the pupil
pilot was not afforded the opportunity to sit beneath a visor,
with an instructor to both advise and keep watch, while building
up experience in flying solely by reference to instruments.
Further, although the flight instruments in the Vampire were
well up to the standards of the day, there were certain foibles
associated with the standard Mk.4F compass that could quite
easily catch out the inexperienced or the unwary. And although
a standby compass existed– the E2-type – this does not seem
to have been fitted to all Vampire aircraft. Besides, the
diminutive E2 always gave the appearance of having come from
a Christmas cracker, and rarely having to be used 'for real',
was not always deemed worthy of attention, for all that it was
to be fitted to Concorde!

The E2 Standby Compass; this
example from Concorde!

   Another, equally fundamental, shortcoming of the Mk.5 Vampire was the lack of an ejection
seat, for a manual abandonment was very likely to result in the pilot striking the tailplane.
Certainly, had he had an ejection seat, Flying Officer Lawrence Beckford, a qualified pilot who
had rejoined the Service and was re-acclimatising to flying at the Refresher Flying Training
School at RAF Finningley, might well have considered ejecting rather than putting his aircraft
down on rough moorland when he lost himself and then ran short of fuel on 25 July, 1951.
   Flying in Vampire FB Mk.5, WA400, Flying Officer Beckford had been airborne for an hour
and thirty minutes on a daytime solo sortie during which he had been authorised to carry out a
series of high- and medium-level exercises including a high-speed, or 'compressibility', run
close to the machine's limiting Mach number: of the order of 0.85M (0.85 of the speed of
sound). The high-speed run, starting at 40,000 feet, would have been straightforward – always
supposing that WA400's airframe had not been overly brutalised by student handling in the
past – but Flying Officer Beckford had also been authorised to carry out aerobatics. And it may
be assumed that he had carried these out with full verve. After which came the recovery to base,
starting off with the call for a homing to the Finningley overhead and finishing with him being
deposited below the cloud base – real or simulated – and on a heading that would have allowed
him to join the circuit visually, and land. But prior to all that, after his aerobatics, and even
before calling for the homing, he should have flown straight and level while re-erecting his
gyroscopically-controlled artificial horizon, and while carefully resetting and double-checking
the synchronisation of his equally gyroscopically-stabilised compass. Only it is just as likely that
he cheated a little, as most people did, and busied himself with resetting his instruments during
the wings-level preparatory descent; straight, certainly, and if not *quite* level – well, levelish.
   For after Finningley had told him the direction to steer for their overhead, subsequent R/T
exchanges showed that he was heading away from the airfield rather than towards it. Naturally
this would have caused mild consternation on the ground, but it was initially assumed that he
had simply misunderstood the instructions. What seems likely, however, albeit in retrospect, is

that in his hurry to descend he had indeed paid insufficient attention to synchronising his gyro-magnetic compass, which was consequently giving him a false heading indication, an error only too easy to make on the compass in question, when it was merely a case of twisting a knob towards either a dot or a cross, and towards the wrong symbol, as often as not, if half-occupied with doing something else – like descending.

The annunciator window but showing Dot, or Cross?

Synchronising the G4 Compass. Dot or Cross? So easy to turn the knob the wrong way … (Photograph by courtesy of MOD, AP129)

Whatever the cause, whether the compass had actually failed, or whether it had been inadvertently de-synchronised, and so sent him off in the wrong direction, the result was that in a short space of time – yet not distance, for he would have been holding 250 knots – Flying Officer Beckford became aware initially that he was totally lost, and then that he was short of fuel.

Chagrined as this ex-operational-squadron pilot must have been at losing himself like a novice, but with almost total cloud cover preventing him from getting a visual fix, Flying Officer Beckford would have realised that, being so low in fuel, he had just two options. To gain height, and using the risk-laden technique recommended for safety, abandon the aircraft. Or to descend through a gap, and put the aircraft down as best he could. Of the two he chose the latter.

In fact, he broke cloud near Strines Moor, in the vicinity of the celebrated Strines Inn, and was recognised as being in trouble by Mr Wilfred Livesey, an off-duty ambulance driver who lived in a cottage in the grounds of nearby Sugworth Hall and was out walking with his five-year-old daughter, Jill.

Mrs Jill Arnall, née Livesey, witness

As Jill, subsequently to become Mrs Arnall, recalled in 2004, 'We were halfway up the drive to the road, and the aeroplane flew over our heads, going to the right of Bents House. What I always remember was the noise – the screaming sound. But Daddy knew it was going to crash, so he ran back, and phoned the fire service. Then he drove round by the cattle grid – it's tarmacked over now – and just where the road kinks, as you approach the Strines Inn, saw the aeroplane on the moor. So he ran up to it, and was just in time to help the pilot away – he'd grazed his knee, that was all – when it caught fire. Then he brought the pilot back to the Hall.'

Whatever the causative problem, the compass, together with the rest of the aircraft, was totally consumed by the flames. But Flying Officer Beckford had clearly drawn upon each of his six hundred or so hours of flying experience by choosing an only gently ascending moorland slope to alight on. Further, having approached at the prescribed 140 knots, albeit choosing to land wheels-up, he had finally had the luck he deserved, for in the course of the aircraft's slide to a halt it had hit none of the moor's ubiquitous boulders.

Regarding Flying Officer Beckford's decision to land wheels up, no criticism is implied, for at that time, 1951, the technique recommended in Vampire *Pilot's Notes* was to select the undercarriage down, 'unless the terrain is unsuitable', and not for some years would an amendment alter this to 'regardless of the terrain'.

The aircraft having burnt out, both the court of inquiry and Higher Authority seem to have flailed around rather. While noting that Flying Officer Beckford had only 52 hours of jet time, they accepted that the aircraft compass had become unserviceable, but loftily observed that, as the cloud cover had not been total, Flying Officer Beckford should have deduced from the sun the direction he was flying in. (True, nothing was said about moss and the northern side of trees.)

Then Air Traffic were castigated for not having ordered a ninety-degree turn, duly noted the change in bearing, and calculated from that what heading the pilot was actually on.

Finally, it was the turn of the Equipment Branch, who, with more credibility, were enjoined to see that E2 compasses were henceforth fitted as a standby to all the Command's aircraft whose primary compass was the G4-type.

For many years the location of this crash site defied detection, particularly as the popular printed sources were so far out, but in September 2004 aviation artist and researcher Mr Alan Jones supplied a reference from researcher Mr John Ownsworth which led to its rediscovery. In fact, it lies some thirty miles from Finningley, on a lift of hummocky, heather-covered and boulder-strewn grouse moor belonging to the Fitzwilliam (Wentworth) Estates but – since the September 2004 'Right to Roam' legislation – normally open to the public. In early 2006 there was still a substantial amount of surface débris left in the form of sheets of molten metal. But although the metal was plentiful enough, the heather growth at any time would be critical to actually locating the site.

Sugden Hall

September 2004; the author at the crash site of Vampire WA400 shortly after the rediscovery of the site following information supplied to aviation artist and researcher Alan Jones by researcher Mr John Ownsworth

The crash site of Vampire WA400, looking back along the line of its approach (Insert: debris from the surrounding area, re-interred)

De Havilland Vampire FB Mk.5 VV602, Torgate Farm, Wildboarclough (west of the Cat and Fiddle Inn)

SJ 98612 71930 306m crater
SJ 98443 71980 384m pilot
No.613 Royal Auxiliary Air Force Squadron, Ringway (Manchester), No.12 Group, Fighter Command
1 May, 1954

Pilot: killed, unsuccessful manual bale-out:
Flying Officer Jocelyn Francis Baverstock Davis, Royal Auxiliary Air Force

The de Havilland Vampire FB Mk.5 – FB denoting a fighter-bomber – was the version modified for the ground-attack role, having secure-points for rockets or bombs, a strengthened airframe, and clipped wings.

In addition to the many first-line RAF squadrons which were equipped with the Vampire FB Mk.5, it was also flown by the Royal Auxiliary Air Force. This organisation, raised in 1925, had received the 'Royal' prefix in 1947 for services rendered, not least during the Second World War when, together with other accomplishments, the Auxiliary Air Force accounted for a third of all enemy aircraft downed. Among the Royal Auxiliary Air Force squadrons to fly the Vampire FB Mk.5 was No.613, the City of Manchester Squadron.

After wartime service, in part as No.69 Squadron, No.613 Squadron had reformed again on 10 May, 1946, only this time as an Auxiliary Air Force fighter squadron. The Squadron motto was *Semper parati*, 'Always ready', an admirable claim, and one it had long lived up to. But an assertion too that set the very highest of expectations. Not least on the 1 May, 1954, when two of its Vampire FB Mk.5s took off to carry out a cinema-gun combat practice at a briefed 'above 25,000 feet'.

Flying Officer Jocelyn Davis, a South African, who, outside the Auxiliary Air Force, was an engineer employed by Metropolitan Vickers Electrical Company, and who had been married some months before, was to fly in the Number Two position to Flying Officer George Parker. The sky that day was dominated by heaped cloud, estimated at between six- and eight-eighths cover, which was giving heavy rain: indeed there was thundery activity in the area. Accordingly, having settled after take-off, Flying Officer Parker turned towards the less threatening south-easterly sector. However, as the section passed 6,000 feet, still in thick cloud, Flying Officer Davis, losing station, made the advisory call, 'Breaking', following this a short while later with an unclear transmission which was almost certainly 'Baling out', after which nothing more was heard from him.

Mr John Bowler, of Torgate Farm, just under a mile west of the Cat and Fiddle Inn, later gave evidence to the coroner. Interviewed again in late 2004 the memory was still vivid. 'The aircraft', he said, 'was diving almost vertically. And I fully expected it to pull up, the way aircraft did. Only this one didn't. It carried straight on down and disappeared behind the intervening rise. Then there was an explosion, and a cloud of dirt and smoke rose up into sight. Before the plane actually crashed, though, I'd seen something white appear. A parachute, it turned out, but it stayed with the plane for some time, then came free and spiralled down. Only it never opened properly.'

Mr Bowler had been walking with his dog when the accident occurred. 'I ran over the fields', he said, 'to the Stanley Arms– it was a farm still, but a farm-cum-pub even then – where there was a phone. Eileen, my sister, ran straight to the wreck.' He paused. 'And so, halfway down the hill to the site, she came across the pilot's body in the field, where it had fallen ...'

The board of inquiry were able to ascertain that the crash had occurred only five minutes after the section had become airborne, but in flight conditions that might well have caused a far more experienced pilot than Flying Officer Davis to lose station. In fact, although Flying Officer Davis had done just over four hundred hours' total flying, he was only claiming thirteen hours of flying solely with reference to instruments in cloud.

Whereas having broken formation, as he had found it necessary to do – itself a severe shock to the system – and finding himself in thick cloud, it was then required that he instantly transfer his attention from the misty-brightness of the neighbouring machine's wingtip to the gloom of his own cockpit. Not only this, but it was also necessary to both interpret and assimilate what the flight instruments were telling him, all the while totally ignoring his instinctive senses, and firmly controlling his aircraft.

The investigators would have appreciated that the transition Flying Officer Davis was forced to make was not an easy one, requiring him to switch from the essentially mechanical and instinctively controlled

Vampire flight-instrument panel (courtesy of MOD, *T.11 Pilot's Notes*)

operation of holding station, to flight on instruments in which all often overwhelmingly compelling 'seat-of-the-pants' sensations must be not only ignored but fiercely contested.

It was therefore concluded that, having been forced to break away – and cleanly – from the neighbouring machine, a manoeuvre that would have been achieved by banking steeply, then hauling back on the stick, Flying Officer Davis would already have placed his machine in a relatively extreme attitude. True, he might have been expected to cope. But having assessed the situation for himself he clearly felt that discretion was called for, and sensibly decided to bale out, advising his leader accordingly.

It was evident, however, that the manual evacuation had not gone to plan. For it became obvious that while the cockpit canopy had fallen away – it was recovered from the edge of the Macclesfield Forest – the parachute had, somehow, been opened in the cockpit! An upset that could only have hampered the pilot's departure, causing more vital seconds of delay. Further, it was found that the material had subsequently been badly ripped. All this aside, however, medical evidence established that Flying Officer Davis had actually been killed by striking the high-set tailplane, an only too-well-known hazard prior to the installation of ejection seats.

Understandably, the findings fixed the blame upon Flying Officer Davis's lack of 'actual' instrument flying, an arbitrary record of experience logged by the RAF – but not by professional civil aviation – and built up by the Service pilot estimating how much time in any sortie he actually spent in cloud; as opposed to time spent on simulated instrument flying which, be it in Link, simulator, or 'under the hood,' is precisely timed. To that end the board called for the provision of a dual Vampire on single-seater squadrons in which pilots could receive regular exposure to flight solely on instruments while under the eye of an instructor or a safety pilot. Hopefully it was a recommendation that was to be embodied.

The coroner, in his own court, paid handsome tribute, saying, 'We must admire the public-spirited actions of men like Davis who undertake such hazardous training and risk their lives to be ready to defend their country in time of need.'

Recalling those frenetic days, Mrs Sheila Bowler remembered a whole crowd of RAF investigators taking over her kitchen, one of them demonstrating how the aircraft should have been turned inverted in order to allow the pilot to drop out cleanly; she also remembered them deciding that the lightning which had been in the area would only have been a factor had it caused Flying Officer Davis to panic.

Mr John Bowler, standing on 'the green field' where the pilot's body landed. The crater site is just on the far side of the gully, but shards of wind-borne wreckage reached the distant hills.

Crash site of de Havilland Vampire FB Mk.5 VV602

Indeed a memento of that long-gone conference still existed in 2004, for one of the rigging lines from the hapless Flying Officer Davis's parachute served to hang out kitchen cloths. Not only that, but as Mr Bowler had stood, watching unbelievingly as the smoke rose and the débris settled, so the cushion from the Vampire's seat-well had drifted down, swept out by the airflow after the pilot had vacated the cockpit. 'We used it for years afterwards', Mr Bowler smiled, 'on the tractor seat.'

A characteristic sidenote to the investigation – indeed to virtually any aircraft-crash investigation – was provided when two farmers working on an adjacent hill reported having seen a fireball in the sky before the aircraft crashed. The RAF investigators, however, having weighed all the evidence, discounted any notion that the aircraft had been on fire before impact. Nevertheless, as Mr Bowler said, 'Both maintain their version to this day.'

But Mr Bowler also remembered that after the aircraft exploded the other Vampire appeared and carried out a wide orbit to the right, overflying the still-smoking crater, before flying off. He recalled too that the next day the pilot of that aircraft, the erstwhile section leader, Flying Officer Parker, brought Mrs Davis to see where her husband had died. And he remembered her murmuring brokenly, 'At least he found a green field'.

For such a small aircraft the spread of débris was astoundingly wide. Where it fell it left a crater, but the explosion not only demolished a section of stone wall – which was never replaced – but also spread shards of metal across the fields as far as the Cuckoo Rocks, just under half a mile distant. Indeed Mr Bowler remembered that although his father was desperate for pasture for his cows, the area downwind of the crash site could not be used because of the metal scraps littering the area; also that even after RAF personnel had spent many days picking up tiny pieces, his father still had to put lime on the ground to prevent the cows eating the yet hazard-laden grasses.

As for the major wreckage, not all that long after the event a group of Air Training Corps cadets spent some considerable time digging down to locate the engine. They eventually found it, but only at a depth of eighteen feet, and embedded in rock. Whereupon they back-filled the hole, and departed, leaving the engine where it was.

By 2006 little remained at the scene, just a grass-covered depression inside the barbed-wire boundary fence of the private holding of nearby Broughsplace. But a metal-detector search positively located the impact site, if only through minor fragmentary, mainly molten, scraps. Yet scraps consistent, at that, with the violence with which the ill-fated VV602 impacted on that squall-hagged day in May 1954.

Vickers Armstrongs Wellington Mk.1C Z8980, Burbage Moor, Rud Hill

SK 26149 83798 414m
No.27 Operational Training Unit, RAF Lichfield, No.91 Group,
Bomber Command
17 July, 1942

Crew: five, all injured:
Sergeant Thomas Frank Thompson, Royal Australian Air Force, pilot
Pilot Officer J.W. Moore, navigator
Sergeant J.H. Levett, wireless operator/air gunner
Sergeant Kennington John Hythe Harris, RAAF, air gunner
Sergeant Jacob Henry Roden, RAAF, rear gunner

The Wellington first entered RAF service in October 1938 and in its various roles was to remain on the strength until 1953, long after both its contemporaries – the Hampden and the Whitley – and many of its intended replacements were the vaguest of memories. It owed its longevity in harness to the durability of its basic structure and to its overall dependability, but also to the respect it engendered in all who came into contact with it, those who directed its use, those who serviced it, and those who flew it. Certainly not least those who brought it into being, as Mrs Stella Crofts, in the war years a Vickers' worker at Brooklands, testified in 2005.

'For a start,' she asserted, 'nobody at Weybridge ever called it by a nickname. To us it was always "The Wellington". It was respect. And that's what I feel for it to this day. Of course, what made it special was the geodetic. The fuselage, the tail, the wings, they were all geodetic. Bar the wingtips which were ordinary metal.' Using an envelope Mrs Crofts sketched out a geodetic section. 'There were wooden strips, pre-drilled with screw-holes, and in places we'd press these into shaped recesses in the geodetics. Then we'd lay the fabric over the area and use pump-action screwdrivers to screw it in place. Next we'd tape over the screw heads. In other places we'd lay wire along the geodetic over the fabric, and use hooked needles to secure the skinning with waxed string. We'd bring the needle up, over the wire, and down again, all along ... And finally the whole skin would be doped. We were so proud of those aircraft.'

Whether Sergeant Thomas Thompson of the Royal Australian Air Force and his largely Australian crew felt quite that same pride is not known, but certainly they had nothing to reproach the machine with when they left Lichfield for a cross-country training exercise in Wellington Mk.1C, Z8980, on the night of 16 July, 1942.

The details of the route they flew are no longer known, apart from the fact that it began with a leg towards the east coast. At one stage, however, they made a significant navigational error, peering down at blacked-out Nottingham and mistaking it for Leicester, which they had unknowingly overflown some time before. A significant error, but not a surprising one considering the effectiveness of the blackout and the relative unfamiliarity of most of the crew with the United Kingdom's urban sprawl. However, from then on the misidentification caused them to believe they were twenty-three miles south of where they actually were. A belief which helps to explain why they were still trying to edge under a cloud base that varied, according to their subsequent report, from 1,400 to 1,500 feet when, thirty minutes into the morning of 17 July, and while maintaining a 173 mph (150 knots) cruising speed, they flew into the 1,400 feet-above-sea-level surface of Burbage Moor, just to the north of Upper Burbage Bridge.

The Wellington, sturdy though it was, splayed across the moor, and burst into flames; notwithstanding which all five crew members were able to get clear of the immediate conflagration, although Sergeant Thomas, the pilot, had suffered a significant head injury, Sergeant Jacob Roden, the air gunner in the rear turret, had sustained a broken leg, and the others had less serious injuries.

First on the scene were members of the Home Guard, who, by mere chance exercising in the area, must still have made good time in their trek across what, even then, would have been a most unpleasant stretch of bog and hummock-grass. For on arriving at the site they are accredited with having actually pulled some of the crew clear of the flames! Thereafter, having escorted the still-mobile crew members from the moor to the road, they used débris and parachute harnesses as makeshift stretchers for the non-walking casualties. Gratifyingly, their senior NCO, a Sergeant Lowey, later received a well-deserved King's Commendation on their behalf for the service rendered that night.

The court of inquiry attributed the accident to a navigational error, noting that the aircraft had been skimming below the cloud base. But in dealing with the root cause, the misidentification of the two cities which had thrown out the subsequent dead-reckoning, they decided that a snap judgement had been made, and accordingly indicted the crew for overconfidence.

Having suffered diverse injuries the crew were unable to complete the course together, and as each became fit, so he joined a fresh crew, all eventually completing their training. Yet their subsequent careers serve as a salutary reminder that, while attrition rates were high among crews under training, they were even higher once training gave place to operations.

So air-gunner Sergeant Kennington Harris was to be killed on an Essen raid in January 1943, when a night fighter downed his Lancaster. Rear-gunner Sergeant Roden was killed in a Wellington in September 1942, when serving with No.150 Squadron. And Sergeant Thompson, the pilot of Burbage Moor Wellington Z8980, who subsequently transferred to the Air Transport Auxiliary, was killed in August 1944. There are also sources which hold that Pilot Officer Moore, erstwhile navigator on Z8980, was another who failed to return from operations, but this assertion is refuted by the Commonwealth War Graves Commission. Even so, a compelling rate of wastage – of sacrifice.

The crash site is close to an unnamed mere with the twin-humped minor prominence of Rud Hill on the horizon, and in early 2006 there was still a patch of burnt ground strewn with fragments of the molten remains of Wellington Z8980. But this is another of those sites whose location, although not on particularly undulating ground, might well

Looking slightly north-eastwards, towards shallow, twin-humped Rud Hill

call for a little casting about among the cotton grass and heather, no matter how skilful the map reader. (Scornful sheep should be ignored during the process.)

Vickers Armstrongs Wellington 1C DV678, Lindup Low, Chatsworth Park

SK 25436 69112 161m
No.14 Operational Training Unit, RAF Cottesmore (6 miles north-east of Oakham), No.92 Group, Bomber Command
11 June, 1943

Crew: three, all slightly injured:
Flying Officer Leo Braham Patkin, Royal Australian Air Force, pilot
Two other crew members, as yet unidentified

No.14 Operational Training Unit (OTU) which, in 1943, was based at RAF Cottesmore, north-east of Oakham, was typical of the units which employed the Wellington as a crew trainer. The type was generally dependable but mishaps did occur, as was instanced when one of the OTU Wellingtons, DV678, experienced engine trouble an hour and a half into a training exercise which took it over Derbyshire.

The pilot, Flying Officer Leo Patkin, of the Royal Australian Air Force, was flying at 6,500 feet when both engines began to splutter. Evidently he judged it politic to set the machine down rather than attempt to struggle on in the hope that one engine, at least, would keep going. Accordingly, finding a gap in the cloud, he was able to select a wide expanse of grassland which happened to be in the park of the Chatsworth Estate. Approaching from the south-east, the aircraft flew low over the village of Beeley and was then brought to a wheels-up belly landing beside the road at the brow of Lindup Low. The aircraft was not severely damaged but all three crew members were injured to some degree, one suffering facial lacerations.

The Lindup Low crash site

Retired estate worker Mr Charles Roose, then a teenager living with his parents in the singular walled-about Keeper's Cottage – and in late 1944 accepted for RAF aircrew – arrived at the scene with his father just minutes after the aircraft had landed. 'It had come in over Beeley', he recounted in 2005, 'and it appeared virtually intact, although the belly had been damaged. One of the crew had smashed his face rather badly. Either he'd been sitting on the floor for the landing, or had been thrown there by the impact, but his face actually came into contact with the ground. The rest were fine, though. As for the aircraft, it wasn't left there long. In fact, Queen Mary trailers arrived, and the whole thing was gone by that afternoon.' He smiled. 'And what little there was left, I suppose us lads made pretty short work of.' Reflecting, he added, 'It wasn't all that badly damaged, of course, for the pilot had done such a good job ...'

The court of inquiry was less generous. For it felt that, having 6,500 feet in hand, Flying Officer Patkin should have been able to fly onwards to an airfield; that in putting down on unprepared ground he had displayed poor airmanship. However, his station commander was able to argue that since the incident Flying Officer Patkin had lost an engine on another machine, and on that second occasion had made a successful landing despite having to put down on a strange aerodrome. In the light of which both the Air Officer Commanding (AOC) and his superior, the AOC-in-Chief, recommended that no disciplinary action be taken.

Flying Officer Patkin successfully completed the OTU course, was promoted to Flight Lieutenant, and duly went on to bomber operations with No.467 Squadron. However, on the night of 1 January, 1944, he was killed when his Lancaster (LM372) was shot down near Celle in the course of a raid on Berlin.

In 2006 the site of the Wellington forced landing showed no trace of the incident. But then the aircraft had not suffered any serious damage, and being within feet of a road, the site was easy for the salvage crews to access. Notwithstanding which, in 2005, after some rounds of ammunition were discovered, a comprehensive site clearance was carried out by a research and safety group supervised by the Chatsworth Estate.

Left: Belted machine-gun ammunition, removed for safety

Above: Mr David Robinson, the Chatsworth Estate's Head Park Keeper, who supervised a 2005 safety clearance of the site

Right: Mr Charles Roose, who attended the 1943 crash

Vickers Armstrongs Wellington Mk.1C L7811, Conksbury Bridge, Youlgreave

SK 21099 65770 146m
No.149 Squadron, RAF Mildenhall (south-east of Ely), No.3 Group, Bomber Command
12th February, 1941

Crew: six, baled out successfully:
Sergeant Turner, pilot
Sergeant Campbell, second pilot
Sergeant McKnight, observer/bomb aimer
Sergeant Pates, wireless operator/air gunner, sprained his ankle
Sergeant Piper, air gunner
Sergeant Rae, air gunner

The Wellington was undoubtedly one of those aeroplanes which engendered loyalty in all who came into contact with it. And yet, this loyalty notwithstanding, there were occasions when crews were obliged to leave the machine to its own devices. As occurred on the cloudy night of 12 February, 1941, when Wellington Mk.1C, L7811, returning from a raid on Bremen, was abandoned by its crew in Derbyshire, lost over 100 miles from its base.

Just after 1800 hours the evening before, No.149 Squadron had begun dispatching its Wellingtons from RAF Mildenhall as part of a Bomber Command operation against Bremen comprising 45 Halifaxes and 75 Wellingtons. Of these, two of each type were to be posted missing in action, but there was to be another casualty, for having successfully returned to the United Kingdom, Sergeant Turner and his crew, flying Wellington L7811, found themselves hopelessly lost above cloud.

The official report on the incident having gone astray, there is no means of knowing why Sergeant Turner's crew, among so many who safely returned to base, were unable to employ any of several emergency procedures that might have brought them to a suitable airfield. All that can be said with certainty is that Sergeant Turner, having found himself inexorably running short of fuel, made the eminently sensible decision to abandon the aircraft rather than descend blind through cloud. Accordingly, at about 0200 hours, he took up a south-westerly heading and ordered his crew to bale out.

With its crew gone the aircraft fell into a gradually descending left-hand spiral, eventually impacting near river level on Lathkill Dale, just yards upstream from Conksbury Bridge, between Upper Haddon and Youlgreave.

The crashing aircraft itself caused no significant material damage, but some of the crew caused more than a little stir having floated from the sky. One landed innocuously enough in a tree at Swiss Cottage, in Chatsworth Park, another in a field near Sheldon, a third by Beeley Bridge, and a fourth in Park Lane, Rowsley. Sergeant McKnight, however, a Scot, found himself just outside a village which turned out to be Upper Haddon. Making his way from the fields he knocked on the door of Manor Farm Cottage, rousing its incumbent, a lady, who took him to the (then) post office where the local Home Guard had set up their picquet. Only here he found himself under the levelled rifles of a group headed by a highly suspicious Mr Bill Bebbee, none of them able to decide what to make of the unintelligibly broad accent – he was not to be the last Peakland-area survivor to find himself in this predicament! Whether he truly found the situation more fraught than laughable is not known but when another of his crew was ushered through the door, having landed nearby, he instantly threw his arms around him in – it is to be hoped – theatrical relief.

Mr Joe Oldfield, Upper Haddon

With the passage of time many people began to regard the story of 'an aeroplane landing on the Lathkill islet' as something of a myth, but Mr Joe Oldfield, of Upper Haddon, a Lathkill farmer, was able to indicate exactly where the aircraft fell. And Mrs Joan Dale, of Youlgreave, also remembered the crash, for her brother, John, a flight engineer on Halifaxes, was on leave from operations at the time and visited the crash site, bringing back some perspex which he then fashioned into rings for her and her mother (The first instance of this practice the author had come upon!).

In 2006 there was nothing left to even hint at the fact that a forsaken bomber had crashed at the site, by then a wide, hard-surfaced, very popular footpath towards the upstream end of an island in the River Lathkill just above Conksbury Bridge. Indeed the heavily wooded slope, the rush-bordered bank and the deepened channel combined to hinder the writer's search for evidence. But débris enough to prove the site was found in 2004.

Such fragmented remains were discovered in the first twenty feet of the slope, with more in the riverside rushes, and yet more – some only after plunging an arm through ice!– in the deep muddy bed of the river itself. But it seems there was a time when plans were formulated to recover an engine believed to remain in situ.

Site-proving débris, 2004

The impact spread of Wellington L7811, facing Conksbury Bridge

Notwithstanding all of which the site tends to hold its secret, albeit not the greatest national secret the seemingly sleepy Upper Haddon area was to hold. For resident Mr John Oldfield, the brother of the aforementioned Mr Joe Oldfield, was to be knighted, and appointed 'M'. Yet neither the one occurrence nor the other now draws the attention of any but a trifling number of the thousands who annually throng to walk, fish, or merely dally alongside the, at least, seasonally sparkling – but on occasion, dry-in-parts – Lathkill.

Nor are these the only associations the walker's Lathkill Path has with aircraft, and with security. For in April 1958, at the Dale's distant end, towards Monyash, Canberra bomber WT207 exploded at a great height when engaged in secret trials, débris falling over a wide area around the village, with a wing and engine actually landing on the path itself.

Vickers Armstrongs Wellington Mk.1C DV732, Eyam Moor (eastern end of Sir William Hill Road)

SK 22285 78097 373m
No.11 Operational Training Unit, RAF Westcott (Aylesbury), No.92 Group, Bomber Command
2 June, 1943

Crew: all survived, uninjured:
Sergeant R.H. Trangmar, Royal New Zealand Air Force, pilot
Other crew members presently unidentified

Long before October 1943, when it was withdrawn from bombing operations over Europe, the Wellington had proved its worth as a training aircraft, and from then on it was to become the mainstay of the Operational Training Units (OTUs) preparing aircrews for both twin- and later four-engined first-line bombers. Similarly the machine had proved its dependability. Yet dependable and worthy as the type was, the all-year-round training of crews, many of whom had done their basic training over the uncluttered plains of Canada or Rhodesia, always had inherent risks.

This was well illustrated on 2 June, 1943, when Wellington DV732, of No.11 Operational Training Unit, located at RAF Westcott, near Aylesbury, crashed at 0230 hours in the course of a night-navigation exercise when it was flown into high moorland above the celebrated plague village of Eyam. The aircraft had to be written off, although none of the crew sustained any injury.

The investigation into the crash submitted that Sergeant Trangmar, of the Royal New Zealand Air Force, had simply flown into the hillside in the dark, seemingly without either mechanical or weather complications. The finding, subsequently concurred with at all levels, was that bad navigation had caused the aircraft to be off track, and that it had been flying 'unnecessarily low'. The Air Officer Commanding encompassed the whole as, 'bad captaincy'.

In early 2005 Mr John Hancock was able to point out the site. 'I was about fourteen, and cycled over here with friends,' he said, tramping the heather much as he had done sixty years before. 'The Wimpy was pretty whole, although the trellis-like geodetic showed through where its back had broken, and the nose was somewhat skewed off. But none of the crew had been hurt.' He indicated the skyline ridge, descending from the nearby trig point. 'How on earth it missed that! But I suppose it was already in a shallow easterly descent, for there was hardly a mark on the heather back along its way, no furrow or anything. It must simply have brushed it, and slowed, until it actually struck.' He smiled. 'We were able to look around inside. But it was so whole that all I remember taking away was a piece of broken perspex which I picked up off the ground.'

In mid-2006 the crash site, in flourishing heather and hardly fifty yards from a public footpath, showed no surface evidence of the crash. But then Mr Hancock has vouched for how little the aircraft had fragmented, while the proximity of the Sir William Hill road would have eased the salvage task considerably.

Sixty-two years on, and Mr John Hancock revisits the scene

Vickers Armstrongs Wellington Mk.3 HF613, Hope (near Castleton)

SK 16179 83030 161m
SK 15999 83418 roadside monument, A625, Castleton
No.22 Operational Training Unit, RAF Wellesbourne Mountford (east of Stratford), No.91 Group, Bomber Command
15 February, 1943

Crew: all killed:
Sergeant John Douglas Kester, Royal Canadian Air Force, pilot
Sergeant Richard Foote Cairns, RCAF, navigator
Sergeant Bernard Elliott Wilkinson, RCAF, bomb-aimer
Sergeant William Arthur Billy Marwood, RAF Volunteer Reserve, wireless operator/air gunner
Sergeant William James Hackett, RCAF, air gunner

Although the Operational Training Units (OTUs) were fundamentally non-operational, there were occasions when OTU personnel, both instructors and crew under training, would be called upon to swell the numbers on such special operations as the high-profile one thousand bomber raids. So it was that No.22 OTU, based at RAF Wellesbourne Mountford (just east of Stratford), provided aircraft for three such raids in May and June 1942, in the process losing six Wellingtons, each with its six-man crew.

But such operations were only incidental risks, and in the workaday training role the swiftly-changing British weather was a factor as high as any of those prevailing. Indeed it quickly became a truism among crews and authorising officers alike that the weather was predictable only in its unpredictability. And despite the best endeavours of both, it was a truism that could become only too bitter. As was the case on 15 February, 1943, when Wellington HF613 was lost in a weather-related crash at Hope in Derbyshire.

On that wintry day Sergeant John Kester, of the Royal Canadian Air Force, and his mainly Canadian crew, were briefed for a solo cross-country flight from RAF Gaydon, No.22 OTU's satellite airfield, six miles east of Wellesbourne Mountford. That the route took them to the north is the only detail now known regarding the cross-country itself, except that, in view of the unstable weather pattern, Sergeant Kester, with only twenty hours solo on type, was specifically briefed to keep an eye out for storms, and to go round shower clouds, rather than enter them. However, at just after one o'clock in the afternoon, Wellington HF613 was heard over Hope, in Derbyshire, eighty miles north of Gaydon.

At the time young Noreen Beverley, later to become Mrs Eric Robinson, was on her school lunchbreak having arrived home at a run to try and miss a sudden cloudburst. 'It was like a blizzard,' she remembered, speaking in early 2006, 'violent gusts of wind, pelting snow – really awful. And then, hardly ten minutes later, there was a clear sky again.'

Mr and Mrs Eric and Noreen Robinson, Hope

But those ten minutes had proved only too protracted for Sergeant Kester and his crew.

As Noreen's husband, Mr Eric Robinson, confirmed. 'We saw him coming from the Bradwell direction, not that high above the Earles' Cement Works chimney, before we lost him in the cloud. But just then the storm really broke, and we couldn't see anything for snow. Only you could tell from his engine note that he was trying to turn back again.'

Except that just moments later the Wellington, its engines at high power, plummeted out of the downsweeping snow flurries, struck the ground, skidded on across a ford, and exploded.

'We could see the flames from the house,' Noreen said sombrely, 'and the black smoke. But my mother wouldn't let me go over there ...'

And just as well, for as those arriving at the scene were to find, the fire had burnt fiercely, and there was nothing to be done for the crew.

There seems to be little doubt regarding the essential train of events during those fatal moments of cloud penetration. Evidently Sergeant Kester had entered what had looked like an innocuous enough cloud, not realising that a storm cell, shielded from him by the veiling stratiform layer, was just about to boil over. But although clouds, once penetrated, invariably tend to be far wider in extent than they appear on the approach, it would not have been long before the suddenly increasing turbulence alerted him to the fact that there was more to this woolly-edged seeming-stratocumulus than had shown itself moments earlier.

With snow suddenly darkening the windscreen and – it being midday – with no cockpit lighting turned on to show him, in this extremity, what he was about, he would have had to make an instant transition onto instruments. And not simply to accommodate a change from a visual to an instrument straight-and-level cruise. For he was called upon to bank the unwieldy bomber hard over and then pull it around to the reverse direction as expeditiously as possible in order to regain clear sky and an area of proven terrain clearance once again. It would have been rather a lot to ask of himself even in smooth flying conditions. So one hardly has to postulate a gust under his upgoing wing suddenly increasing the bank to appreciate that, in the event, he found it quite beyond his capabilities. Or that he then lost control, was unable to take remedial action, and spiralled into the ground under full power.

The court of inquiry did investigate the alternative possibility that ice had played its part in the loss of control. But as the aircraft's penetration, including its one hundred and eighty degree turn, could hardly have taken longer than a few minutes, any ice accretion could only have been secondary to the failure to accommodate the demands of instrument flight. Appreciating which, every reporting officer up the chain was quite unequivocal in his condemnation of the conduct of the flight.

The unit's commanding officer pointedly proffered his own briefing forbidding the pilot to 'enter heavy squalls or showers, but to avoid them'. At best a rather impracticable authorisation under which to dispatch an inexperienced Canadian crew on a lively mid-February English day.

For his part the station commander fumed, and scribbled, 'Disobedience or disregard of orders in entering a cloud'. A cloud! While the chief instructor commented testily, 'This form of disregard of orders is frequent'. And from their cerulean heights both the Air Officer Commanding and the Air Officer Commanding-in-Chief concurred.

A savage condemnation, surely! Of an inexperienced pilot who had clearly been taken unawares by the ferocity of a storm which witness evidence showed only lasted ten minutes at the most. And even then, a pilot who had tried his level best to rectify the error. Yet there is the larger picture to be taken into consideration.

No.22 Operational Training Unit came into being on 14th April, 1941, and by the time it was disbanded on 25th July, 1945, it had trained 9,000 aircrew; indeed at its peak, in 1944, it was turning out 113 operationally ready crews a month. But this was never to be without a cost, and between Wellesbourne Mountford and Gaydon the training cost was high, with 315 aircrew killed, and a further 80 injured; figures reflecting the deaths of one WAAF, one Australian, two Belgians, nine New Zealanders, fifty-nine RAF, and including Sergeant Kester and his crew, two hundred and forty-three Canadians. Additionally, ninety-six Wellingtons lost to the war effort. All in all, some attrition rate for a single training unit!

So perhaps it is understandable that while living with such losses took its toll upon the nerves of the aircrew and ground staffs, it wore equally, at least, upon those of the senior officers responsible for producing the crews so desperately needed. Remember, too, that each of the 9,000 aircrew trained was a volunteer. Additionally that nearly all were very young, and it could be to an above average degree imbued with all the impetuously adventurous qualities engendered, not only by their own years, but by the tumultuous times they were living through. Accepting this, it can be appreciated that to condone a shortfall in discipline might well have led to even higher casualty rates. In which context the severity of the report into the loss of just one of the ninety-six aircraft, Wellington HF613, might become a little more palatable. Notwithstanding that the individual human hurt remains. But at least it can be measured against the overall human cost at stake.

As for Wellington HF613, having fallen out of control from that untimely snowstorm the stricken machine had plunged into a field just short of the northern bank of Peakshole Water – even then, locally known as 'The Styx'!– and disintegrated as it ground its way onwards to encounter the slope beyond the stream.

Mr Robert Stamper of Hathersage was an early visitor to the scene. 'I found it horrible,' he said in 2005. 'There were body parts still lying there, but aside from both wheels in the stream, nothing that looked like an aeroplane.' Robert's wife, Dorothy, who had lived nearby, also remembered how violent and short-lived the lunchtime snowstorm had been.

Yet with the wreckage cleared the scars soon healed, and the ford became a drinking place for stock once more. And also a playground for picnicking children. Until 4 April, 1982, when the night-time peace was rudely disturbed. As indeed, were Mr and Mrs Eric Robinson, long since married, and both now domiciled in nearby Marsden Farm. For although the ill-fated Wellington had been on a training sortie, dangerous ordnance had suddenly come to light, discovered by a walker one Saturday afternoon.

'I saw these lights out in the field,' said Mr Robinson, 'which turned out to be the police. For two practice bombs had been found. Unbelievable! Because so many people had been over the place, even with metal detectors. And of course, children regularly played there.'

The practice bombs turned out to be very corroded, but fused, and still potentially lethal. Notwithstanding which Mrs Robinson observed: 'Yet when the bomb disposal people blew them up they sounded very small, although all doors and windows had to be opened as a precaution.'

In the interim, a Mr Stephen Lewis had researched the crash and subsequently contacted the Canadian relatives. As a result of this Sergeant Bernard Wilkinson's sister came on a visit from Canada, after which she faithfully exchanged Christmas cards with the Robinsons. In due course, Mr Robinson had a plaque made by a foundry in Birmingham which he placed on a wall on the Castleton Road at the extension of the field where the crash occurred. Only yards, in fact, from the Canadian Maple, planted on her visit by Sergeant Wilkinson's sister as a tribute to the memory of 'Bunny', her brother, and erstwhile bomb-aimer of the ill-fated Wellington, HF613.

The field-wall pattern in the vicinity of the crash site has been altered since the war, but in early 2006 the ford was still a reliable locator, just to the south of the initial impact point, the terminal site being only yards downslope from a public footpath. Nothing was evident on the surface, however, with sheep-cropped pasture rising gently from the brook. But evidence enough was found to show that this pastoral slope was not always so tranquil; that despite its sunny aspect it is forever overshadowed by associations altogether more sombre than the banner plume issuing even then from Bradwell's lofty chimney.

Mention of the Bradwell chimney admits a wartime anecdote from Mrs Margaret Brown (née Dakin), who grew up in the Hope Valley. 'After our parents had gone upstairs,' Mrs Brown recalled, 'warning us against running the accumulator-powered wireless flat, we used to crowd around it with the volume turned low. Only one night Lord Haw Haw [William Joyce, the American-born, Irish-nurtured English traitor who made regular propaganda broadcasts from Germany and was eventually hanged] said, "You people in the Hope Valley think you are so snug and safe. What you don't realise is that the moment we cross the coast we can see the smoke from the Earle's chimney." We were quite literally petrified. I'm sure we all felt that the Germans could see us even as we sat there. So we switched off the radio at once, scarcely daring to move or make a noise.'

Far left: The terminal crash site of Wellington HF613, beyond the brook, viewed from the initial impact point

Left: The memorial on the Castleton Road

Vickers Armstrongs Wellington Mk.3 X3941, Gladwin's Mark Farm, Screetham

SK 30376 66211 328m
No.27 Operational Training Unit, RAF Church Broughton, No.91 Group, Bomber Command
30 January, 1943

Crew: five; two killed, three injured:
Sergeant Kenneth Barton Killeen, Royal Australian Air Force, pilot, killed
Sergeant William Alan Catron, RAAF, second pilot, on pre-operational experience, killed
Navigator, wireless operator/air gunner, and rear-turret air gunner: identities presently not determined; all injured

The overall task of No.27 Operational Training Unit (OTU) was to train aircrews on the twin-engined Wellington, normally prior to further training on four-engined types. In doing so, however, this OTU particularly accommodated Australian crews who had done their training in Canada under the Empire Air Training Scheme and were now being introduced to European flying conditions. Certainly the weather was to prove a prime factor on 30 January, 1943, when Sergeant Kenneth Killeen and his trainee crew were dispatched on a night exercise from RAF Church Broughton, a satellite of RAF Lichfield, the headquarters of No.27 OTU.

The exercise prescribed was a bombing and navigational sortie known as a 'Bullseye', in which the task was to navigate to, and locate, a target, then to simulate a bombing run by use of photography, although 'Bullseye' exercises might also involve OTU aircraft being sent part-way towards enemy-occupied coasts to lure enemy fighters away from a real raid.

The weather that night, starting as extremely unstable with strong winds and an abundance of rain clouds, steadily worsened, until at about midnight a general recall was issued. Evidently Sergeant Killeen's wireless operator did not receive the message, for there was no acknowledgement. But two hours later, their detail completed, the crew had made contact once again, and furnished with a track to fly, had turned inbound to Church Broughton, and were actually descending. Except that when they were still twenty-two miles short of the aerodrome their aircraft struck a line of trees then plunged into a field. Both pilots were killed, and the other three crew members injured.

The field belonged to Gladwin's Mark Farm, Screetham, to the west of Chesterfield, in Derbyshire. But as the farm was hidden from the wreck by a clump of trees, the rear gunner, the fittest of the injured men, seeing a random flash of moonlight on a distant roof, set out across country, eventually raising the alarm at Mr Lomas's Moor Farm (to become Darley Forest Grange), on Flash Lane, half a mile to the south-west.

Mr David Fearn, the 2005 incumbent, was told how the rear-gunner's arrival was remembered from childhood by Kathleen Lomas, subsequently Mrs Kathleen Dixon, and residing in Australia. 'This German pilot, covered in blood,' as she had put it on a visit to her old home, 'arrived at the door in stormy weather in the middle of the night, giving a terrible fright to my father.'

In 2005 Farmer Mr Ernest Dronfield could personally vouch for the foulness of the weather that

Moor Farm, where 'the German pilot' arrived covered in blood ...

night. 'We'd been to Home Guard in Ashover,' he remembered. 'Farming all day, then Home Guard at night! But what a rum night that was! I never saw such weather: rain, low cloud, and such rough winds! The road to Gladwin's Mark is very exposed but as we turned onto it that night we had to get off and push our bikes. Well, I was only too glad to get indoors and to bed. So I didn't hear about the crash until next day. But then I went over there. I believe they were all Australians ...'

Mr Dronfield was to get to know the wreckage well. 'It crashed in the "Second Ten-Acre field"– some people now call it "Aeroplane" field. The RAF soon cleared the 'plane away. But for years after I was ploughing up bits.' Mr Sam Bown, his stepbrother, remembered that too. 'It was 1955 before I started ploughing "Aeroplane" field, but I was always turning up pieces of crumpled aluminium.' Yet clearly such regular ploughing had its effect, for Mr Jack Dart, who had ploughed the field since the mid-sixties, and as a champion competition-ploughman had the keenest of eyes for the soil, could never remember seeing a trace of aircraft-derived metal.

Mr Ernest Dronfield resumed his account, 'The 'plane had come from the Chesterfield direction, took the tops off the trees, skimmed over the road and drystone wall, and into the field where it broke up. We always supposed they'd had something wrong with their engines.'

In fact, plotting out the line of flight, from Chesterfield, and beyond the crash site, it becomes clear that Sergeant Killeen and his crew were reasonably on track for RAF Church Broughton. But Mr Dronfield, cycling home, had experienced the worsening violence of the westerly surface wind. It follows, therefore, that the aircraft would have been bucking a significantly higher headwind aloft. So if the crew had failed to detect the marked increase in wind strength they would not have appreciated the reduction in their speed over the ground. A reduction which meant that they were not as far along the return leg as they had thought. So that as they descended through cloud, thinking they were well clear of any high ground, and with their altimeter showing a comfortable 1,000 feet or so – comfortable for that era, at least – they would not have expected the ground beneath them to be at just that height above sea level. As, unhappily, it was.

The terminal site, looking back along the approach

As late as 2006 the field in which the aircraft crashed was still harbouring enough fragments of the singular geodetic construction to prove that it was indeed a Wellington that crashed there. Essentially, however, there was nothing to see, for thanks to the labours of Messrs Dart, Bown and Dronfield, the field had long since put aside its fatal aspect and taken on once more its customary pastoral mien.

Armstrongs Wellington Mk.3 BJ652, Smerrill Grange, Middleton

SK 19948 62065 205m
No.27 Operational Training Unit, RAF Lichfield, No.93 Group, Bomber Command
21 January, 1944

Crew: six, all killed:
Flight Sergeant Lloyd George Edmonds, RAAF, pilot
Flying Officer Keith Jobson Perrett, RAAF, navigator
Flight Sergeant James Kydd, RAAF, bomb aimer
Flight Sergeant Frederick Popsham Deshon, RAAF, staff wireless operator
Flight Sergeant William Thomas Barnes, RAAF, wireless operator
Sergeant Thomas Dudley Murton, RAAF, air gunner

The normal crew complement of the Wellington was six, but on training units the various aircrew categories would be shuffled to suit the need of the exercise in hand. A need which had changed markedly, for although in pre-war days only pilots and observers had been full-time aircrew, by 1944 the various specialities had long stabilised. But there was still dual tasking, with wireless operators, in particular, almost invariably being trained to double as air gunners.

As for communications, the pilot could speak over the High Frequency transmitter-receiver Mk.9 (TR9), whose regrettable short range at least allowed a common Bomber Command frequency to be used without undue interference between stations. In addition, the short range facilitated the 'Darky' pass-you-along-and-get-you-down system.

For longer-range communication there was the W/T (wireless telegraphy, or morse) transmitter-receiver 1082/83; although from mid-1941 this was supplanted by the more versatile T1154/R1155 morse-cum-High Frequency voice installation. The range of both sets was extended by the use of a trailing aerial weighted by lead beads, with direction finding being afforded by a rotatable loop aerial, such sets being the province of a wireless operator.

Indeed on 21 January, 1944, when Flight Sergeant Lloyd Edmonds, of the Royal Australian

Air Force, and his all-Australian trainee crew, were dispatched on a night cross-country exercise, there were two wireless operators on board, for a staff wireless operator was to put their own operator through his paces.

The crew were training at No.27 Operational Training Unit (OTU) prior to being posted to heavy bombers, and operations, and were presently flying out of RAF Church Broughton, near Uttoxeter, a satellite of RAF Lichfield, the OTU's headquarters.

The detail seems to have progressed satisfactorily with periodical W/T contacts – comprising position reports, weather updates, fixes, and bearings – attesting to the fact that there were no navigational problems. However, towards the end of the sortie it appears that the aircraft ran into cloud, forcing the pilot to revert to instruments.

Whether Flight Sergeant Edmonds experienced difficulty in making the transition, and although fixating on the blind-flying panel, nonetheless entered an almost imperceptible descent; or whether he decided that he would be better off edging below the cloud base and flying visually as best he could over the blacked-out countryside, can never be known with any certainty. But the last few moments of the flight were witnessed by several people, and are well documented.

The Wellington was seen to fly at an extremely low level past the high-set township of Youlgreave, after which a cottager in the village of Middleton, next along the line of flight, reported being so startled at how closely it passed across his roof that he had hurried out to gaze after it as it skimmed its way down the valley.

In fact, had the aircraft not continued its gradual descent, but carried on along its track, it would have overflown Ashbourne and so arrived at RAF Church Broughton. Except that at 2210 hours it entered the curved, bluff-sided gully carrying Rowlow Brook and impacted at speed just below the 700 feet-above-sea-level rim.

The Kenworthy family at Lowfields Farm, on the far side of the gully, were just getting their daughter, Pat, to bed when the crash alarmed them. Seeing unlooked-for lights infringing the blackout, they phoned across to Smerrill Grange Farm, and on hearing what had happened, Farmer Bernard Kenworthy, a Gallipoli veteran, hurried to the site. 'Doctor Ivers was there,' daughter Pat, subsequently Mrs Hollingsworth, remembered him reporting later, 'but there was nothing anyone could do.'

Mr Colin Rowland, then on leave from the Irish Guards, also made his way to the site where he joined other villagers, including members of the Gregory family who actually farmed Smerrill Grange Farm, situated just a hundred yards beyond the rim.

It was found that the steep slope immediately beneath the rim itself had completely contained the wreckage, leaving the drystone wall on the gully's edge unbroken. But from first glance it became evident that nothing could be done for the crew. Accordingly the would-be rescuers turned to the task of extricating the bodies from the wreckage and carrying them to the nearest of the farm's outbuildings. Meanwhile the RAF authorities were being contacted. Which led to a hiatus. For it then became clear that one crew member was unaccounted for.

Guardsman Rowland, in company with one of the Gregory family and a policeman, once more clambered down between the oak and the ash tree to the slope encompassing the bulk of the wreckage and realised that the tail, with the missing gunner still in his turret, was projecting out beyond a prominent limestone crag.

Locating the gunner was all very well, but getting him down was to prove no sinecure, for the tail was not only well above their heads but teetering. Yet undeterred the three men persisted in their hazardous endeavour.

'When we finally got up, and I tried to drag the gunner from the turret,' Mr Rowland said soberly, speaking in 2004, 'his boots came away in my hand. The policeman was worried that he might still be alive. But I knew better.'

Guardsman Colin Rowland, Middleton by Youlgreave

The impact point, looking upslope   The crag over which the tail teetered

The RAF were quickly on the scene and for the next few days busied themselves clearing the wreckage – demolishing part of the drystone wall in order to gain access – and attempting to stop the souvenir-hunting village children from doing an even more thorough clearance job.

In the course of time the investigating officers submitted that the accident was probably due to faulty instrument flying which had caused the pilot to inadvertently descend too low, thinking he was still in cloud. Higher authority having concurred with that, the incident was closed, but in 1995, fifty years after the end of the Second World War, a tastefully modest memorial was erected, commemorating the loss of these six Australian lives.

In 2006 the oak and the ash tree still framed the impact point, with the crag below overlooking the vegetation-choked gully and Rowlow Brook, where one of the mainwheels of Wellington BJ652 came to rest. But there were no visible scars, and only pram frames and plastic bags protruded above the rank grass and wiry brambles which carpeted the almost precipitous slopes. Just the same, a careful search turned up sufficient evidence to prove the location in the shape of a fragmented piece of geodetic, with its bonding wire attached.

Notwithstanding which, as no public footpath followed Rowlow Brook, the site seemed set to remain a lonely one, allowing Smerrill Grange Farm, just feet above the rim, and only yards along the projected line of flight, to brood upon what might have been the outcome had the aircraft struck just that few feet higher than it did.

Left: The oak, and the ash, and – a single piece of geodetic

Left: Smerrill Grange Farm, from the drystone wall above the impact site

Vickers Armstrongs Wellington Mk.2 Z8491, White Edge Moor (north-east of Froggatt)

SK 26987 77406 358m
No.12 Squadron, RAF Binbrook (south-west of Grimsby), No.1 Group, Bomber Command
6 February, 1942

Crew: six, four injured:
Flying Officer Colin Arthur Barnes, DFC, pilot (broken ankle)
Sergeant Jack Seaman, second pilot, on operational experience (frostbite)
Sergeant Bob Coldwell, navigator
Sergeant Brian Lunn, bomb aimer
Sergeant 'Kit' Carson, wireless operator
Sergeant John Blute, air gunner (concussed)

That it was deemed worthwhile recovering Vickers Wellington 'R' Robert from Loch Ness, a bomber since displayed at the Vickers' Museum at Weybridge, says much for the soundness of the geodetic construction developed by Barnes Wallis. Further, the ruggedness that helped many Wellingtons limp home despite severe battle damage also helped save some of those crews who found themselves unexpectedly brought to earth.

Vickers Armstrongs Wellington 'R' Robert, from Loch Ness, displaying the partially-skinned geodetic construction (courtesy of Vickers, Weybridge)

Certainly Flying Officer Colin Barnes, DFC, and his crew found cause to thank that basic robustness of the Wellington on 6 February, 1942, when they were dispatched from RAF Binbrook, near Grimsby, to the westernmost extremity of Brittany to bomb German installations in the French port of Brest.

The round trip would have taken the No.12 Squadron crews some four and a half hours, but as Wellington Z8491 approached the Brest area it became obvious to Flying Officer Barnes that thick cloud was going to prevent them from identifying the target. True, by 1942 there would no longer have been any restriction on their dropping, or even jettisoning, their bombs anywhere over Germany if faced with such conditions, but indiscriminate bombing over Occupied France was unthinkable; consequently he aborted the operation, and keeping his bombs on board, faced about for home.

On making a landfall in the region of Start Point, the crew still had some 265 miles to go to reach Binbrook. But as it was a route they had so recently transited they were familiar with the weather pattern and would have had as up-to-date a wind as any. So, although it was a seasonable February night, with low cloud, no moon, and with the blacked-out ground made even more featureless by deep snow, the flight would have presented no problems. Accordingly they seem to have settled onto their north-easterly heading and patiently awaited the navigator's estimate for Binbrook.

The lapse time to Binbrook would have been some eighty minutes from leaving Start Point, so that with ten minutes to go – representing thirty-five miles – they would have anticipated being in the area of Newark. Which meant that the only terrain of note ahead was the Wolds, a ridge of low hills not that much higher than Binbrook, itself standing at a mere 370 feet above sea level. Surely then, there was no danger in easing down through the cloud? And no reason at all for breaking W/T radio silence, or bothering any emergency service, even the HF 'Darky' get-you-home organisation.

Except that as they commenced their descent, and with their altimeter still reading some 1,200 feet, they struck the ground. The aircraft bounded high, struck again, then, having hung as if suspended for long seconds on end, impacted for a final time, only now with such violence that it broke its back. Providentially, there was no fire, nor did the bomb load detonate, despite a main ordnance comprising seven 500 lb bombs.

Once those who were able to had managed to scramble clear it was found that the tail had twisted, rope-like, then come to rest fin downwards. However, despite the basic integrity of the rest of the machine, a hasty muster failed to account for two crew members. Air gunner Sergeant John Blute was quickly located in the tail turret, but there was no sign amidst the wreckage of the second pilot, Sergeant Jack Seaman.

With that mystery shelved for the present it was found that Sergeant Blute, although uninjured, was trapped upside down in the turret from which, despite all efforts, none of the crew were able to extricate him. For the rest, the captain, Flying Officer Barnes, was now immobilised with a broken ankle, and the bomb-aimer, Sergeant Brian Lunn, who had been stationed in the front turret, was concussed.

Eventually, although with everyone still at a loss to account for the second pilot, some sort of order was established, and Sergeant 'Kit' Carson, the wireless operator, and the only one presently capable of the undertaking, was dispatched to try to summon assistance.

Not surprisingly, Sergeant Carson found the going tough, having to force his way across pitch-dark, heather-choked and largely hummock-grassed moorland where the footing was made yet more treacherous by deep snow. Nor were these the only hazards, for when Mr Bill Sayles, the resident water inspector, spotted him from his doorway, the airman, heading for the water-control tower, dimly silhouetted against the whiteness, was perilously close to blundering onto the only thinly-iced Barbrook Reservoir.

The Sayles family house, from which the rescue effort was launched

Sergeant Carson was swiftly handed into the care of Mrs Margaret Sayles while Mr Sayles set about organising a search party. Indeed it is to be hoped that the family received some recognition for their night's work, for in addition to organising the rescue, Mr Sayles himself made two journeys to the crash site, first leading rescuers, then assisting a crew member back.

The trapped gunner was eventually released and along with the others remaining at the site was escorted down the moor to the house. But only later, as the day drew on, was the missing second pilot discovered. He had been thrown clear, it transpired, and being badly shocked, had assumed that he was, in fact, in Occupied France, after which, doubtless taking to heart his escape-and-evasion lectures, he had lain low until daylight. He was found to have cracked ribs, with frostbite subsequently costing him some fingers.

But not least among the casualties was to be an unidentified member of the local Home Guard who, gallantly making over his greatcoat to one of the crew at the crash site, then fell victim to exposure, from which he was never to fully recover.

Just a few days later the bombs had been disposed of and the site cleared of all wreckage. On the administrative side, similarly, the inquiry worked swiftly. They were reporting, after all, on an operational sortie, and operationally qualified crews were precious commodities. Accordingly the Binbrook Station Commander merely noted that, in his opinion, his pilot had 'lost height thinking he was over low country'. Nor was there anything but the tiniest suggestion of mild reproof in the investigators' summary that the aircraft 'flew into high ground owing to navigational errors in bad visibility'. Consequently, with the inquiry's findings submitted and approved, the incident was closed.

With their injuries healed, and having had their survivors' leave, the various crew members went their separate ways. Sergeant Lunn and Sergeant Blute were later to be killed on ops; as was Sergeant Coldwell, although by then he had been awarded a Distinguished Flying Medal, been commissioned, reached the rank of Flight Lieutenant, and received a Distinguished Service Order, the latter no mean distinction for an officer so junior. Sergeant Seaman flew on as a captain in his own right, surviving the war, while, with his ankle mended, Flying Officer Barnes transferred to instructing on Heavy Conversion Units, eventually leaving the Service as a squadron leader.

But that night in February 1942 was not quite the last he was to see of White Edge Moor. For after the war he returned, by daylight, accompanied by his wife, and walked out to the crash site where he duly photographed his lady standing beside a singularly kinked sapling with Barbrook Reservoir as a backdrop.

Then again, Sergeant Carson, the erstwhile wireless operator of Wellington Z8491 who also survived the war, painted the machine as he remembered it from that night; twisted, battered, and buckled, tail awry, but with its integrity not essentially compromised, for all that it would never fly again.

And yet for many years it did seem that Z8491 might well have taken wings once more, gathering itself phoenix-like from any ashes left by the salvage crew, for no physical evidence of an impact site had been found despite exhaustive searches. In August 2005, however, Mr Ken Adlington, of Shepherd Flatt Farm, generously driven onto the moor by Eastern Moors Estate Warden, Mr Danny Udall, was able to throw light on the lack of débris.

A post-war photograph taken by Squadron Leader Barnes of his wife, with Barbrook Reservoir to the rear; the terminal impact site is some hundred yards out of shot to the right (Photograph by courtesy of Mr Roni Wilkinson, Pen & Sword Books)

The crash of Z8491, by Sergeant Carson, used by courtesy of Mr Roni Wilkinson, Pen & Sword Books

'At the time of the crash,' Mr Adlington explained, 'I was Head Shepherd for the Water Board, who owned the moor. First thing next morning we followed the wall from the Grouse Inn to the Hurkling Stone and then to a spot adjacent to the single tree to where the main wreckage was. Beyond that there were two scars a few hundred yards back where it had touched and bounced – on a line back towards where the trig point is. The Wellington had obviously descended over White Edge, but then come down where the ground flattens, touching a time or two before finally stopping, breaking its back to leave its tail resting on its fin.' He reflected. 'I can't remember seeing any bombs, but then on that first visit the Holmesfield Home Guard had gone and the army were there – busily pointing their rifles! After that, however, it seemed to be a salvage gang who dealt with the wreck, for they weren't in uniform. But a friend of mine, Richard Crossland, had a Fordson tractor, the only one in the area, and as the wreckage was dismantled it was dragged off the moor and along the reservoir walls to the access road near the Swales' house. As for the lack of débris since, people took souvenirs at the time, of course – in particular, I remember the two Gamekeeper's sons from White Edge Lodge: nothing was too big or heavy for that pair!– but when it was all done there wasn't a nut or bolt left; an absolutely swept-up job.' But he then produced a tiny fragment. 'Even that,' he said, just a little wryly, conscious suddenly, it might be, of the passage of time, 'I probably picked up thirty years ago, for it must be that long since I've been out here ...'

Mr Ken Adlington
As it transpired, Ken was to die within days of passing on the exact location of this site; at that juncture, information only he still possessed. Which makes this an opportune place to pay grateful tribute to all those who, in furtherance of this research, supplied knowledge that, by dint of time, only they were still privy to, and by 2006 were no longer with us.

A 2005 photo-match of the one taken by Squadron Leader Barnes, with the singularly kinked tree, age-bowed, and having twisted, now revealing its twin forks. To the right rear, the drained Barbrook Reservoir. Again, the terminal impact point is some one hundred yards to the right out of frame.

2005, at the terminal impact point, Estate Warden Danny Udall and Mr Ken Adlington. The drained Barbrook Reservoir is in the background.

2005, and Mr Ken Adlington displays a fragment of debris found some thirty years before

An impact-fractured section of aircraft fuel pipe discarded by souvenir hunters on the Barbrook Bridge track and found by the author early in 2004

Vickers Armstrongs Wellington Mk.10 MF633, Kiveton Park (south-east of Sheffield)

SK 49898 82909 110m
No.201 Advanced Flying School (AFS), RAF Swinderby (near Newark), No.21 Group, Flying Training Command
29 June, 1951

Crew: three, all killed:
Pilot Officer Thomas Andrew Blair Bond, pilot
Flying Officer Ryland Leonard Luffman, navigator
Sergeant Bernard Leslie Curson, air signaller

Despite the comprehensive process by which the RAF has selected them, one of the prime concerns of the majority of pupil aircrew has always been that, having started training, they will fail to meet the standard and be 'chopped'. As a corollary of this, when a fellow pupil is taken off his flying course, and particularly if 'the chop' falls towards the end of the course, it is invariably felt that someone so keen might surely have been given just that little bit more time in which to improve. Yet for instructional staff the decision to continue training in doubtful cases is a fine one, and with the best will in the world, the wrong decision is sometimes made.

Sadly for all concerned, this seems to have been the case on 29 June, 1951, when Wellington MF633 of No.201 Advanced Flying School, RAF Swinderby, near Newark, was lost with all four members of its trainee crew.

Pilot Officer Thomas Bond and his crew were returning from a four-hour night cross-country exercise, the final one of their course, and having advised air traffic that they would reach Swinderby in six minutes, were homing on a bearing when their aircraft emerged from cloud and crashed at Red Hill, Kiveton Park, near Sheffield, catching fire and killing everyone on board.

The alarm was raised by Mr Oswald Ilsley, Kiveton Park's grocer, who phoned 999, while other witnesses testified to having seen the aircraft break cloud with both engines going, then make a steep right-hand turn in the course of which the nose dropped and the aircraft spiralled into the ground.

In inspecting the location, the investigators turned their attention to the bright lights of Kiveton Colliery. After which, having collated all the evidence, they deduced that, regardless of the fact that his navigator's estimate had placed him a good five minutes from Swinderby, Pilot Officer Bond, on breaking cloud, had immediately assumed that the lights below were those of the airfield and commenced a robust visual turn. They further deduced that, having ceased scanning his instruments, he had become disorientated as he tried to reconcile the lighting pattern below with what he expected to see at Swinderby, that as a consequence he had lost control, allowed his turn to steepen into a spiral dive, and crashed.

Pilot Officer Bond, his record showed, had done a total of 277 hours' solo flying, including 23 hours on Wellingtons, 12 hours of night flying, and in addition 45 hours practising instrument flying on the Link trainer: his total number of hours being noticeably higher than might have been expected for a pupil at that stage of training. Additionally, his record showed that he had made heavy going of the course from the outset. 'Throughout training,' the court of inquiry revealed, 'the pilot has made erratic progress and at best only reached low-average standard. He appears to have been of highly strung and nervous disposition.' They added: 'Pilot's reaction to emergency open to doubt.'

But it goes without saying that Pilot Officer Bond would have been keenness itself to carry on and to eventually achieve his goal – the RAF motto specifically has *Per Ardua*, after all! And clearly his aspirations had persuaded his instructors to permit him just those few hours more. Poor fellow! Poor hapless crew! Yet the understanding of even the higher echelons showed through in the rider they added to the findings of the court: that 'no blame [is] attached to [the] instructors for persevering with [the] pilot's training.'

In 2006 the crash site on Red Hill had long since been built over with houses, few of whose occupants were aware of the tragedy that had visited the hillside. Among those who had vivid memories of the crash, however, was Mr Jack Clark, occupying a bungalow which was built only yards from where the Wellington struck a tree and was scattered up the slope. 'Nobody had a chance, of course,' he observed, indicating where the aircraft had impacted.

The crash site, taken from the houses before the arrival of the RAF party (courtesy of Mr Les Gibson of Wales)

The crash site (courtesy of Mr Les Gibson of Wales)

Three other long-term residents were also able to point out the site. 'There was a big tree just where it hit the ground,' said Mr Raymond Taylor. And Mr Derek Mills and Mr Eric Clark, the latter ensconced in an electric scooter, nodded agreement. 'Now all the houses up Dandy and Trinity Roads have been built over where the wreckage was.'

Mr Len Gibson, of Wales, adjoining Kiveton Park, an RAF corporal engaged in crash and recovery duties at the time of the accident, was sent to carry out an independent inspection of the team detailed for the task and recalled that because one of the engines had proved to be over twenty feet down, it was left in situ.

Left: The Kiveton Park triumvirate, Messrs Eric Clark, Raymond Taylor and Derek Mills. The arrow shows the descent path.

Above: Mr Jack Clark, of Red Hill, indicates the impact point

Right: The impact site near the junction of Dandy and Trinity Roads

Unidentified trainer, Lower Crossings, Chapel-en-le-Frith

SK 05141 80301 232m
1942

Pilot: Charles Bowen, probably RAF Volunteer Reserve, slightly injured

2005, Mr Ron Lomas, of Chapel-en-le-Frith

Mr Ron Lomas, of Chapel-en-le-Frith, witnessed this accident, and in June 2005 was able to point out the locations involved. 'At the time,' he explained, 'I was working at Crossings Garage at the junction of the old A6 and the Crossings Road [SK 04995 80457] – it's a tarmac company now. The pilot was a Charlie Bowen from one of the big houses that were then spaced along the road. Whether he was dropping in for a visit, or taking off again, I've never been sure. But as the plane came towards us it hit a tree some fields back from the road, and crashed. My boss, who was ill in the upstairs room, yelled for me to take a fire extinguisher to it as a precaution. But when I balanced the extinguisher on the first drystone wall I came to it toppled and fell: the foam, I remember, stayed there for months. So I ran on, over what was a marshy patch, then over another wall, and found that the plane didn't seem all that damaged. But Mr Bowen had a cut nose. And that was it, really. I just went back to work.' Mr George Barratt, of Chapel, also remembered the aftermath of the incident, having seen the aircraft pushed to the edge of a nearby lane in order to facilitate its removal by Queen Mary low-loader.

As Mr Lomas pointed out, the still-extant tree line where the Magister struck had since become the boundary between Chapel-en-le-Frith High School and the adjacent housing estate. The place where the aircraft came to rest, however, had been built over, but was some 200 yards into the estate from the former garage. By chance, this setdown took place in the same field as that chosen for a precautionary landing by Magister L6909 on 27 August, 1941.

Below: 2006, the tree line at the impact site, facing in the direction of the former Crossings Garage

Unidentified twin-engined aircraft, near Gladwin's Mark Farm

SK 31670 66800 334m
Late Second World War

At some stage during the wartime years, a forced, or precautionary, landing was made in the location given, near Gladwin's Mark Farm, Screetham. By mid-2006, however, research had failed to progress beyond the account given by Mr Ernest Dronfield, of Gladwin's Mark Farm, in 2004. As a member of the Home Guard he had stood sentry over the machine until the duty was taken over by regular troops. The machine stayed on the ground for two days or so, and was then moved away by road. Mr Dronfield remembered it as a twin-engined machine: 'A Blenheim, perhaps. Or an Oxford or Anson. The two chaps in it were all right, though.'

Another rather unsatisfactory inclusion, but incorporated for the record, again, in the hope that more details will emerge in the future.

The site of the precautionary landing by a twin-engined aircraft

Unidentified type at Flash Dam, near Screetham (west of Chesterfield)

SK 31157 64438
Date unknown, but Second World War

In mid-2006 this incident, though widely sourced, remained a mystery. Mr Selwyn Elliot, formerly of the Ordnance Survey, knew of the aircraft from his grandfather, who had always held that it was a light communications machine and that there had been something hush-hush about it, someone having been on board who should not have been. What has been verified is that the location given above was an open quarry at the time, and only later became overgrown with trees and brush. Other sources have the type as both a Magister and a Wellington. The incident is included here against new information coming to light.

The site of the Flash Dam crash: warranted by Mr Selwyn Elliot, of the Ordnance Survey

Unidentified Type, Kiveton Hall Farm, Kiveton Park

SK 49828 83210 120m
*c.*1936

In late 2005, while being interviewed regarding the crash of the Wellington at Red Hill, Kiveton Park, Mr Jack Clark, of Red Hill, tendered: 'Of course, the Wellington was not the only bit of aviation history in Kiveton Park, for in about 1936 a passenger plane put down into the field at Kiveton Hall Farm. It was one of those which carried about eight in its cabin, and it had either got lost or run short of fuel. But although

1930s setdown site at Kiveton Park

the field was big enough for it to land in, it couldn't be taken off again. Or perhaps it had been damaged. But after a day or so it was taken away by road. As for the type, I couldn't say; I probably didn't know even when I went to see it. But it wasn't a biplane.'

Unspecified type, near Coal Aston (Norton) Aerodrome, Sheffield

Exact site undetermined
Delivery Flight, No.2 Northern Repair Depot, Royal Flying Corps Coal Aston
10 August, 1917

Pilot: solo, fatally injured:
Captain H.E. Dixon, Royal Flying Corps

On 10 August, 1917, Captain H.E. Dixon was tasked to deliver a machine to its designated unit. Shortly after taking off from the No.2 Northern Repair Depot at RFC Coal Aston, however, he crashed, suffering injuries from which he died a week later.

   The type of aircraft Captain Dixon was flying is not recorded, but it is known that in 1917 the types dispatched from Coal Aston included RE8 corps-reconnaissance aircraft, and FE2b and BE12 two-seater fighters.

RAF Coal Aston crash (spurious)

20 January, 1919

In January 1919 the *Sheffield Daily Telegraph* reported the funeral of Sergeant Pilot A.W. Ellis, of Sheffield, recording that it was attended by 'two other sergeant pilots from Coal Aston'. Some enthusiast sources tender this as a Coal Aston crash. In fact, the fatal accident occurred in Dublin.

In the course of researching the Peakland series of books it became evident that folk were prone to believe that any fallen wartime aircraft had been German. However, the truth of the matter is that the only German-aircraft sites positively identified by the author in the Peakland Central area were those of the V1 Flying Bombs at Burbage, Dove Holes, and Langley, and of the Heinkel He.111 ('one-eleven') at Hazel Grove. Just the same, that more German aircraft did come down in the area seems likely, for on 16 December, 1940, for example, the *Sheffield Telegraph and Independent* reported that five German airmen had baled out at Penistone two days before, and two more near Doncaster; that on 8 May, 1941, a raider had crashed in flames, with three of the crew being taken prisoner. Similarly, on Saturday 19 April, 1941, the *Holmfirth Express* had reported that three German airmen had been caught hiding, having been shot down some nights before. It is further recorded that downed enemy crew members were taken into custody by personnel of RAF Harpur Hill, near Buxton. This section then, aims to record what was known of both the positively identified sites, and the other, somewhat nebulous reports, following research carried through into 2006.

Equally often proffered during research were German bomb craters, invariably explained as bombs intended for Manchester or Sheffield but 'jettisoned' as enemy bomber crews made good their escape. Which, if true, would be a damning indictment of German aircrews. Perhaps, then, these partisan beliefs should be weighed against post-war bombing analysis which showed that, even by 1944, by which time Allied aerial bombing techniques had been well honed, over half the RAF's bombs still fell in open country; that in late 1941, when the *Luftwaffe* was most active, only three out of five RAF bombs fell within five miles of their targets; and that as a comparable measure of enemy bombing accuracy, the very centre of the Peakland moors is hardly five miles from the nearest then-blacked-out city.

Much guidance was given regarding these possibly-supposed sites by Mr John Ownsworth, of Penistone, who was active as a walker and crash-site researcher in the 1970s and 1980s. By 2005, unfortunately, a knee condition precluded him from accompanying the author to the locations.

But in this context a late-2005 communication has bittersweet relevance. Mr Gordon Taylor, of Connecticut, but formerly of both Tinsley and Abbeydale, Sheffield, wrote, 'I was always interested in aircraft recognition, and just before the first Sheffield blitz, I was nine, and in the street at Tinsley with my mother, when a plane came over so low that the pilot waved to us. My mother said it must be a hospital plane because of the cross on it. I explained to her that it was a Heinkel He.111.' (The Taylors were to lose their Tinsley home on 15 December, 1940, when it was bombed during the Sheffield blitz.)

Heinkel He.111 No.2871 GI+LH, Springfield Farm, Hazel Grove, Stockport

SJ 94476 87665 122m
Luftwaffe Kampfgeschwader (Bomber Group) No.55, Soesterberg,
Utrecht (Netherlands, due east of Southend-on-Sea)
8 May, 1941

Crew: parachuted successfully: one, broken ankle; others, minor abrasions:
Oberleutnant [Flying officer] Adolf Knorringer, pilot
Oberfeldwebel [Flight sergeant] Karl Kohlhepp, observer/bomb aimer
Unteroffizier [Corporal] Ludwig Rathsam, wireless operator
Oberfeldwebel [Flight sergeant] Aloys Kloos, flight engineer

On the night of 7 May, 1941, Heinkel He.111 No.2871, GI+LH, based at Soesterberg, Holland, was part of a *Luftwaffe* force dispatched from occupied-Dutch airfields to bomb targets in the

West Midlands. GI+LH was subjected to anti-aircraft fire during its bombing run on Manchester's Old Trafford Industrial Estate – then largely devoted to military production – and having turned away south-east, towards Stockport, was seen to catch fire. At 0125 hours, the four-man crew having baled out and suffered only minor injuries, the burning aircraft impacted and exploded upon open farmland at Hazel Grove. Initially it was supposed, even by members of the crew, that the Heinkel had been disabled by anti-aircraft fire, but it was later established that it had been shot down by a Defiant night fighter.

With a raid in progress over Manchester, Air Raid Precaution (ARP) wardens, fire watchers and aircraft spotters in the Cheadle, Bramhall and Hazel Grove areas of Stockport were fully alert, so that not only was the aircraft's fall closely monitored, but the individual crew members were swiftly located, and – very nearly as swiftly – taken into custody.

When British or American aircraft crashed during the Second World War newspapers were permitted to carry little, if anything, of the story, for fear of 'giving comfort to the enemy', as the phrase went. This incident, however, was amply covered by the local newspaper, the *Stockport Express*.

'It was like a streak of fire crossing the sky,' an ARP warden told the paper. 'Suddenly it tilted and disappeared downwards.' After which, as the *Express* described, it touched down inverted and finally blew up as the fuel exploded.

One of the witnesses interviewed by reporters was Mr Edward Price, of Cheadle Heath. Indeed he was photographed standing by the main impact crater. 'I saw the plane light up as it was hit,' he said. 'It flew over Cheadle ... and I could see the four men bale out.' He then described how the abandoned machine curved across Bramhall towards Hazel Grove. And he described the scene at Springfield Farm. '[The plane] was scattered all over the place ... covering a couple of acres.' 'A huge area,' as another witness observed.

Then-schoolboy Mr K.J. Daniels of Hazel Grove also visited the site, and in 1978 would write, 'I cycled there the following morning and, risking the attentions of the Home Guard, I obtained some bullets and a petrol cap (which I still have).' Others among the visiting crowds described how the oil covering the ground turned the pasture a dirty yellow.

The crew members, abandoning in disciplined order, the pilot last, fell between Cheadle and Hazel Grove. One broke his ankle on landing, and required an ambulance, but none offered resistance, so that within minutes all were accounted for. Just the same, the treatment accorded one of them by a local

Mr Price is on the left, viewing the central portion of the wreckage (Photograph by courtesy of the *Stockport Express*)

dignitary led to controversy; as Mr Daniels recalled when he observed, in 1978, 'I remember the fuss it caused when Councillor Herbert Walls offered "hospitality" to the captured airman.'

The worthy councillor, it transpired, had seen one of the parachutists coming down, and set off by car to capture him, taking with him three other men, among them, as he would argue later, 'an air raid warden, and a "high Air Cadet Officer" who had a revolver'. Having located and picked up the airman – *Unteroffizier* Rathsam, the wireless operator – Councillor Walls then decided to take him home to be given first aid by Mrs Walls. The detracting *Express*, deriding the minor nature of the cuts on the German's lip, nose and the backs of his hands, observed pointedly, 'but no shrapnel wounds'. The airman was then regaled with tea and sandwiches. And a full forty minutes after the crash, having confided in the course of chatting that this was his twenty-first birthday, and having displayed personal photographs, he was delivered to the local police station and the authorities.

The *Express* criticised the councillor for departing from government instructions on the handling of downed enemy aircrew. In contrast, it praised the action of two fire watchers who apprehended another similarly injured crew member who was 'very dazed ... and was more afraid than we were'. As the newspaper spelled out, although this enemy airman landed beside their own homes, they very correctly took him to the chief warden's house nearby, to phone for the police. 'The man was lame, and had to be helped to walk,' the men reported. Other than this the airman was virtually cold-shouldered. Even when he asked to be allowed to bathe his bleeding mouth – he had landed badly, on his head, besides losing one of his flying boots in the descent – both men accompanied him into the scullery for fear he would escape. Nor was the shocked airman offered as much as a hot drink, although he was permitted to consume his iron rations, 'a small round tin of chocolate and a few caramels'. Before the police arrived a German speaker had elicited that this had been the airman's third raid over Britain, and that his wife was a nurse. However, what made all this the correct course of action, the *Express* pointed out, ignoring the 'inappropriate questioning' (a heading under which they criticised the councillor), was that the kinder treatment of the first airman, and the forty-minute delay in turning him over, meant that, with his shock diminishing and his morale burgeoning, he would have been far less likely to give information to the authorities.

Seen from 2006 the wrangle smacks rather more of local point-scoring than partisan support for government directives, or fear of evaders contacting fifth columnists, but after exchange and counter-exchange the matter, together with the crash itself, dropped from the news.

The crash, however, was to be resurrected in 1978 when the newspaper called for reminiscences of the incident: an initiative which rekindled enthusiast interest, for in 1981 an excavation was organised to recover the engines.

Farm owner Mrs Florence Wilkson, who, together with her husband, Roger, came to Springfield Farm not that long after the crash, remembered the preamble to the excavations. 'Mr Hankison', she recalled, 'was tenant farmer here when the plane came down, and people had often asked to dig in the field for remains. For although there has always been talk of the plane landing on the golf course, just over the hedge, it didn't, but came down in our field. Anyway, in 1981 it was finally agreed. Only when they came to dig they discovered that the engines had already gone.'

Mrs Wilkson's son, named Roger after his father, had known the site all his life. 'We'd frequently plough up bullets, and pieces of aircraft metal,' he recalled in 2005. 'But I can't remember seeing anything of note for something like twenty-five years.'

The general impression having been that the Heinkel had been hit by anti-aircraft fire, the German wireless operator, as Councillor Walls reported, 'kept repeating that it was "flack" [*flak*] which brought them down'. However, at least one witness who had watched the crew abandon had reported hearing 'what sounded like a burst of machine-gun fire in the distance' before the Heinkel passed overhead, 'burning and apparently on one side'. And indeed the kill was claimed by a Defiant night fighter crewed by Flight Lieutenant Christopher Deanesley, DFC, and air-gunner Flight Sergeant Jack Scott, DFM. In 1978 the former communicated with the previously mentioned Mr Daniels, confirming that he had been flying a No.256 Squadron Defiant from Squires Gate, Blackpool, and specifically referring to his 'very skilful' New Zealander air gunner, at that time still resident in Auckland.

The author was unable to locate any Combat-in-the-Air report. Therefore the reference to the air-gunner's skill intrigues. For if, as some sources have it, the Defiant's attention was drawn to the He.111 by the anti-aircraft fire, the procedure would then have been for the Defiant pilot to dive beneath the enemy bomber, chancing fire from its single belly-gun, and simply have the gunner rake it from below, paying particular attention to the engines: the *Express* records that in this case some 800 rounds were expended in a diving pursuit, with both the Heinkel's engines catching fire.

Of course, using the word 'skilful' might have been the pilot's supportive way of giving credit to his colleague, crew members – even modern all-important back-seat systems operators – being so often forgotten as the plaudits are heaped upon the pilot.

On the other hand, if the Defiant was one of those equipped with the early form of Airborne Interception radar (AI), the rear-crew member would indeed have had to exercise considerable skill in encompassing the interception, guiding his pilot into an attacking position, and then leaving his radar scope at the last moment, to man his turret and his guns. Certainly, if such were the case, any publicity would have followed the pattern already set for the kills engineered by Sergeant J.R. Philipson, and later, navigator Flight Lieutenant Cecil Rawnsley, for their pilot, then-Flight Lieutenant 'Cat's-eyes' Cunningham, when the fable of a carrot diet to improve night vision was invented to screen the existence of the still-classified airborne radar. Nor is it significant that ex-Flight Lieutenant Deanesley did not put the record straight, even as late as 1978, for many ex-servicemen of his era would have held that oaths of secrecy have no term.

The area of the main impact site, with Stockport Golf Club – formerly Torkington Golf Club – beyond the poplars

In mid-2006 no evidence of the crash was to be seen at the site, although Mrs Wilkson remembered that for many years there had been a faint depression where nettles grew in profusion. But that had long since filled up, the field being most often used for haylage (silage – fodder – made from only partly-dried grass), so that although a public footpath bordered one end of it unauthorised incursions onto the unharvested site would be a discourtesy, at the very least.

As an historical footnote, 8 May, 1941, proved costly for the *Luftwaffe* force sent out against the West Midlands, for two other KG55 machines were lost, together with Junkers Ju.88 No.6213, of KG76, the latter coming down in The Roaches, in the area covered by the southern volume of this series. Perhaps it should also be mentioned that one source has KG55's aircraft based at Melun-Villaroche, near Paris, as part of *Luftflotte* (Air Fleet) No.3, which, if correct, would have faced them with an enormously long flog.

V1 (*Vergeltungswaffe 1*) Flying Bomb, Tunnel Farm, Burbage, Buxton

SK 02998 73723 448m
Luftwaffe: launched by Heinkel He.111s of No.53 *Kampfgeschwader* (Bomber Group)
24 December, 1944

The V1 Flying Bomb had a range of only a hundred miles or so, which meant that while the south-east of England was within range of the launching ramps on the French and Dutch coasts the Midlands area was little bothered. However, as the launching sites were imperilled by the advancing Allies after the invasion of Europe, the Germans began mounting their V1 weapons below Heinkel One-Eleven bombers, and launching them towards the industrial Midlands from the North Sea.

The major attack, and the last of the war, as it transpired, came in the form of an onslaught by some fifty Heinkel-launched Flying Bombs on Christmas Eve 1944, the impact sites being officially recorded, and later listed by Peter J.C. Smith, in his book, *Flying Bombs over the Pennines*. One of the Flying Bombs launched against the Midlands fell on farmland bordering the open moorland of Burbage Edge, above Tunnel Farm, Burbage.

In 2005, residents at Wormhill, who had just been setting about their daily tasks on that 1944 morning, remembered the distinctive, intermittent note of the pilotless aircraft's pulse-jet forcing itself upon their attention as it throbbed its way, very low, overhead. Just two miles further on, at Waterswallows, the young Bob Sie was actually awoken from his sleep. 'My iron

The area of the Tunnel Farm V1 impact site, looking south

bedstead', Mr Sie recalled, 'was shaking so much I thought someone was in the room riding his motorbike. And when I looked out of the window the whole sky seemed to be lit up by the flare from the Doodlebug's back end.'

Mr Bernard Minshull, of Goslin Bar Farm, on the old Macclesfield Toll Road at Burbage, near Buxton, remembered that Mr Tom Bell, for many years Head Keeper on the Estate, who lived at Tunnel Farm, would tell of the V1 having dived directly over him to land in the field above the farm. 'Tom would say', related Mr Minshull, 'that it was lucky it came down just over the brow of the hill, for otherwise it would have caught him in the open. Even so, although he was shielded by the slope, the blast blew his hat off.'

Mr Minshull was able to indicate on the map the general area above the farm where the V1 exploded: beyond the boundary wall of the top field, 'on the downslope, but short of the Burbage Edge wall and the moor proper.' In truth, the depression at the reference given, and upon which the photograph is centred, might well be just one more of the mining depressions along the Edge. Yet the one selected had the general shape of known V1 craters on local moorland, albeit not flooded. It could well be, however, that a metal-detector search would, even at this juncture, positively determine the site.

V1 (*Vergeltungswaffe 1*) Flying Bomb, Hob Tor, Black Edge, Dove Holes (north of Buxton)

SK 06178 77911 471m
Luftwaffe: air-launched by Heinkel He.111s of KG53
24 December, 1944 (officially, but probably earlier)

Ex-WRNS plotter margaret Herbert

Officially-derived sources hold that the V1 which exploded on Black Edge, south of Chapel-en-le-Frith, was one of the fifty air-launched on Christmas Eve, 1944. Local remembrances, however, insist that it fell earlier than that, a conviction supported by former WRNS Margaret Herbert, of Derby, a plotter throughout the assault. 'V1s started coming over in June,' she asserted, 'and at least 800 were air-launched.'

Mrs Henrietta Craven, of Rye Flatt Farm, Combs, recollected being shocked into wakefulness by 'A terrible pulsing noise which abruptly cut off. Followed by an unearthly silence. Followed then, by this tremendous explosion.' An explosion still remembered by her then-infant daughter, Carol (in 2005, Mrs Bill Barratt), while Mr George Barratt, then of Marsh Green Farm, recalled, 'It shifted a great marble slab in our farm.' 'But,' insisted Mrs Craven crisply, 'it was certainly not on Christmas Eve.' And Mr and Mrs Bill and Jean Hollinrake, of Peak Forest, had an especial cause to doubt this date, 'For earlier that night we'd been out to celebrate our engagement.'

Indeed it was their son, Mr Stephen Hollingrake, who re-identified the site in February 2005. 'In the sixties,' he asserted, 'I came upon a section of jet pipe, and threw it back into the water.'

By early 2006 there was no sign of metal in or around the crater. Yet, being shallow, it was singularly different from the area's myriad disused mining pits, the peat having dissipated the effects of the ton or so of amatol high explosive which detonated on the spot back in 1944.

The V1 crater, at the north – Lady Low – end of Black Edge

V1 (*Vergeltungswaffe 1*) Flying Bomb, Clough House Farm, Langley, Macclesfield Forest

SJ 95501 72672 276m
Luftwaffe: air-launched by Heinkel He.111s of KG53
24 December, 1944

When the Luftwaffe employed Heinkel He.111 bombers to launch some fifty V1 pulse-jet Flying Bombs against Manchester on 24 December, 1944, one of the pilotless machines overflew Macclesfield Forest and exploded at Langley on land belonging to Clough House Farm.

In 2005 Mr Bill Cantrell, of Clough House Farm, remembered that he and his father, John Thomas Cantrell, were up and about when they heard a stuttering engine sound approaching from behind the hills to the east. With their attention engaged, they then saw a machine, and flames, and began to think they were watching an aircraft in trouble. Only seconds later, there was an abrupt cessation to the engine noise. There followed a few moments of anticipation, and then the concussion of a massive explosion not that far up the hill. 'It was not a case of immediately running to see what had happened,' they would explain later, 'but of waiting until the light improved somewhat. For nobody knew what might have come down.' Just the same they clearly did not delay unduly, for when they arrived at the intervening Crooked Yard Farm, the incumbent, Mrs Frances Barnes, was only just emerging from the wreckage. Her house had lost its roof, and taken much of the blast, but she was quite unhurt, although her dignity was severely ruffled.

For as she had been on her knees lighting the fire when the 'Doodlebug' exploded, chimney soot had showered all over her.

There was damage too, to one of the barns of Clough House Farm, but the house itself was untouched, as were other nearby holdings, the contours of the ground having protected them from the blast.

Mr John Cantrell, Mr Cantrell's son, and the 2005 incumbent, was able to show the crater left by the bomb, just over the fence from the public footpath, and impressive even after all this time. 'Until the seventies,' he remembered, 'there was a metal tube around the place – the jet pipe. But that has long gone.'

2005, Mr John Cantrell standing in the flying bomb crater, with Clough House Farm to the rear

German bomber, Little London Road, Sheffield (spurious)

A persistent tale, sometimes printed, has it that a German bomber, hit by anti-aircraft fire, fell in pieces in the vicinity of Stoke's paint factory in Little London Road, Sheffield. Contacted in 2005, the managing director of the company remembered his father, Mr J.B.W. Stokes, refuting this years before. He then explained that the rumour had spread after two of a stick of bombs had hit the factory, one igniting the white-spirit store, the other burning out the company's stock of labels. It seems, however, that Mr Stoke, senior, always spoke benignly of the bombing. 'It was our best advert,' he would maintain, 'as the labels that went up in the initial blast did not ignite, but drifted over and landed throughout Nether Edge!' A spurious report then, as a bomber crash-site, but possibly something for the urban walker to ponder over.

Junkers Ju.88 of KG106

3 July, 1942

This report, naming crew members Bergman and Majer, was listed by author Ron Collier, but although he specified the names and the date, he gave no location. The report is included here against future information coming to light.

Heinkel He.111, Buxton Area, 'above Burbage'

17 March, 1942

The list, said to have been compiled by author Ron Collier in preparation for a projected (but never completed) White Peaks crash-site book, also records that a Heinkel He.111 came down 'above Burbage', and that two members of its crew, *Leutnant* [pilot officer] Frishau, and *Hauptmann* [flight lieutenant] Ernst Fraden were taken into custody by personnel from No.28 Maintenance Unit of RAF Harpur Hill. The very specific date, the details of the crew, and the involvement of RAF personnel, suggest that there is substance to the report. However, extensive inquiries from Burbage to Flash – where a German headstone was erroneously held to exist – brought nothing to light.

SITES SUPPLEMENTAL TO THOSE IN *PEAKLAND AIR CRASHES: THE SOUTH*

Bell B206B Jet Ranger Mk.3 G-NORM, Brook Close Farm, Parwich

SK 18489 54104 214m
Norman Bailey, Southampton
13 May, 1984

Occupants: two pilots, operating pilot killed:
Major Simon Hugh Codman Marriot, Greenjackets
Mr Peter Bradley Banks, killed

On 13 May, 1984, Mr Robert Shields, of Parwich Hall, Parwich, had arranged to have a Bell Jet Ranger helicopter carry out an aerial survey of his holdings in the Longcliffe area. Accordingly, Major Simon Marriot, a Greenjacket (Rifle Regiment) officer, a close family friend, and a pilot with some 3,000 flying hours qualified on both rotary- and fixed-wing aircraft, had flown for the greater part of the day, including carrying out a lift for the senior members of the Shields family, Mr and Mrs Donald and Rosemary Shields. In the late afternoon, with the overall task completed, Major Marriot brought the helicopter down on a field belonging to Farmer Mr Reginald Twigge, of Brook Close Farm, above Parwich. Mr Robert Shields disembarked, and Major Marriot took this opportunity of offering the forthcoming take off to his associate, Mr Peter Banks, the holder of a Private Pilot's Licence for both rotary- and fixed-wing machines, but with under 200 hours total experience, albeit with a healthy-enough 23 hours on Jet Rangers. In the interim, Mr Shields had perceived the interest taken in the proceedings by haulage contractor Mr Frank Dale, and a youthful villager, Mr Peter Evans, and as Mr Dale recounted in March 2006, offered them both a flight.

'I'd always been interested in aircraft,' Mr Dale said, 'so when Robert made the offer – he's now High Sheriff of Derbyshire, you know? – I jumped at the chance. But then Major Marriot pointed out that they were rather too low on fuel. So Robert apologised to us, and said it would have to be some other time.'

Mr Dale, standing on the crash site, reflected for a moment. Then he indicated the singular ridge-and-furrow undulations of the field, a legacy of early-medieval tillage. 'You can see how pronounced the launts are [elsewhere, the 'balks', the tops of the ridges, and at Parwich standing eighteen inches above their furrows]. Well, the helicopter started to lift, but one of its skids had backed into a launt, so that, with its engine still going full blast, it heeled over, both rotor blades hitting the ground.' He paused again, then continued. 'One of the blades broke off and a two-foot-long piece came flying over our heads to land down at Staines Cottage, Margaret Lees' place at the foot of the hill. But the rest smashed back into the right-hand side of the machine. The Major seemed more shaken than hurt, and seemed to spill himself from the wreck. The other pilot wasn't that lucky, for, as it turned out, the blade had killed him instantly.'

He eyed the ground. 'At the time,' he said flatly, 'we didn't know that, of course. The engine was still howling away, the tail rotor was spinning wildly, and fuel was pouring out, worrying us that the whole thing would catch fire. But we had to get him out. So while Robert and I lifted up the helicopter, Reg and the Major managed to reach in, switch off the motor, and then drag him clear.'

No mean effort by the four of them! And what a risk! Yet for all that, related as being too matter-of-fact to be worthy of note. But then, as Mr Dale stolidly observed, 'What else could you do?'

Mr Frank Dale, near-passenger, at the impact site of the Jet Ranger

Bell 206B G-MONK (Photograph by courtesy of the *Derby Evening Telegraph*)

Mr Robert Shields

'I heard Major Marriot say,' Mr Dale continued then, 'that if only he had been able to get at the controls soon enough, he'd have been able to stop the helicopter tipping up, but that he had been unable to. So I suppose the other pilot was, in a sense, getting his hand in. As it was, when an official group arrived to investigate the accident and interview everyone, they used Reg Twigge's kitchen.'

The Air Investigation Board's investigators, assembling in Mr Twigge's kitchen, observed that the site raised definite problems for helicopter operations, that besides the pronounced undulations from the furrows, the sloping ground would have made it difficult for Mr Banks, as the operating pilot, to find a horizontal reference. They also noted that to bring the machine into wind had called for him to make a positive turn immediately after lift off. Just the same, they concluded that the take off should have been well within his capabilities. The accident had been occasioned, they found, by a slight backwards motion which had caused one of the helicopter's skids to touch the ground. This had imparted a rolling motion to the rotors, a consequent diminution of lateral control, and had faced the relatively inexperienced pilot with the potentially catastrophic condition known as dynamic rollover.

Major Marriot, asked about the tragedy in March 2006, and speaking from an experience level swelled to some 7,000 hours, was able to supply the detail.

'I knew Peter was competent, within his experience,' he said, 'But I still made a point of taking him over the problems the site presented.' He paused. 'It was just one of those moments in flying we all come across – you'd agree? I'd momentarily dropped my eyes to the map, when I realised that a correcting input had become necessary. But before I could assume control the aft end of a skid had hit the ground, so that immediately we had a dynamic rollover on our hands. Believe me, it was the work of an instant. But it was a lesson, bitterly learnt, that I've held in mind ever since.'

The March 2006 visit to the crash site was permitted by the courtesy of Mr Owen Bradbury, successor to Reg Twigge as incumbent of Brook Close Farm, although, as might be expected, there was no longer any evidence of the crash. That notwithstanding, the public footpath of the Limestone Way ascended the hill only one field distant from the crash site, the view across Parwich to Parwich Hill, and its singular cross-shaped wood, behind which a forced-landing Spitfire had a very much more benign upset in 1949, being well worth the climb.

Europa G-KWIP, Holly Meadow Farm, Bradley, Ashbourne

SK 23050 44822 162m
Private owner
12 March, 2000

Occupants: two, both seriously injured:
Mr Graham Singleton, pilot
Mr Isaac Porat, passenger

During the afternoon of Sunday 12 March, 2000, aircraft engineer and private pilot Mr Graham Singleton planned to fly Europa G-KWIP to Tatenhill Aerodrome, in Staffordshire. However, in the course of taking off from Mr Tom Lawton's strip at Holly Meadow Farm, Bradley, the Europa's engine lost power coincident with smoke coming from the engine bay, after which the aircraft stalled into the ground, grievously injuring both occupants.

At the time of the accident Mr Singleton had some 500 hours' flying experience,

The Europa at Holly Meadow Farm, Bradley (Photograph by courtesy of the *Derby Evening Telegraph*)

including 250 on type, and was also an approved inspector for the Private Flying Association. As such, he had played a major role in building G-KWIP which, when it crashed, had flown some 210 hours. In the course of this flying, and during construction generally, the basic design of the kit aircraft had been objectively developed with several technical modifications being incorporated; all, it should be stressed, in accordance with manufacturer's advice, and not least when it came to diluting the water–glycol mixture for the engine's cooling system.

Beyond such engine and airframe adaptations, one quite novel addition to the actual equipping of the machine was the development of a Light Aircraft Glass Cockpit (LAGC) system which would, in essence, supplement the normal instruments with a sophisticated 'plug-in' computer-based display. This was a project upon which Mr Singleton had been collaborating with the passenger, Mr Isaac Porat, a university professor and a specialist in the electronics and computer fields. Already the pre-production version had proved itself during three hours of flying, the intention on this particular occasion being to have the installation inspected and to carry out calibration.

Because both occupants were so severely injured, witness testimony by other light-aeroplane pilots who happened to be at the Holly Meadow strip played a significant part in the deliberations of the Aircraft Accident Investigation Bureau (AAIB). Mr Jonathan Tye, for example, of Holloway, spoke of how, during the time G-KWIP was being prepared for flight, its engine had been heard to stop after running normally for some minutes; that a delay had then followed, which those waiting presumed to be while adjustments were made, after which the engine had been restarted and Mr Singleton had taxied the aircraft to the northern end of the strip, passing out of sight in the process. Mr Tye then spoke of a far more protracted delay during which it was assumed that the instrumentation computer was being set up. Eventually, however, as he explained, the aircraft had come into sight and lifted off the grass strip.

His testament to the AAIB aside, Mr Tye was also able to supply the *Derby Evening Telegraph* with details of what he saw. 'As the Europa took off,' he was reported as saying, 'I saw a stream of smoke coming from the engine bay. The aircraft didn't seem able to climb any higher than about 50 feet. I saw Graham struggling at the controls, but he couldn't stop it diving into a ploughed field some hundreds of yards from the strip.'

The AAIB inspectors were to establish that when the loss of power occurred the aircraft began 'a gentle turn to the left', from which they deduced that wooded areas on its nose had ruled out the classic 'land straight ahead' dictum. However, they noted that, despite the power loss, 'the aircraft remained in the same nose up take-off attitude' as it commenced this turn. Except that, just as the turn was begun, and in what must have been a disconcerting further development for Mr Singleton, the watchers saw the smoke disappear and heard the engine pick up. By that time, however, the left wing had dropped, with the nose following in an incipient spin which took the aircraft heavily into the ground.

Mr Tye had been one of those who ran to the scene. 'When we got there,' he told reporters, 'we found them both so seriously hurt that all we could do was comfort them until the fire service arrived. Indeed one of them had to be cut free from the wreckage.'

The impact had left the broken aircraft pointing back towards the runway, its state such that the AAIB inspectors could only wonder that the crash had proved survivable.

Farmer Mr Tom Lawton, a private pilot in his own right, and owner of both Holly Meadow Farm and the landing strip he had set up, had been absent when the aircraft crashed, but in 2006 he was able to make a valid appraisal of the good fortune that had seen Mr Tye and others on the spot. 'They'd planned to take off earlier,' he said, 'but had waited to see G-KWIP get away, although the pre-takeoff delay had been so protracted that they had very nearly taken off anyway. Thanks to changing their minds, they had not done so. Therefore they were on the spot, and able to phone for the emergency services while they ran.' As Mr Singleton, also speaking in early 2006, was able to confirm. 'By good fortune,' he said, 'the helicopter just happened to be airborne when John's call was passed to them, so I'm told it was with us in an estimated fifteen minutes, and that we were both in operating theatres inside forty minutes. And just as well for both of us, for when the inspectors viewed the wreckage they deemed it to have been a non-survivable accident.' 'Moreover,' as Mr Tye pointed out, 'had they not been seen to crash down there below the dip it could have been a very long time before anyone realised that anything untoward had happened.'

Exhaustive technical tests were carried out to determine the cause of the loss of engine power, as a result of which it was decided that, probably due to an increase in engine temperature during the atypical lengthy delay on the ground, there had been an over-pressuring of the liquid-coolant system during takeoff, with some of the water-glycol mix escaping to be ingested into the engine. This would have answered for both the smoke and for the power loss, each effect lasting only until the ingested coolant was exhausted, but proving drastically untimely, with the aircraft caught in that parlous attitude, and at that pivotal phase of flight.

During the weeks the two injured men were hospitalised in Stoke, where both were in a critical state for a considerable time, Mr Tye spoke to the newspaper of his friend's background in aviation. 'Mr Singleton is known all over the world as an authority on the Europa,' his account read. 'He is a self-employed aircraft engineer, and a very competent one.'

Mr Graham Singleton
(*Derby Evening Telegraph*)

Indeed Mr Singleton was to live up to this reputation, for working in conjunction with other interested parties from Europa Aircraft, he was able to show a flaw in the technical findings arrived at by the AAIB. 'The engine had a closed-circuit cooling system,' he explained, 'with normal excess pressure being safely released through a valve. But although we had clearance to dilute the cooling mixture, and although we had stayed well below the permissible engine temperature for ground running, it transpired that a secondary-relief hole in the system's collector bottle was too small, which led to such a build-up of pressure that a hose failed and allowed coolant to escape into the engine bay.' Not only did Mr Singleton reason this out, and then demonstrate how it could happen, but he presented his findings with such competence that the AAIB, in what has to be a very rare move, actually issued an addendum to their official report.

Notwithstanding this incidentally-gratifying outcome it was an accident that cost both men dearly, particularly Mr Isaac Porat. So that Mr Singleton would later affirm, 'Isaac's lap strap attachment did fail. I think the whole structure failed in compression. I was lucky; lighter weight I guess. Isaac was not so lucky.'

Mr Singleton's return to flying was to be long delayed; indeed by early 2006 he had still not quite regained the fitness required to once more exercise his pilot's licence. Just the same his lifelong zest for aviation had clearly sustained him throughout this traumatic period. His zest, that is, and the support of his lady, Joan, who until 1971, as Miss Joan Mosely, had been Chief Air Hostess for British Midland Airways. Mr Singleton, for his part, undaunted by the vicissitudes consequent upon the crash, and although by 2006 regarding himself as being 'pretty well retired,' was – judging by a peeping inspection through his workshop window – also 'pretty well involved', for his inventiveness had not been in the least curtailed, with the result that his ongoing Composite Aircraft Development concern was clearly flourishing.

As might be expected with such a recent crash, particularly one investigated so minutely, nothing is to be seen at the site, which, besides being on private farmland, is relatively remote from all public footpaths.

Mr Tom Lawton, the owner of the landing strip, stands on the impact site of Europa G-KWIP at Holly Meadows Farm, Bradley. The arrow indicates the line of take-off from the strip prior to making the left turn.

Mignet Flying Fleas: Hartington, never registered; and Congleton, G-ADVU

SK12769 60409 97m Hartington construction site, 1935
SJ 80158 65165 93m one Congleton crash site, 1936

The Flying Flea build-it-yourself aeroplane which burst upon the aviation world in 1934 was designed by Henri Mignet in France and introduced in his book, *Le Pou-du-Ciel*. Published in translation within the year for the Air League of the British Empire as *The Flying Flea: How to build and fly it*, it was warmly recommended by Air Commodore H.A. Chamier, of the League, one of the first pilots to discover how to recover from a spin: by 'doing everything wrong', that is, by pushing the stick towards the rapidly approaching ground instead of hauling desperately away from it.

The Mignet book – packed, as it is, with gems!– was written by the Flying Flea's enthusiastic inventor after just ten hours of test-flying in Flea Number Four, a machine he began to build on 6 August, 1933, and took into the air exactly a month later. After some months of adjustment he then did the ten hours of flying 'in mid-winter, in bad weather, in rain and in storm' during which 'Ugly clouds … scudded under its wheels. Fatigue and excessive cold gave me hallucinations in flight.' Among the claims he makes are that 'The Flea flies on its own. It cannot side slip. It cannot get into a spin. It cannot stall. It can fly at angles beyond the stall. I felt I could pilot it at the end of an hour's flight! If I had had an instructor I would have been a pilot at the end of five minutes.' And he assures the would-be constructor-flyer, 'A belt, a petrol filter, and a strong undercarriage are the aviator's safeguards [which] render aviation safer than motoring. You must also have a flying helmet, a rev counter, and an airspeed indicator. With these … you have nothing to fear.' And is the Flea suitable for a woman? The French gallant has no doubt whatsoever on that score. 'The woman? ... Her light weight (don't make me say her small brain) invites her particularly to the sport of the air! A woman's strength is in her intuitions … Ladies, the Flying Flea is made for you.'

Mignet's overall enthusiasm caught on and Flea construction became a craze in which hundreds were soon abuilding in both France and Britain, any family car being ousted from the garage while the aeroplane – they cost a healthy £90 to build – took shape according to the detailed instructions in the book. True, few of the Fleas embarked upon were ever completed, and not that many were as much as pointed towards the sky, let alone taken into it. Just the same, among those that did fly there were many crashes, some of the most spectacular being captured on cine film. And there were fatalities. So that in 1936 the French government banned the Flea, the Air Ministry in London following suit in 1937, wind-tunnel tests having shown that an inherent aerodynamic instability could throw the machine into an uncontrollable, ever-steepening dive.

In 2006 few in Hartington remembered that a Flying Flea was actually constructed in the village. Fortunately local historian Mr Ronald Riley had all the details. 'Wilshaw Basset,' he explained, 'who had taken over the garage, always wanted to build a flying machine, so when the Flying Flea came along, he funded the enterprise while Walter Birch, from up the Dale, did all the woodwork. As the work neared completion onlookers would gather about the shed in the evenings, some of them having a narrow escape when the propeller flew off! But eventually the Flea got built, only then the builders couldn't get it into the air. In the end they hitched it to a Ford Eight and towed it up to the Ashbourne–Buxton Road, by the Jug and Glass, to get more breeze. Yet even that didn't do the job. After which the pair of them used to exhibit it at the local shows. They'd just drive it around, not attempt to fly it. True, at one show a bump threw it about twenty feet into the air, but that was the nearest it got to flying. And then, of course, Flying Fleas were banned as being too dangerous, and that was that. For some while their Flea was stored in the Village Hall and used by the Air Training Corps, then, I rather fancy it was sold off.'

Local historian Mr Ronald Riley indicates where the shed stood in which the Hartington Flying Flea was built

1935, the Hartington-built Flying Flea, courtesy of Mr Alan Shipley

Mr Alan Shipley, of Raikes Farm, Hulme End, who served a full twenty-two years in the RAF in the time-honoured, but now long-since defunct, trade of Blacksmith, was able to supply a photograph of the Hartington Flying Flea.

A markedly more successful Flea was that built on the Peakland's western border by members of the Burns family of Congleton. Although their Flea, registered as G-ADVU, was constructed in their Park Street Garage premises by four members of the family – Mr Bob Burns, senior, his two younger sons, Alan and Robbie, and his eldest son, Harold – it fell to Harold to play the aviator when the time came. He made his first flight on 13 January, 1936, ascending from the Somerford Park Estate, and learning to fly as all of them had learnt how to build the machine, namely, with no other assistance than Mignet's book. Despite this, this first flight was successful. Possibly getting rather too ambitious on his second essay, however, the young pilot was forced to turn to avoid a tree, and promptly crashed, sustaining a black eye. Notwithstanding which, a month later the Flea got airborne again, when Harold made two successful flights. During a third, however, he ran out of fuel, and was forced to set down to the rear of Davenport Methodist Chapel where he actually struck a tree. The editor of the *Congleton Chronicle*, one of those who chased after the Flea on this occasion, later published a doggerel verse:

'Flea, fly, flow, flop,
We saw it start, and we heard it stop,
Be he alive, or be he dead
 – he's crashed his 'plane, and bumped his yed'.

In his column the editor also urged Harold to give up, especially as he had now had 'two useful little crashes', but undaunted, the intrepid Harold continued to take the Flea aloft. However, two months later still, at Meir Aerodrome, after several successful flights, Harold crashed from an estimated 70 feet and this time was lucky to escape with a few stitches in a badly gashed knee.

In early 2006, Mr Ian Burns, of Wincle, Harold's son, was able to catalogue what happened then. 'Of course,' he explained, 'Dad'd had several other mishaps. But he'd also done a fair amount of flying. So that sometimes he flew from local parks, and on other occasions from the flat ground below Bosley Cloud. But eventually his mother, Patience, my grandmother, put her foot down and said enough was enough where the Flea was concerned, and that if Dad wanted to continue to fly he should get lessons on a proper machine. Which is what he did. Besides which, shortly afterwards the government imposed its ban on all unmodified Fleas.' He paused. 'And then, of course, war broke out. Dad had his pilot's licence by that time but for some reason a medical condition – nothing associated with his Flea crashes – meant that he was unable to join the RAF. Both Alan and Robbie were accepted, however, and flew throughout the war. Just the same Dad undoubtedly had the better time of it, for he spent the wartime years serving with the Air Transport Auxiliary, flying anything and everything, indeed logging time on 82 different types. Nor did his interest wane post-war, for as well as serving as both borough councillor and Mayor of Congleton, he flew on for some years with the local flying club.'

The crash site behind the Methodist Chapel (SJ 80185 65165 93m)

1936, Mr Harold Burns at the controls of Flying Flea G-ADVU

Parts of the Flea, Mr Burns confirmed, lingered on for years: the instrument board, two of the propellers constructed for the machine, and the wheels, which the family pressed into service on a wheelbarrow. But as a flying machine the Congleton Flea had had its day. Only in 1993 it saw a resurrection of a sort, when a team sponsored by Burns' Garages, and led by a Mr Ken Fern, built, and then exhibited in the family showrooms, a reconstruction of this most celebrated of Fleas.

De Havilland DH60G Gipsy Moth, Mountain Ash Farm, north of Parwich

SK 18923 57389 323m touchdown
SK 18743 57385 326m terminal site
Privately owned
*c.*1928

Pilot: successfully forced-landed:
Mr Norman Styche, not seriously hurt

In researching this incident in 2005, the writer was initially led astray. The RAF crash report on Spitfire PK488 had it crashing 'One and a half miles north of Parwich'. So that when Mrs Annie Walker, an endearing ninety when interviewed, was questioned about an aircraft crash nearby, she responded at once. Except that, as it transpired, Mrs Walker was talking about the Moth that came down in about 1928, and not the Spitfire of 1949, about which she knew nothing. The mistake only came to light after publication of *Peakland Air Crashes: The South*, when Mr Charles Fearn, then of Market Rasen, took the trouble to advise that the Spitfire had crashed very much closer to Parwich.

So it is that Mrs Walker's recollections, accurate as they were, are now to be applied to the Moth. 'When it happened,' she had said, 'I was at Cobblersnook Farm, where I was brought up, working near our field barn with my brother. The plane began to circle overhead. Then suddenly it came down in one of Kirkham's fields – they had Mountain Ash Farm at the time. It seemed to land all right. But later, when I went to have a look, I could see it was broken. So a day or so later it was taken away.'

Mrs Annie Walker, witness

Mr Asa Kirkham, in 2006, of Ashbourne, a lifelong quarry owner-cum-farmer, whom Mr Fearn had recommended to the writer as a source for the Gipsy Moth, proved well able to fill in the pieces.

'I was born in 1920,' he said, 'and brought up at Mountain Ash Farm, and I fancy the Moth came down in the August of 1928. I say the August, because Dad had already cut the Long Meadow and stacked the hay by the barn just over the wall at the far end: the stack would feed the fourteen calves we'd keep in the barn. The pilot was a Mr Norman Styche – ask me yesterday's date, and I'm lost, but the pilot's name has always stuck in my mind. He was a civilian pilot, and he was flying from Lincoln to Liverpool when he got lost. He decided to land, find out where he was, then get on his way again, so having circled the area a time or two, he chose Long Meadow. Mind you, it looked a lot different then.' He indicated the ruinous state of the walls, indicative of how farming practice has changed. 'Back then, if there was as much as a stone off, Dad would want to know why. And although the walls weren't that high, they kept cattle contained. Anyway, the pilot was wary of catching his wheels in the near wall as he came down, but this took him further than he'd planned into the field. He'd no brakes, only a skid on the rudder, and so when the slope of the field began to take him to his left, he had no way of straightening out.

'Dad and my brother were working in a nearby field, and had been watching him come down. But the moment the slope took him, Dad was alarmed. "The bugger's going to crash into my hay," he shouted, and both of them began to run. But even as they got under way they saw that the pilot, too, had realised that he was likely to end up crashing into the stone barn. So next thing, they saw him leaping from the cockpit and letting the plane carry on. In fact, it ran out of space just short of the barn, hit the drystone wall, and tipped over it, the two-bladed wooden propeller breaking off as it and the engine hit the ground on the far side, the tail rearing straight up into the air. At first Dad was more concerned over the petrol catching fire and destroying his hay, but when nothing happened, he turned his attention to the pilot. To find that, although he was basically all right, he'd banged his head on the tail as it passed him, leaving him a bit dazed and headachey.'

Mr Kirkham smiled. Then continued. 'Anyway, they took him back to Mountain Ash, and mother took care of his head. And a little later Dad drove him into Parwich – he'd got a 1920 bull-nosed Morris – where there was a phone, so that he could call his people. When that was done, Dad brought him back again and he stayed with us until about ten. But he needed accommodation for the night, and we were too cramped to put him up, so Dad took him to Mr Etches, at Royston Grange Farm. Next day, though, he was back again.' Mr Kirkham paused, then continued. 'I say he was civilian, because when he was brought into the house, and took off his helmet and his overalls, he was dressed in ordinary clothes. But it was an Air Ministry vehicle with three men that arrived next day, a driver and two mechanics. They were able to bump their way over to the plane, and having taken off the wings, they loaded the body, and tucked the wings down the side. And that was it, really.' He paused again, then smiled. 'A little later we got a letter, from his mother, I believe it was, thanking us for the help we'd given. Indeed my older brother might still have it. Another of the family had laid claim to one of the rod-like struts that held the wings up above the actual cockpit, so Dad fitted it with a brass knob and a ferrule and it was used for years afterwards as a walking stick – again, it's probably still around.'

In the course of this 2006 visit there was nothing to show that an aircraft incident had ever occurred, although Mr Kirkham remembered that back in 1928, the Moth had left indented wheel tracks where it had first touched. The 2006 incumbent of Mountain Ash Farm, Mr Jim Rushton – not to forget his three-year old grandson, Ashley – proved extremely helpful, and spoke of welcoming walkers using the footpath which, even in 1928, intersected the meadow.

Wies White, Mr Asa Kirkham, witness, with Ashley, Frank and Jim Rushton at

Mr Asa Kirkham indicates the terminal site of the Moth, with Mr Jim Rushton of Mountain Ash Farm

Certainly, and quite unlike Pater Kirkham of 1928, he does not deliberately tether a bad-tempered bull near one of the stiles.

Regarding the status of the pilot, Mr Norman Styche, it is not unlikely that he had associations with the Service, at the very least, particularly as the recovery team were clearly RAF. Neither is his wearing civilian clothes under his flying overalls particularly meaningful, for it was commonplace even into the 1980s to dress in civvies when on a weekend jaunt, space in any trainer's cockpit being limited. And Moths are known to have been in use by the RAF from 1927 onwards.

From a research point of view, it has to be noted that a not too diligent trawl through the Ashbourne newspaper from 1926 through to 1932, and through the Derby one from June to September 1928, found no reference to this interesting, if relatively minor, incident.

North American Harvard KF570, Postern Hill Farm, Hazelwood

SK 32480 46372 153m touch down
SK 32151 46180 132m terminal site
No.6 Service Flying Training School, RAF Ternhill (near Market Drayton, Shropshire), No.23 Group, Flying Training Command
16 January, 1947

Occupants: two, both injured:
Flight Sergeant George King
Flight Sergeant Robert William Baird

At 1520 hours on the afternoon of 16 January, 1947, Sergeant Pilot George King, accompanied by Sergeant Robert William Baird, got airborne from RAF Ternhill to carry out an envisaged half-an-hour's air test on Harvard trainer KF570. The January weather, however – it was the year of the big snow!– was such that he became lost, and after failing to establish radio contact with any ground station, was forced to begin a visual search for the first available airfield. Sergeant George's search proved fruitless, and at 1845 hours, having been airborne for nearly three and a half hours, with the winter's darkness intensifying, and the fuel gauge reading empty, he decided upon setting the aircraft down before the engine cut altogether. Chancing to overfly the lights of a hamlet he found himself skimming a flat pasture near a farmhouse, and realising that few more such opportunities might offer themselves, he hastily closed the throttle. What he had not realised was that beyond the pasture the ground, although flat enough in appearance, fell away sharply, the subsequent need to drop the nose more than expected, allied to the unfamiliar attitude required to settle to the ground without his undercarriage, causing him to strike hard. The aircraft then bellied on, to clip one tree then bury itself in a hedge just short of a second, having sustained severe damage to the wings and propeller.

Extracting themselves, the two shocked occupants took stock, and found that, while suffering from bruises and superficial cuts, they were not seriously hurt. They realised too that the farmhouse they had overflown, although now hidden by the slope above, was only a matter of three hundred yards away. And as they began to make their way uphill through the gloom, and met nobody hurrying down, they realised too that the crash must have gone unnoticed.

Indeed this had been the case. Having been busy in the milking shed, the men of Postern

Harvard KF570 (courtesy of the *Derby Evening Telegraph*)

Mr Herbert Slater, Duffield

Mr Arthur Chadderton,
Cowers Lane

Hill Farm, farmer Frederick Job Spendlove and his hands, had heard nothing. Mrs Elizabeth Spendlove, however, although engaged in baking in her kitchen had at least heard an aeroplane go over, but after the sound died away had thought no further of it. Therefore it came as a total surprise, when she answered a knock at the door, to find herself confronted by two shaken and bloodstained airmen. Just the same, rising to the occasion, she at once ushered them in, put on the kettle, and got out her first-aid things. And only when, with their cuts bandaged, and as they sat there at her kitchen table cradling cups of tea and confronted by a hastily assembled spread of farm food, did she turn to the task of alerting the police and the RAF at Burnaston airfield, near Derby.

A guard was mounted on the Harvard, and the two pilots were taken to Burnaston for the night, returning to Ternhill, just over forty miles from the crash site, the next day.

The court of inquiry submitted that Sergeant George, having become lost, should have made a decision earlier and carried out a forced landing before darkness overtook him, or alternatively, that he should have ordered an abandonment, and baled out. Sergeant George's commanding officer interviewed him with a view to entering an endorsement in his flying log book, but beyond that no further disciplinary action was taken. The court had also taken note, however, that Sergeant George had been unable to make contact with ground wireless stations, so as a consequence, as the RAF crash report summary records, up-to-date VHF (very high frequency) radios were subsequently fitted to the Harvards.

Mr Herbert Slater, then of nearby Overlane Farm, but in 2005 of Duffield, recalled the crash. 'It was some time before we found out what had happened, although the plane had finished up not that far from the farm. It was only a light aeroplane, of course, and it had come down in what was then a hayfield. So that, by the time we got to it, it was already well guarded, and airmen kept us away. After which it stayed there for nearly three weeks. How they actually got it away, I never saw, but there was easy enough access to the road.'

Mr Arthur Chadderton, in 2005 of Cowers Lane, but in 1947 working at Postern Lodge Farm, below the crash site, remembered seeing the aircraft on the hill and was able to point out the site. 'We saw it lying there next day,' he said, 'but knew the crew had been taken away, so didn't bother to go up.'

Mr Roy Robinson, in 2005, of Allestree, agreed that the guards had been swiftly posted. 'But not swiftly enough,' he ventured, 'for the two Bridges brothers, David and John, who then lived at Brook Farm, got there quickly enough for John to get one of the magnetos off the engine.'

As might be expected, in early 2006 there was no trace of the incident, and both the farm and the pasture overflown before touchdown had been extensively remodelled. On the other hand the site is relatively remote from public footpaths, and on strictly private ground.

The touchdown area of Harvard KF570   The terminal site

Miles Magister Mk.1 L8227, Long Lane, Lees, near Derby

SK 26711 38036 98m
No.16 Elementary Flying Training School, RAF Burnaston
(Derby), No.51 Group, Flying Training Command
21 June, 1942

Occupants: instructor and pupil:
Pilot Officer Godfrey Harry Grantham, RAF Volunteer Reserve, killed
Corporal J.P. Ward, army, pupil pilot, injured

At just after 1600 hours on 21 June, 1942, flying instructor Pilot Officer Godfrey Grantham
got airborne with his pupil, Corporal J.P. Ward, a soldier, on a
navigational cross-country. It would seem that the navigational
side of the exercise had proved satisfactory, for having been
airborne for fifty-five minutes, and as they returned to the
vicinity of RAF Burnaston, Pilot Officer Grantham initiated a
forced-landing drill, closing the throttle and leaving Corporal
Ward to select a landing site and carry out an approach. The
setting-down area Corporal Ward chose was a very adequate
pasture just to the north of Long Lane, at Lees, but in the course
of positioning, he carried out a gliding turn, and at only an
estimated two hundred feet from the ground, stalled the aircraft.

The impact point of Magister
L8277, Long Lane, Lees

To be stalled that close to the ground was a dire predicament.
The wings needed to be unstalled, but any lowering of the nose to do so would have further
steepened the dive. Similarly, to have increased power before the nose was up would have
exacerbated the situation even more; further, to attempt to lift the nose while the aircraft was
still stalled would have simply deepened the stall. In the event, whatever action was taken was
ineffective, and the nose drop following the stall-judder took the aircraft heavily into the ground,
killing Pilot Officer Grantham and injuring Corporal Ward.

Two witnesses held that the engine had been spluttering before the crash, but in the face of
Corporal Ward's evidence the investigators ruled out an engine failure as the basic cause. The
unit's commanding officer did suggest that a contributory cause might have been the fouling of
the plugs during the idling approach, but went along with the court of inquiry's finding that the
primary cause was an error of judgement by the instructor in not assuming control before the
situation became critical. It was noted that Pilot Officer Grantham, the instructor, had only
some three hundred flying hours.

In late 2005 a witness from Lees, who asked that his name be withheld, was able to locate the
crash site, and to describe what he saw. 'I was seventeen and a half,' he remembered, 'and riding

west down Long Lane on my motorbike when I saw this Maggie in the hedge. By the time I got there a man who lived locally, a former fire chief, had already got the pilot's body from the cockpit and was laying it out.'

A daunting encounter for anyone, but the witness was clearly of stern mettle, for little more than a year later he had begun the first of the thirty operational sorties he was to fly as a Lancaster navigator: a full tour, and during the most testing time of all for Bomber Command. His name is reluctantly withheld here, but at the same time borne in mind with both deference and respect.

Miles Magister Mk.1 L8258, Cheddleton, Staffordshire

4 September, 1940

It is known that this aircraft suffered a complete engine failure, and that in the course of the resulting forced landing it hit overhead cables and crashed. This seems to accord with the reference in *A Moorland Dedication* (Marshall S. Boylan, 1992, page 59) to a Magister leaking fuel over crops in Brund Lane, with the pilot emerging unhurt, but nothing more came to light during research in early 2006 either in Brund Lane or in widespread canvassing of the Cheddleton area.

Miles Magister Mk.1 L5950, Blakelow Farm, Draycott in the Moors, Staffordshire

SJ 98381 36400 197m
No.16 Elementary Flying Training School, RAF Burnaston (Derby), No.51 Group, Flying Training Command
2 July, 1941

Pilot: pupil pilot solo:
Leading Aircraftman Wells, survived

On 2 July, 1941, pupil pilot Leading Aircraftman Wells, with a total of just thirteen hours' solo experience, was sent off on a further solo training sortie. In the course of this, however, and seemingly without warning, a violent thunderstorm developed and swept across the airfield at Burnaston. Leading Aircraftman Wells judiciously cleared from the area, but got lost, and with his fuel running low, attempted a precautionary landing in open country near Draycott in the Moors, Staffordshire. In doing so, however, he struck a tree and the aircraft crashed, although without catching fire. The accident was attributed to the weather, with no blame attaching to the pupil pilot. Apart from that, however, little more is known, besides which the microfilmed copy of the accident report available in 2005 proved too poor to fully decipher.

In late 2005 farmer Mr John Brassington and his brother, Victor Brassington, whose family took over Blakelow Farm shortly after the crash, were able to point out the field concerned, each identifying it as 'the field with the bump'.

The 'field with the bump' in which Magister L5950 crashed

Miles Magister Mk.1 N3813, Roston, near Rocester

SK 14141 40577 161m
No.16 Elementary Flying Training School, RAF Burnaston (Derby), No.51 Group, Flying Training Command
18 August, 1940

Pilot: badly injured:
Flying Officer R. Hope

Flying Officer Hope, most probably newly posted to the staff on the Elementary Flying School, and engaged in something like a refresher course, had amassed over three hundred flying hours, but only five on the Magister. He was carrying out a detail of aerobatics and forced-landing approaches when he realised that he was short of fuel. He selected a substantial enough field in which to make an actual forced landing but stalled in the process, crashing and sustaining severe injuries.

The crash site of Magister N3813, Roston

The inquiry found that Flying Officer Hope had taken off without sufficient fuel to carry out the sortie, and had then allowed the aircraft to stall while carrying out a forced landing. Before flight, of course, Flying Officer Hope would have signed the Form 700, the RAF's 'technical log', thereby accepting full responsibility for the aircraft, and certainly for ensuring that it carried sufficient fuel for the task in hand. The only blame the court found, however, was that his instructor, named as Sergeant Greenup, had not entered into the Flight Authorisation Book the specific details of the exercises to be carried out. Heinous omission! And duly upholding the court's finding the Air Officer Commanding the Group directed that disciplinary action was to be taken against Sergeant Greenup.

In early 2006 Mr Alan Wood and his wife, Viola, of Bank End Farm, Roston, were able to indicate the field in which the crash had occurred. 'Every August,' Mrs Wood remembered, 'my three cousins, two lads from Manchester and one from High Wycombe, used to come here on a month's visit. And when they heard that an aeroplane had come down on the far side of the Dumble they all ran off to see it. Each brought back some souvenir, one of them a compass, I remember. But Dad made them take everything back. Only when they came up out of the Dumble again, guards had been posted.'

The Dumble, it transpired, is a vegetation-choked gully separating Roston from the fields where the aircraft crashed. Even at the time the adjoining fields above the gully had been sufficiently large to accommodate a light aircraft, but by 2006 the wall pattern had been changed to combine them into one large field known as the Ten Acre. As might be expected on working farmland, no trace of the crash was to be seen.

Of possible interest to the walker, the most direct access to the field, having branched off a public foot-path, required the negotiation of the deepest field ditch one is likely to encounter. Indeed the 2006 owner of the field, farmer Mr Jeff Chadfield, of Grange Farm, Darley Moor, told of a bullock that had gone missing, only to be discovered a full twenty-four hours later, trapped, and barely visible in the depths of one of these naturally formed, water-excavated ditches.

Miles Magister Mk.1 N3876, Culland Hall, Hollington

SK 24516 39062 102m (area of)
No.30 Elementary Flying Training School, RAF Burnaston (Derby), No.51 Group, Flying Training Command
21 September, 1939

It is believed that this aircraft was carrying out manoeuvres at an illegally low level, for it struck the trees when attempting to recover from a dive and crashed. At present no further details have become available, and exhaustive canvassing of the area in late 2005 found nobody who had any recollections of the incident. Once more, the crash is recorded here for posterity.

Reputed to be the area of the crash site at Culland Hall

Miles Magister L8277, Hollybush Farm, Moorwood Moor, South Wingfield, Alfreton

SK 35845 56754 166m area of successful landing run
SK 35915 56689 157m area of impact into hedge on attempting take-off
No.16 Elementary Flying Training School, RAF Burnaston (Derby), No.51 Group, Flying Training Command
Mid-1942

Occupants, two, both uninjured:
Sergeant Pilot Louis and presently unidentified passenger

Sergeant Pilot Louis, a staff pilot at RAF Burnaston, became lost during flight and decided to set the machine down in a field to check his position. He chose wisely, a long, ten-acre field belonging to Hollybush Farm on Moorwood Moor, at South Wingfield, and duly made a successful landing. Having ascertained his position, he then prepared to get airborne once again. However, he failed to take into account the unprepared surface of the flat field, was unable to gain flying speed, and crashed through the boundary hedge, his aircraft keeling over onto one wing in the process. Although both Sergeant Pilot Louis and his passenger clambered out unscathed, the aircraft was badly damaged and had to be transported off by road.

Speaking in late 2005 Mrs Jean Ludlam, of Ludlam's Farm, South Wingfield, the sixth generation of that family to farm the holding, had good cause to remember the scare the failed take-off had given her. 'I was newly married,' she recalled, 'and working part-time in Woolworths at Alfreton. Someone came into the store and told me that a German plane had come down near our place. Of course, knowing I'd have to walk across the fields going home, I was very worried that I might run into some Germans. So when a friend met me off the bus I asked about them. She was surprised that I'd already heard, but assured me that it hadn't been a German bomber but a British training plane, and that the two men on board had been all right. As we walked towards the farm I could see a wing of the plane stuck up in the air in Hollybush Farm's Ten-Acre Field, but I never bothered going over to it, just got on with my jobs. Although when I got indoors I found my mother-in-law, Pamela Jane, had got seven or eight soldiers crowded into the room and was feeding them. They guarded the aircraft, probably overnight, after which the RAF moved it to the road and took it off in long trailers.'

Mrs Ludlam was able to confirm that the field pattern had changed little over the intervening years. 'In front of Thanet House on Pit Lane', she explained, 'is Hollybush Farm's Eight-Acre Field, and beyond that, Ten-Acre Field, which is where the plane came down.' In mid-2006, understandably, there was no indication that farmwork had ever been interrupted.

Mrs Jean Ludlam, Hollybush Farm, witness

It might be noted that the RAF crash report locates this incident, patently recorded-as-heard by the field investigators, at 'Maud' instead of 'Moorwood', reconciling the two requiring no small measure of lateral thinking in research.

Finally, there is a caveat regarding the actual aircraft matched to this incident, for although an enthusiast list holds that the aircraft involved was Magister L8277, *Air Britain* records, nearly always dependable, show that L8277 never had an accident, that it served at North Weald and was subsequently sent to the Middle East, latterly to Amman.

From the area of impact along Ten-Acre Field, with Colliery Farm to the left

Miles Master Mk.1 M7836, North Wingfield (near Chesterfield)

SK 42256 65307 147m
No.7 Operational Training Unit, RAF Hawarden (Chester), No.10 Group, RAF Fighter Command
12 October, 1940

Pilot: student pilot, killed:
Sergeant Malcolm Parker

Sergeant Malcolm Palmer

The function of No.7 Operational Training Unit (OTU) was to convert newly qualified pilots into operational fighter pilots using both Spitfires and Miles Masters. On 12 October, 1940, shortly before the unit became No.57 OTU, Sergeant Malcolm Parker, a student with just under two hundred hours' experience, was briefed for an hour of local flying and sent off in Master M7836. Nothing more was heard from Sergeant Parker until the news came in that he had crashed fatally at Highfields, North Wingfield, over sixty miles east of Hawarden.

It was quickly ascertained that Sergeant Parker had lived at North Wingfield, and that he had deliberately flown there in order to carry out some low-level stunting.

One of the many witnesses of the crash on that Saturday afternoon was miner Mr George Searston, who described what he saw to the *Derbyshire Times*. 'It was at about four', he said, 'when I was drawn outside by this very low-flying aeroplane. It flew backwards and forwards several times and was doing aerobatics. It kept coming very low and then zooming upwards. It banked very steeply on one occasion, and once or twice it started a loop which developed into a roll. [A layman witness showing a nice eye for a 'roll off the top'.] The last time, after about twenty minutes, it did not come out properly but went straight into a dive, narrowly missing the row of houses and crashing within yards of the railway line with a terrific impact, bursting into flames which were so intense that nobody could get near.'

Mrs Betty Houghton, of Highfields, interviewed in early 2006, had some personal knowledge of aviation – not particularly broad, but noteworthy nevertheless – for as a girl she and two other members of her family had crammed into the back cockpit of Alan Cobham's machine for a joyride during his circus's visit to Ollerton; 'No straps,' she smiled, 'just an open top with the three of us squashed down on the floor.' She was well aware of the Master crash, however, responding immediately, 'Yes, the pilot was Malcolm Parker – and at the time so many people rushed to the crash that they broke down the fencing between the house here and the railway. In fact, it was my Pop, Arthur Pollett, who brought Malcolm's body to the morgue. Pops worked at the colliery as chauffeur and mechanic, as well as ambulance driver and medical attendant, so he was hardened to grim sights. Just the same, after that accident he was physically sick for four days.'

And it had clearly been a grim experience, although Hawarden's medical officer, Flying Officer John Watts, who had travelled to the inquest by air and whose aircraft had landed in a field nearby, was able to assure the relatives that Sergeant Parker would have been killed instantly.

Regarding the final moments of the crash, both the coroner and the RAF investigators also heard the testimony of a Police Constable Cole, who saw the machine approach from the west and begin its cavortings. From this, together with what miner Mr Searston had told them, they were able to ascertain that Sergeant Parker had eventually pulled up into a left-hand climbing turn but had stalled at an estimated 800 feet, after which the aircraft had spun into the ground and burnt.

Mrs Betty Hutton, Highfields

The finding was clear; the Operational Training Unit's commanding officer recording 'Pilot disobeyed orders – only one hour of local flying had been authorised'. A clear-cut case. Low flying to impress, and thereby destroying an aircraft, and losing the Service a student in the final phase of becoming a useful operational pilot. As the Chief Instructor spelled out, 'disobedience of orders, low flying, and stunting over his house'.

Tragically enough, the whole of Sergeant Parker's display had been watched by his father, William, who, knowing that his son had progressed to flying Spitfires, had failed to connect him with the trainer. Mr Parker was to tell the coroner that his son had been at home on leave less than a week before.

And yet Sergeant Parker's mother was to be struck even harder by the tragedy, illumining with poignancy the appalling waste involved in all such incidents, for the RAF accident report particularly notes that the sergeant had been stunting *at his mother's request.* Clearly Mrs Parker had said as much to the investigators. But what a dreadful burden for her to carry ever afterwards!

Again in 2006, Mrs Janet Hague, of Holmeswood, was able to speak of just how grievously the mother must have suffered for her proud incitement. 'Edith idolised Malcolm,' she said. 'She was a great Chapel member, and after all, he was her only son.' The stricken mother's regard for her son is amply illustrated by the memorial she erected for him in nearby Heath churchyard, not settling for the standard Commonwealth War Graves stone but for a substantial structure of bluish hue, recording that he was 'Accidentally killed on active service.'

The crash site, a potato field bordered by the colliery railway at the time, remained farmland in 2006, although the rails had long since given place to the 'Five Pits Way', a stile at the first sharp bend from the road offering access into the field. As for positively proving the precise impact spot, it is held that the field itself was scraped over as part of the landscaping when reclamation of the colliery site was carried out. Even if that were not the case, determining the exact site would call for a diligent metal-detector search. Just the same, local feeling is that the reference given here is very close to the impact area.

To find this wartime accident reported in the *Derbyshire Times* was unexpected, but gratifying. And it is interesting to note the care that was taken to blur the facts. Thus the Master is merely 'a British trainer', Sergeant Parker is stationed 'in the North-West of England', the crash occurred 'in an East Midlands mining village', and his parents, Mr and Mrs William Parker, lived 'in the village near which the plane crashed'; finally, it is explained that 'owing to war restrictions the story of the aeroplane crash was held over from last week.'

Left: Impact area of Master M7836, Highfields

Miles Master Mk.1 T8685, Denby Common (west of Heanor)

SK 40800 47150 107m touchdown
SK 40902 47226 138m terminal site
No.5 Service Flying Training School, RAF Ternhill (Market Drayton), No.21 Group, Flying
Training Command
25 September, 1941

Pilot: pupil pilot, solo:
Leading Aircraftman G.B. Garland, injured

On 25 September, 1941, pupil pilot Leading Aircraftman G.B. Garland, with just under one
hundred hours' flying time, was sent on a solo sortie from RAF Ternhill to practise spins, steep
turns and forced landings. During the exercise he became lost in poor weather and had to make
a forced landing in earnest. Unfortunately the field he selected, on the edge of Denby Common,
the outlier of Denby, and some 46 miles from his Shropshire base, was not only planted with
anti-invasion stakes – vertical poles intended to deter landings by German troop-transporting
aircraft – but rose steeply. The upward slope, imperceptible from the air, proved Leading
Aircraftman Garland's undoing, for he suddenly found himself easing the nose up to avoid too
heavy a touchdown. This, however, took him skimming beyond the area he had earmarked for
touchdown, with the space ahead rapidly running out. Finally, he managed to touch his wheels,
only to become aware of the obstructing poles looming before him. At once he applied full

From the initial impact
point, looking upslope
towards the cottages

Mrs Mavis Mills, Denby,
witness

In 2005 Mrs Mavis March
indicates where the nose
of the Master impacted

power, but with his speed purposely brought back to a minimum,
and with not all that much power available at best, he was unable to
climb swiftly enough, and struck one of the poles. The impact, it is
thought, took off one of the aircraft's wings, but certainly it left the
machine incapable of further flight, and having brushed through a
hedge, the nose of the Master drove into the yard of the first of a pair
of cottages, was stopped short by the dividing wall, and burst into
flames. The RAF accident report recorded that Leading Aircraftman
Garland was injured, notwithstanding which he was able to make his
own way clear of the machine.

Upon investigating the crash site the RAF court of inquiry deemed
the field chosen to be quite unsuitable for the purpose, and further
ruled that Leading Aircraftman Garland, having become lost, had
failed to make a 'reasoned and systematic attempt to establish his
position'. However, as no recommendation for disciplinary action is
recorded it would seem that the incident was put down to a natural
hazard attendant upon flying training, and that Leading Aircraftman
Garland continued with his course. Certainly he is not among those
aircrew surnamed Garland who failed to survive their operational
tours.

In late 2005 Mrs Mavis Mills (née Hartshorne), of Hill Farm, Denby, remembered the crash well. 'The aeroplane came down on Lands Hill,' she explained. 'It's one of the few areas in that area that still looks as it did then, bearing in mind the opencast mining operations and the subsequent reclamation which has smoothed off so much of the land. But then it had telegraph poles planted all over it. The plane hit one of the poles, and then crashed into the end of the Bardells' cottage, where my schoolfriend, Marie, lived with her mother and father.' She paused. 'I remember the flames rising up above their roof.'

Still living in the neighbouring, non-involved cottage at Denby Common, Mrs Mavis March (née Orme) also remembered the crash. 'My parents had just got the keys to move in here – it was The Hollies then, now it's No. 7 – and Mrs Bardell from next door – Elizabeth Bardell – was in what was to be our upstairs bedroom when the plane suddenly arrived in her yard. We always said that if she'd been in her own kitchen, getting the tea ready, as she might well have been, she wouldn't have survived. Nor would she, for the nose of the plane was right up against her kitchen door so that the flames burnt through the door and kitchen window and up the back wall to the bedroom windows. Where the wing was – probably back in the field – and what happened to the pilot, we never did find out.'

The wreckage was swiftly removed, and the rear of the house repaired. Certainly in 2006 there was no trace of the incident. The house remained, of course, a strictly private residence, but a good viewpoint was obtainable from the public footpath which still ran across the field in question, passing roughly midway between the touchdown point, and the house. From the footpath the near-impossible task Leading Aircraftman Garland had set his relatively low-powered aircraft can readily be appreciated: to be throttled up from touchdown speed and still outclimb both slope and obstruction poles.

Airspeed Oxford N4597, Elm Farm, Little Eaton, Derbyshire

SK 36007 41364 54m
No.21 (Pilots) Advanced Flying Unit, RAF Seighford (north-west of Stafford), No.21 Group, Flying Training Command
13 July, 1945

Pilot: solo, killed:
Flight Sergeant Lancelot Percy Williamson

On the afternoon of 13 July, 1945, Flight Sergeant Lancelot Williamson, an instructor on No.21 Advanced Flying Unit at RAF Seighford, was authorised for a staff-continuation-training flight in Oxford N4597. His RAF record shows him to have flown a substantial 142 hours solo on the Oxford, with 217 hours solo on all types, which means that he probably had a total of something over 600 hours' flying experience.

He took off at 1345 hours, and in the course of carrying out some general handling exercises evidently made his way eastwards, for an hour later his aircraft was seen in the area of Little Eaton, just outside Derby. Approaching from the direction of Derby, Flight Sergeant Williamson descended as he neared the village, then carried out a sustained dive to make a pass over a specific row of thatched cottages (since demolished). He failed to check his dive, however, and in brushing through the upper branches of a tree his aircraft was tipped nose down so that it crashed and disintegrated across the fields immediately beyond. There was no fire, but Flight Sergeant Williamson did not survive the impact.

In late 2005 Mr John Easter, of Little Eaton, a retired senior manager from Rolls-Royce Aero Engines Division, was one of the few residents who still remembered the crash. 'My mother', he explained, in the course of reprising a boyhood visit to the crash site, 'was working in a nearby engineering office when this aircraft came from the Derby direction and passed very low and very fast overhead. It then passed out of her line of sight behind the roof of Elm Farm –

John Salt's place now, although the Oakdens had it as tenant farmers then – and hit one of the trees in what we know as The Lawns, with wreckage spilling over into Brickyard Field where the pilot's body finished up.' He indicated the adjoining, low-lying field. 'Of course, us local school-lads rushed to the scene and I wouldn't be surprised if there are still some souvenirs around the village. But the RAF were here very quickly, and sealed the area off. After which the wreckage soon disappeared. The pilot's body, I remember, was initially taken to a room in the railway station.'

Mr John Easter revisits the impact site

By 2006 it was enshrined in village lore that this was not the first aerial visit Flight Sergeant Williamson had made; further, that he had a friend in the immediate area whom he wished to impress. Be that as it might be, the RAF were most definitely not impressed by the flight sergeant's undisciplined flying. Indeed, the court of inquiry went out of its way to castigate Flight Sergeant Williamson. The bare bones of the accident were recorded as: 'While carrying out unauthorised low flying pilot allowed aircraft to hit a tree, causing the aircraft to disintegrate', with the further observation that the pilot had either misjudged his height or too tardily pulled out of his dive. But each reporting officer in turn, the unit's commanding officer, the Air Officer Commanding (AOC) No.21 Group, and his superior, the AOC-in-Chief, concurred with the finding that the accident had been a 'flagrant disobedience of orders', each upholding the court's recommendation that, 'full publicity should be given this accident throughout the RAF'– a singularly unusual recommendation! Virtually unheard of, in fact. But clearly, with the war manifestly in its last stages, the Service was anxious to ensure that flying standards were maintained, that no slackness was to be allowed to creep in.

The tree in 2006, vouched for by a closely involved villager

In 2006 the tree the Oxford struck was vouched for by a villager who retained intimate details of the crash. On site, however, there were no indications that any such accident had occurred, and although metal detectors had been employed in the field at some stage it was not known whether they turned up any aircraft débris.

Airspeed Oxford (probably), RAF Darley Moor, Ashbourne

SK 16453 41654 176m
Possibly January 1943

In late 2005 Farmer Mr Jeff Chadfield, of Grange Farm, Darley Moor, described an aircraft which crashed having suffered an engine failure on taking off from Darley Moor airfield. 'It wasn't a bomber,' he remembered, 'or not one of the big ones we were used to seeing here. It had taken off from the cross runway, but turned this way and hit a tree on putting down. I didn't see it until some time later, but when I did, it was just sitting there, slumped over. There wasn't even a guard on it, possibly because it was a Sunday afternoon.'

It is very likely that this was a visiting Airspeed Oxford trainer; certainly one is known to have come down in similar circumstances in January 1943.

Above: The crash site of the Darley Moor Oxford

Left: Mr Jeff Chadfield, Grange Farm, witness

Supermarine Spitfire Mk.22 PK488, Hilltop Farm, north of Parwich

SK 18832 55374 286m touchdown
SK 18785 55155 290m terminal site
No.502 (Ulster) Squadron, Royal Auxiliary Air
Force, Reserve Command, RAF Aldergrove;
detached to RAF Newton, Nottinghamshire
25 June, 1949

Pilot: successfully forced-landed:
Flight Lieutenant A. MacDonald, Royal Auxiliary Air Force

As the 1949 air defence exercise 'Foil' moved into its second day, Derby became the target for the 'enemy' bomber forces comprising American B-29 Superfortresses and B-24 Liberators, supported by some RAF Lancasters and Lincolns. This force mounted attacks that varied from intrusions at 30,000 feet to low-level penetration raids; but it was held that few got through, the ground-control organisations directing the defending fighters being assessed as more than a match for them.

The defenders were drawn from units all over the United Kingdom, not only from regular RAF squadrons but also from those of the RAF Auxiliary Air Force, and not least from No.502 (Ulster) Squadron with its Spitfire Mk.22s from RAF Aldergrove – long since the shared Civil/RAF Belfast International Airport. Such intense flying, being scrambled in real Battle of Britain fashion, demanded intense concentration on the part of the ground controllers. For at combat power settings the Spitfire virtually guzzled fuel, and with the pilots focusing upon the airborne task it was vital that the machines should be closely monitored, and speedily recovered to their exercise bases as fuel states dwindled.

At 1810 hours on Saturday, 25 June, Flight Lieutenant A. MacDonald, one of the No.502 Squadron pilots, airborne from the squadron's exercise-detachment base of RAF Newton, Nottinghamshire, in Spitfire PK488, suddenly became aware that he had not heard from ground control for some while. At the same time he realised that his fuel state was worryingly low. He also realised that, being over unfamiliar terrain, and despite an almost cloudless sky, he did not know where to turn for the nearest airfield. He had obtained navigational fixes at intervals throughout the sortie, but now that he had occasion to apply them to the ground features below, and to his map, he could make no sense of them. Accordingly, after deliberating, he decided he had no option but to make a precautionary landing. And clearly it was a timely decision, for having flown a visual pattern around a suitable-seeming field, made distinctive by a singular cross-shaped wood, and near enough to both a farm and a village to ensure succour, his engine cut from lack of fuel at the very moment of touchdown.

The forced landing was successful in that Flight Lieutenant MacDonald was able to walk away unhurt. But towards the final stages of his landing run the aircraft suffered damage as it encountered hitherto unseen rough ground; indeed from witness evidence it seems likely that the undercarriage collapsed. (Even as late as 1949, Spitfires would commonly have been operated off grass, therefore it is almost certain that Flight Lieutenant MacDonald would have made his approach with his wheels down.)

It is clear that with so many aircraft in the sky all attempting to use the limited communications channels of the day, the airwaves had been somewhat frenetic. Further, Flight Lieutenant MacDonald had found that the three secondary channels available to him were either overcrowded – and therefore swamped by aircraft closer to the receiving stations – or were being deliberately blocked by defensive radio countermeasures as part of the exercise. But it transpired that, beyond all this, the frequency-controlling crystal in his radio had failed, preventing him from making contact even had he managed to squeeze his way between the other callers.

In the course of the following investigation a court of inquiry was recommended, but this was overridden, the refreshingly pragmatic view being taken that it would have served no useful purpose.

It is evident that the parts played by the faulty frequency-controlling crystal and the cluttered airwaves could be set aside, but it might seem strange that the reason for false bearings being given was not made the subject of such an inquiry. But, in fact, this was a matter which fell under the security cloak and which would have been fully investigated in a separate, restricted, technical and operational Signals inquiry.

As it was both the pilot and the local air traffic service were held to be blameless. For its part, the Spitfire had been officially assessed as 'Category B', denoting 'Beyond repair on site, but repairable at a maintenance unit, or at a contractor's works', and had duly been recovered to a maintenance unit.

Mr Charles Fearn, 2002, witness

In early 2006 Mr Charles Fearn, of Market Rasen, but brought up in Parwich, read the account of the incident as published in *Peakland Air Crashes: The South*, and was good enough to write, correcting the location given. Having left Parwich to serve fifteen years in the RAF police, followed by five in a civilian force, Mr Fearn remembered the incident well. 'Wakes Week', he recalled, 'was in full swing, with Mr Jack Sykes' fair there, as always, when word came that an aircraft had crashed at Hilltop Farm, right above the village. So, many of us immediately set off up Parwich Hill; my cousin, Dennis Evans, and Ronnie Calladine, Roy Ratcliffe, Vernon Parker, and quite a few more. And as we came clear of the wood, there in the field between us and Hilltop Farm, which the Wheldons farmed, facing uphill, was a hardly damaged Spitfire. PC Parker was already in attendance and keeping the growing crowd back. Just the same I was able to speak to the pilot, and despite PC Parker's protests that the plane might explode at any moment, the pilot overruled him, and let us look around the cockpit and its controls.'

Mr Dennis Evans also described what he saw: 'The Spitfire wasn't smashed, just seemed to have flopped onto its belly. So that we could see into the cockpit quite easily. There wasn't much chance of souvenirs, though. And later the RAF brought long trailers, and carted it away.'

'Certainly not souvenirs,' Mr Fearn agreed. 'Not with PC Parker's eagle eye when the Albemarle crashed at Bradbourne Mill.' He paused, and reflected. 'The team at the Spitfire used a Thorneycroft-mounted Coles Crane and a Queen M of which had to be parked between Parwich Hall and the village shop – when crew bought sweets and cigarettes. They couldn't take the plane out towards .... because the Queen Mary wouldn't have got around the tight turn into Back Lane, and besides, the tail would never have passed under the bridge of the Cromford High Peak Railway.'

'As a point of interest,' Mr Fearn added, 'it was always said that before the war the aviation people asked that Parwich Hill Wood should be left as it was. For being the only wood for many miles around shaped like a cross, it made a perfect feature for aircraft to navigate by.'

It is clear that the hordes of village lads who thronged the site would have scavenged any residual débris once the official recovery had been effected, so that by 2006, with the field having been in constant use, no evidence of the setdown was to be seen.

P-47D Thunderbolt 42-22491, Riverside, Upper Tean, Staffordshire

SK 00786 39584 133m
551st Fighter Training Squadron, 495th Fighter Training Group, United States Eighth Army Air Force, AAF342 (RAF Atcham), Shrewsbury
14 July, 1944

Pilot: killed:
Second Lieutenant Donald M. Pfaff, USAAF

In the early days of the American involvement in the Second World War in Europe, the 495th Fighter Training Group, based at American Air Force Airfield No.342 (RAF Atcham), near Shrewsbury, had been a fighter replacement pool which trained fighter pilots arriving from the United States in gunnery and the operational procedures suited to the European theatre. By July 1944, however, the Group, now comprising two fighter-training squadrons, Nos.551 and 552, had become a dedicated Thunderbolt Operational Training Unit for such tyro pilots.

Throughout a particularly busy July day, some of its aircraft had been operating in the Upper Tean area, but in the early evening Second Lieutenant Donald Pfaff encountered a problem while dog-fighting and was unable to maintain control. His aircraft dived steeply under power and crashed into the centre of a row of four cottages by the bridge at Riverside, in Upper Tean. Second Lieutenant Pfaff was killed, yet although the cottages were badly damaged and fuel and ammunition was scattered widely, there was no major fire, and none of the five people indoors at the time were hurt.

Mrs Evelyn Williams, of Upper Tean, in January 2006 the very brightest of 97-year-olds, demonstrated her clear recall of that day. 'It was in July 1944,' she said, 'early on a Friday evening. My husband, Les, had just gone off to work on the night shift and I was just about to clear away the dishes when I heard this plane coming from the Oakhill direction. There had been four or five of them buzzing around for most of the afternoon, but nowhere near this low. And then there was this most enormous crash. I rushed to the back window, and then everything seemed to come down. I put my hands on my head, and just began to scream. The plane had smashed into the two cottages beside ours, and there was rubble and petrol everywhere.' Mrs Williams paused, then explained, 'At that

January 2006, Mrs Evelyn Williams, with her back to the impact area

...e there were four cottages here. Mr and Mrs Bostock lived at the far end from us. But where the plane hit, next to us, there was old Mr Hill, and beside him, Mr and Mrs Richard Wood, a young couple. She'd gone off to the pictures in Cheadle leaving her husband to look after the two children. Brian, their oldest, was in the kitchen, and Ian was in his cot upstairs, so their dad had nipped around to the shop to pick up an accumulator for the wireless. However, two men from up the road clambered in and rescued the boys, and everyone else in the cottages was all right. But the young American pilot – he was only nineteen – he was killed right away.

'In fact, it was some time before they could get his body out. I simply stayed where I was. So that when a policeman appeared he was so shocked to find me that he yelled, "Mrs Williams, what are you still bloody doing here?"– he actually swore! They were worried that the petrol and the tracer bullets might catch fire, and although neither did, there were bullets all over the place, across the road even. And when they took me outside I saw that all the houses nearby seemed to have chimney pots off and the like. As for the bridge, you couldn't see it for sightseers, though where they all came from … So many, that when my husband arrived back – they'd called him from work – he had to go round by the Little Entry because he couldn't fight his way through them.' Mrs Williams paused, and reflected. 'The cottages were so badly damaged that we had to stay with my mother for eighteen months before the Americans – it had to be cleared by the Pentagon – paid off the landlord and he got them done up. Us tenants got compensation for our personal things – carpets and such. But our local authorities valued them all at 1939 – pre-war – prices! And took no notice of the way things had gone up since. All four cottages were set to rights, but over the years the end one kept being hit by lorries. Until one day, when the lady was on the toilet, a lorry lost control and took away all the other rooms. And after that it was demolished for safety.'

In early 2006 the brickwork renewed in the months after the crash was the only evidence remaining of the tragedy that could so easily have been that much more costly in terms of human life.

Originally the two centre cottages into which the out-of-control P-47 crashed. A fourth cottage, to the left, hazarded by traffic, was demolished later.

De Havilland DH82A Tiger Moth, Morley Lane, Little Eaton

SK 37371 41774 134m
Prior to 12 July, 1942

In late2005 Mr John Easter, of Little Eaton, was able to point out the location where he saw this crashed aircraft. 'I was walking with my mother,' he recalled, 'towards my grandfather's place on Morley Lane, when we came upon this Tiger Moth which had forced-landed, and nosed over a hedge into the field. It was half-turned onto its back, but that was all. Not that badly damaged, by the look of it.'

No further details of this incident have presently come to light. But this was not to be the end of Mr Easter's encounters with aircraft crashes in the

2005, Mr John Easter indicates the hedgerow where the Tiger Moth overran

Little Eaton area. 'Some time later,' he continued, 'I looked up to see this Wellington lose a wing – it was the one doing pressurised-trials that came down in Stanley, not far off. But we never heard anything else about any of the three aircraft at the time, not the Oxford [see Oxford N4597 above], the Wellington, or this Tiger Moth.' [The Wellington mentioned was W5795, which crashed on 12 July, 1942, but is outside the scope of this Peakland series.]

De Havilland DH112 Mk.1 Venom WK390, Handley Bank, Caverswall

SJ 95189 43844 219m
Ministry of Supply
22 February, 1954

Pilot: killed:
Mr Kenneth Burton Forbes, Fairey Aviation Company test pilot

On 22 February, 1954, Mr Kenneth Burton Forbes, a Fairey Aviation test pilot working from the company's facility at Manchester's Ringway aerodrome, was killed when the de Havilland Venom he was testing developed a problem and crashed into a field at Cocking Farm, Caverswall. The machine exploded fierily on impact, creating a sizeable crater and spreading wreckage over three-quarters of a mile. It was deduced from pieces of parachute found in the wreckage that no attempt had been made to evacuate the aircraft.

The crater of Fairey Venom WK390 which crashed on test (newsprint photograph by courtesy of the Stoke *Evening Sentinel*; the original has not survived)

Witness evidence played a large part in the official investigation, among those most relied upon being Mr Nathan Atkinson, of Cookshill, who also told the Stoke *Evening Sentinel*, 'I was attending to my pigeons when the plane just came out of the clouds in a power dive only about a hundred yards from the earth, and crashed. I should say it had come from a great height.'

Days later he would repeat his account in the coroner's court where representatives from both Fairey Aviation and de Havillands were in attendance, the Fairey Aviation works manager from Ringway telling the court, 'This Venom Mk.1 had been under test for the Ministry of Supply. It was a normal test flight, and there is no suggestion of sabotage.' [The Venom crash was coincident with one of the de Havilland Comet jet-airliner disasters, when sabotage was being widely mooted, if only in the press.]

Mrs Valerie Parish, of Cocking Farm, and Mr Cecil Wainright, would-be site visitor in 1954

2006, Mr Cecil Wainright, witness, standing on the backfilled impact crater

In 2006 neither an RAF nor a civilian accident report could be traced, although the latter, at least, almost certainly exists somewhere. However, considering the number of things that could have gone wrong to cause the crash, it might suffice to echo the words of Mr Marshall, the North Staffordshire coroner: 'This is a very brave occupation – this test pilot business.'

Nothing was to be seen at the site in 2006, but in granting permission to visit her land, Mrs Valerie Parish, of Cocking Farm, was also able to indicate where the crater had been, explaining, 'After some time we filled it and levelled it off in order to be able to work the field properly.' To doubly confirm the location, a would-be visitor in 1954, Mr Cecil Wainright, of Caverswall, sought the assistance of a former schoolfriend who had actually heard and seen the Venom crash. 'But I was in the field across the way, working,' the friend protested, 'and you couldn't just get up and leave; it'd have meant the sack.' Nor had Mr Wainright stood on the site before. 'But not for want of trying,' he said feelingly. 'As a lad I rushed all the way up here, but when I got to the top of Handley Bank this airman turned me back. So all I could do was look on from a distance.'

Vickers Armstrongs Wellington Mk.1C DV435, Shottle Hall, Belper

SK 30731 47840 131m
No.14 Operational Training Unit (OTU), RAF Market Harborough,
No.92 (Training) Group, Bomber Command
24 November, 1943

Crew: four; parachuted; one killed:
Flying Officer D.W.A. Stewart, pilot
Flying Officer Joseph Norman Clark, navigator/air bomber, RNZAF, injured
Sergeant J. Ould, wireless operator, injured
Sergeant John Donald Hall, air gunner, killed

On 24 November, 1943, Flying Officer Stewart and his crew had been tasked to fly Wellington DV435 on a training flight. He duly got airborne from RAF Market Harborough at 1650 hours, but on his return, some four and a half hours later, ran into bad weather and encountered such severe icing conditions that he found himself unable to maintain control. Accordingly he issued the order to abandon, but although he and two other members of his crew made successful parachute descents, the rear-turret gunner, Sergeant John Hall, was killed. The abandoned Wellington crashed into a field in the vicinity of Shottle Hall, to the west of Belper, and burst into flames, but caused no collateral damage other than a crater.

The RAF investigators were unable to determine whether Sergeant Hall's parachute had opened at too low an altitude, or whether he had made either a bad exit, or a bad landing. However, as they especially noted 'pilot acted OK' in deciding to abandon, it suggests that they were also satisfied that Flying Officer Stewart had seen his crew away in good time. A snagged-up exit from his turret after acknowledging the 'abandon' order, therefore, would seem to be the most probable reason for Sergeant Hall's evacuation being unsuccessful.

The survivors were soon back on flying duties and completed their courses, but the navigator/bomb-aimer, New Zealander Flying Officer Joseph Clark, was later posted to No.207 Squadron and was killed on 16th November, 1944, whilst engaged in Lancaster operations from RAF Spilsby.

In late 2005 Mr and Mrs Herbert and Myrtle Slater, formerly of Overlane, but then of Duffield, recalled the night the Wellington came

Mr and Mrs Herbert and Myrtle Slater, Duffield

down at Shottle Hall. 'We were still courting,' smiled Mrs Slater, 'and I was just putting something away in the scullery when we heard this crash. And when we looked out, we saw this great yellow flame.'

'It was quite a way to go,' Herbert, by 2005 Myrtle's husband of sixty years standing, took over, 'but we made our way up White Lane, and could see that the plane had come down at the back of the hay barn. There was wreckage everywhere, still burning, but the area had already been cordoned off, and we couldn't get much closer than the barn.' He paused. 'Later, I went to work there, but there was little left. As for the crew, I never really heard, but it was said that two of them were found wandering about near Round Wood.'

Mr David Hurt, of Carrbrook Farm, also had cause to remember the aircraft wreckage. 'My uncle Joe Hurt had a threshing set, but would turn his hand to absolutely anything. He took one of the wheels from the Wellington and put it in a wheelbarrow. It was far too bulky and heavy, of course, but as I say, he'd use anything that came his way.'

Mr Jeff Butler, of Shottle Hall Cottages, however, had become very familiar with the site itself. 'When I began working at the farm,' he said, 'the field had long been cleared. Yet throughout the late 60s and early 70s you'd plough up bits of aluminium, but in a very localised area. Later, a Derby historical group did a dig, possibly recovering an engine, but since then, nothing seemed to turn up. Indeed the field hasn't been ploughed for some eleven years now.'

Mr David Hurt, Shottle

The area of impact, looking towards Shottle Hall

Armstrong Whitworth Whitley, Holly Meadow Farm, Bradley, Ashbourne

SK 23307 44552 146m
No 42 Operational Training Unit, RAF Ashbourne, No.38 Group
Mid-summer, c.1943

Mr Tom Lawton, in 2006 of Holly Meadow Farm, Bradley, was able to locate the spot where a multi-engined training aircraft from RAF Ashbourne came down during the Second World War. 'It was a Whitley,' he said, 'and something had evidently gone wrong after it took off from Ashbourne for it had touched down and simply slid across the field into the corner. I was brought across to see it, but there was a guard who didn't let us come too close. I don't think anyone was hurt, and it seemed quite whole. For all that, farmer Joe Moss was quick off the mark, ladling up petrol as fast as it flowed from the aircraft into the ditch, so there must have been damage enough for the fuel to leak, and the plane would have to have been taken away by road.'

No further details have so far been obtained regarding this successful emergency landing, but this incident too is included against further information coming to light.

Far left: Mr Tom Lawton indicates the direction of

Left: The terminal site of the Whitley

The Royal Air Force crash-report summary, Form 1180

Any RAF aircraft accident generated a plethora of paperwork. Once a finding was reached a summary of the investigation was produced. Often hard to decipher, the summaries are notoriously lax when it comes to recording the location of the incident. The great majority of these reports, reduced to film, have been passed on to the RAF Museum at Hendon by the RAF Historical Branch.

A fruitful source for future researchers in this field will be the original files from which the summaries were derived. Unfortunately, in the course of the periodical, independently assigned, document reviews carried out by all government departments – and large organisations – some material, genuinely deemed of no further interest at the time of the review, was destroyed. This was never done in the nature of a 'cover up', most particularly in air accident investigations, but without such review procedures even the National Archives at Kew, where much detailed crash-site material is stored, would soon have become choked.

Crash-site perspex sculpture

It may be that the urge to collect souvenirs from crashed aircraft entered the human psyche when a fisherman retrieved some waxed feathers after Icarus disobeyed family flying orders and flew too near the sun. Certainly it flourished during the Second World War, when so many sons of Icarus fell within the Peaklands, and indeed after it, judging from post-war pleas made for the return of souvenirs by crash investigators seeking causes for effects.

Most débris filched, then as now, finished up in dustbins, but in researching this series it became evident that perspex from turrets and cockpit canopies was fashioned into artefacts, into cigarette boxes, pendants and, most frequently, rings. Former exponents of the art described how fragments would be pierced through with pokers heated in domestic coal fires, then filed into shape, and sometimes polished. An isolated variation was the use of aluminium tubing, but perspex was the material of choice.

The first instance encountered was that of a Halifax flight engineer who made perspex rings for his mother and sister from the crashed Wellington at Conksbury, but several more were to follow, most related by former-schoolboy creators who then sold – or bartered – their products to local lasses. Despite the various accounts recorded, however, only one example of perspex sculpture actually came to hand. Fortunately that proved to be of prize quality. Only it was made not by a schoolboy but by pupil pilot William Vincent Barrett, who was to survive the war, having flown as a flight sergeant pilot with No.17 Squadron.

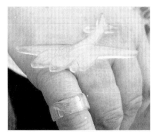

De Havilland Mosquito, and ring with incised RAF shoulder flash, modelled in perspex from a crashed aircraft by pupil pilot William Vincent Barrett, who later flew as a flight-sergeant pilot on No.17 Squadron (courtesy of his daughter, Mrs Trish Lee)

'Darky' and associated emergency homing facilities

Throughout the *Peakland Air Crashes* series various emergency 'get-you-home' systems are mentioned, and 'Darky' in particular. This was a quintessentially British facility which made a strength out of the limited, twenty-five mile range of the airborne R/T (voice) radio installations of the day, the Transmitter Receiver TR1196s and TR9s carried by bombers and fighters respectively. The facility was operated at RAF stations, but also at certain Royal Observation Corps posts, button 'D' being the emergency channel on which a lost aircraft could transmit blind for 'Darky'. Any listening post hearing the call would respond with its position,

The TR9 HF radio set carried in fighters

thus furnishing the aircrew with a location accurate to twenty-five miles, often enough to enable them to plot a course for base. Alternatively, especially if the aircraft needed to land quickly, the ground station could pass it the course to the nearest airfield. This would be followed up by a phone call to the next ground station in that direction, who, when it heard the aircraft call, would take over and refine the lead-in.

Among non-radio aids were 'Occults', aerial lighthouses radiating a white, periodically shaded (or occluded) light flashing a single identifying letter, and visible at thirty miles, which could direct their beams towards the nearest airfield.

'Granite' was supplementary to both facilities, the station sending off red flares to show its position, or alternatively to warn of high ground.

The Royal Observer Corps was able to make the proud claim that over 7,000 Allied aircraft were saved by the use of such systems, with 1,800 other damaged machines being guided to safe landings.

The 'Queen Mary' trailer, the Fordson tractor

The 'Queen Mary' trailer
Throughout the series reference is made to crashed aircraft being towed from the site by 'Queen Mary' trailer. These low-loader trailers were built by Tasker's of Andover in response to a 1938 Air Ministry requirement for a recovery vehicle which could carry a complete fighter aircraft. Within ten days Tasker's submitted not only a design, but a prototype vehicle. Their contract bid was successful, and over 4,000 of their trailers, the largest available, were built.

The Fordson tractor
Another vehicle mentioned in the series is the Fordson tractor which farmers used to help retrieve crashed aircraft. Reference is almost invariably made to the vehicle being a prized possession, and the only one in the area, bringing it home that at the time the term horsepower on most British farms meant just that.

One of the subsidiary outcomes in researching for the *Peakland Air Crashes* series was the substance given to tenets encountered during various Air-Crash Investigation and Flight Safety courses. It quickly became evident, for example, that witnesses do indeed have a very independent perception of any event, and that some, in all good faith, really will believe that an aircraft which was flown blindly into a hill was actually on fire well before impact. Another precept to be frequently proven during research was that if an aircraft has crashed in open fields it will invariably be held that the pilot was trying to avoid the village, the church, the hospital or the school. But although, when challenged, the reasoning is seen to be specious – given even a modicum of control any open space has to be infinitely preferable to any structure – it borrows authority from such popular-press headlines as 'Pilot's Bid to Avoid Houses at Caverswall', notwithstanding that the Venom which crashed at Caverswall was demonstrably beyond control. As was the Flying Fortress which spiralled into Endcliffe Park at Sheffield, despite which a footballing schoolboy was quoted as carolling, 'He was trying to avoid us'. Even a student pilot who killed himself and destroyed his Vampire while 'beating-up' his home was afforded much indulgence: 'The young man's gallantry saved our home,' a neighbour at Rawmarsh told reporters.

Of course, histrionic headlines sell newspapers, but when required, the leads are swiftly revamped, so that after the airliner crash at Kegworth, the 'Captain Hero' of Day One unapologetically gave place to the 'Was the wrong engine stopped?' of Day Two. Personal perceptions, conversely, tend to be more firmly entrenched, so that in 2006 two level-headed witnesses of a Vampire which simply dived into the ground in fifties Wildboarclough remained unshaken in their belief that it had been 'a fireball in the sky'.

There were other outcomes not previously encountered in courses. Among them was the predominant belief that any wartime aircraft which crashed had been 'one of theirs'– a German. Alongside which any large aircraft 'of ours' is held to have been a Lancaster; any little one, a Spitfire. Although one gentleman asserted, 'It was a German Spitfire – but all the crew were captured by the Home Guard.'

Another widely held belief, as observed elsewhere in this Central volume, is that the many German bombs which fell in the Peaklands were all jettisoned by raiders 'trying to escape'; their crews, presumably, having unaccountably turned timorous. The reality is that for a 1941 German crew to manage to get a bomb even that close to the blacked-out pairing of Manchester and Sheffield would have equalled the accuracy of the vastly more experienced Allied bombing forces of 1945, over fifty per cent of whose bombs still landed in open country.

Enemy fliers aside, however, it quickly became clear that folk have the most benign regard for aircrew, notwithstanding that virtually all crashes are caused by their crews – always accepting that when, for example, a pilot stops the good engine instead of the bad one, the fault lies with him and not with those who failed to provide a foolproof 'this-is-the-bad-one' indicator. By this same kindliness of disposition, the public was found to militantly oppose any official finding of 'pilot error', preferring to endow pilots, it would seem, with a near-papal degree of infallibility. Yet flying personnel, whether Service or Civilian, with every facet of their operation being rigorously tested every six months, not forgetting snap check-rides in the interim, can never be under any such illusion. But perhaps the public's faith is rooted in an awareness that, whenever they fly themselves, all their accustomed independence must be surrendered to the crew.

It also became manifest that, prosaic as flying has become since the age-old aspiration was realised by the Wright Brothers in 1903, its aura of romance-tinged-with-danger is still undimmed. Not that many of Peakland's crashed aircrews were ever aware that they were in any particular danger, most survivors being doubly taken aback on discovering that, rather than five minutes from their cosy, low-lying Lincolnshire station, they were on a high and remote moorland forty miles distant.

Gratifyingly, amid these Peakland narratives are to be found several 'Good Shows', where 'navigationally challenged' captains made the decision to abandon having found no safe way in which to penetrate cloud. There are even a very few incidents where the aircraft actually failed their crews, among these being the Ossoms Hill Skytrooper whose wingtip crumpled in the air.

However, that the vast majority of Peakland's foredoomed crews remained providentially oblivious to what cloud and darkness hid from them is too often ignored in crash-site enthusiast accounts. For example, in direct contradiction of the facts established by the official investigators, a popularised account of the 1937 Heyford crash in Edale has the crew aware of their peril and firing off flares in a desperate attempt to locate themselves. In similar fashion, when the tale is told of the American Liberator abandoned to crash on the high moors above Oldham, the exemplary conduct of its actual crew is presented in the manner of the so-excitable actor crew in the shamefully anachronistic 1990s film *Memphis Belle*; the real *Memphis Belle's* crew, and the original wartime documentary, being totally credible. But then this Peakland series, written from the stance of the professional aviator, was unashamedly conceived as a deliberate counter to such enthusiast accounts, the corollary being that there are no histrionics, no 'forgotten heroes of the skies', and few to be singled out for individual praise.

Yet praise is given, and heroism is duly recognised, with ready regret being expressed where no official recognition was given to that heroism, as was so often the case when farm workers risked everything in an endeavour to rescue crew members from burning aircraft, selflessly choosing to discount the imminence of explosion. For the most part nobody knew of this heroism, for when the authorities arrived such homespun heroes simply returned to their farming tasks. Indeed, when just such a former farm worker was searched out in 2004, his family had no inkling of how Grandad had spent that fraught fifteen minutes on a time-hazed wartime day. But 'good' VCs have been won in far less time, and with a risk to life not one whit less extreme. Then again, notwithstanding that police, rangers, fire service, mountain-rescue teams and civilian moor-searchers attend even the most remote of crashes, in the near-300 incidents covered in the Peakland series only three rescue attempts drew the official notice of a King's Commendation, with unofficial recognition being equally sparse, and with rarely as much as a 'thank you' being said to assuage the trauma after the event.

The Peakland series then, contains no mysteries, and certainly no fanciful hints of dark cover-ups; still less of conspiracy theories; nor are heroics entertained. And yet, all aircrew being volunteers, courage underlies each incident. But it was always an unstated courage, besides which few would have exchanged their chosen role – with smart blue uniform, chest-swelling aircrew brevet, and the lure of coloured ribbons – for such other alternatives to the army as labouring on the farm or in the factory; or – dread the thought!– being drafted down the coal mines. Still less, being directed to the domestic kitchen.

Research, however, also revealed a perennial perception of flying as hazardous, but glamorous. Hazardous, despite the fact that 'Beats working for a living, doesn't it?' is a stock conceit to be heard on any flight deck, whether Service or Civilian. Yet glamorous, assuredly, for although it is common knowledge that cabin staff spend their airborne hours in chores not best liked by either nurse or housewife, recruiters are invariably overwhelmed by applicants only too eager, it would seem, to mop up vomit. But then it could be that fliers, as opposed to aviation enthusiasts, tend more to the prosaic than to the romantic. Or perhaps the flier has learned from the outset to keep his head, at least, firmly on the ground. 'Isn't it wonderful,' enthused a pre-solo colleague, 'bursting through the clouds into dazzling sunlight like this?' Drawing the curt response from his instructor, 'I told you to level out at eighteen thousand feet.'

Just the same, nothing seems likely to dent a public perception of the romantic aviator which embraces even those who crash, evidently seeing them all as intrinsically different from the hapless skipper of the crumpled Mondeo. But any aviator writing on the subject would be doing a disservice to Aviation should his work lend credence to such a perception. Accordingly this series deliberately eschews both the sensational and the emotive, fixing its aims instead on directing the interested walker-reader to the site and describing what happened while at the same time critically examining why the incident occurred in the first place. Yet every criticism is made with fingers firmly crossed behind the back, and crossed not only for 'self'– as aircrew denote themselves in their flying log books – but also for those countless others who, unlike the Peakland sons of Icarus featured in the series, did not – and hopefully, will not in the future – come to grief within the Peakland bounds.

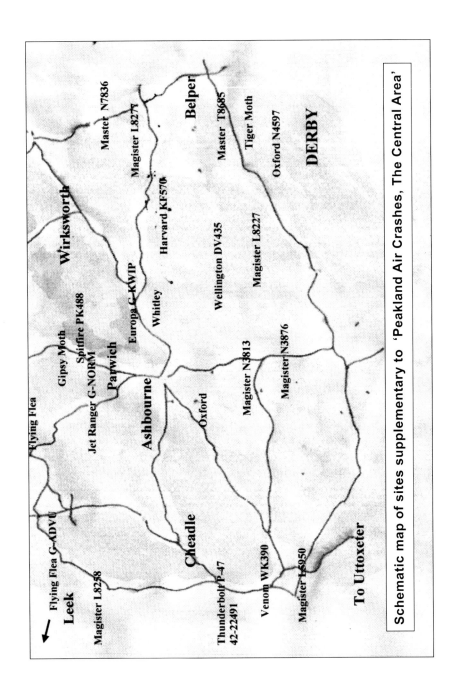

Schematic map of sites supplementary to 'Peakland Air Crashes, The Central Area'

This section aims to provide the walker with a potted guide to the aircraft types introduced in *Peakland Air Crashes: The Central Area*. Details of those already encountered in *Peakland Air Crashes: The South* will be found in that volume. It will be appreciated that only representative details are supplied. The same applies to the performance figures given, for these are never immutable. For example, values quoted in Pilot's Notes always incorporate a healthy safety margin, while workaday machines of a given type often differ significantly. Then again published sources display marked variations, not a few perpetuating values originally enhanced for wartime propaganda purposes. Notwithstanding all of which, the details given here aim to be comprehensive enough to satisfy the passing interest of the walker-reader.

Similarly, it is to cater for this happy non-specialist class of reader that Arabic numbers are employed throughout in designating aircraft marks, the problem of deciphering Roman numerals being left to the enthusiast.

Hawker Audax

The Audax was the army co-operation variant of the Hart (see *The South*, p.177) and could be distinguished from it by its long exhaust pipe and by the message-collecting hook on its undercarriage spreader bar. It first appeared in November 1931 as a replacement for the Armstrong Whitworth Atlas (*The South*, p.185) but 500 were produced under subcontracts alone before production ceased in May 1937. The RAF received the Audax in February 1932 and it then equipped units at home and overseas, including Flying Training Schools, where it was used as an advanced trainer.

Some, in fact, were used during the Second World War, in East Africa with a Rhodesian squadron, and in Iraq in May 1941 when RAF Habbaniyah, then the largest station in the Service, was besieged by Iraqi rebels.

The Audax was typically powered by a 530 horsepower Rolls-Royce Kestrel engine, had a maximum speed of 170 mph (148 knots), could climb to 10,000 feet in some ten minutes, had a ceiling of 21,000 feet and an endurance of three and half hours. It could carry a bomb load of 230 pounds and was armed with a forward-firing Vickers machine gun and an aft-mounted Lewis, both of 0.303-inch calibre.

Auster Autocrat

The Auster Autocrat was a three-seater cabin-monoplane with a high-set braced wing and a fixed, tailwheel-configured undercarriage. Powered by a Cirrus Minor Mk.2 90 bhp air-cooled engine, it took off at 40 mph (35 knots), climbed at 65 mph (56 knots), cruised at 85 mph (74 knots), and was normally descended at 40 mph (35 knots) in a powered approach. Not particularly inspiring to fly, it was nevertheless both dependable and docile.

Canadair Argonaut

The Argonaut was derived from the DC4, developed by Douglas as a civil airliner. When America entered the Second World War, however, the DC4 became the military C-54 Skymaster, and production was diverted. The originally-proposed design had first flown on 7 June, 1938, but its sponsor, United Air Lines, found it to be 'complicated to maintain and uneconomical to operate', a comment future users chose to take as meaning 'ahead of its time'. Indeed it had much to offer, not least a constant cross-section fuselage, with easy access as an incidental benefit of a nosewheel undercarriage.

After the war a number of pressurised DC4s with Rolls-Royce engines were built for the British Overseas Airways Corporation by Canadair. Renaming his new acquisition the 'Argonaut', Lord Thomas, the Corporation's chairman of the day, was to say of it, as the time came for selling on, 'This sturdy, dependable economic and comfortable airliner has been of immeasurable value to my Corporation. Indeed ... it at once began to change the fortunes of BOAC'.

The Argonaut, when powered by four Rolls-Royce Merlin engines, had a cruising speed of 227 mph (197 knots), a ceiling of 22,300 feet, and was able to lift a payload of 11,440 pounds over a range of some 6,500 miles. It had a maximum take-off weight of 73,000 pounds and carried a normal complement of three flight-deck crew, with standard seating for 44 passengers.

Boeing B-17 Flying Fortress

The Boeing B-17 first flew in July 1935, when its perceived role was that of a long-range outpost capable of defending America beyond the range of its shore defences, hence 'Flying Fortress'. However, after it was tested in action with the RAF such modifications as self-sealing fuel tanks and an increased amount of protective armour were called for. With these installed the B-17 then became the mainstay of the United States Eighth Army Air Force's bombing campaign which began in August 1942.

The enormous tail fin ensured that it was stable at great heights, while the fact that it had formidable defensive armament and that it proved capable of absorbing a considerable amount of battle damage was held to make up for its relatively small bomb load.

The upgraded B-17G version, introduced into Europe a year or so later, relied for its defence on up to thirteen 0.5-inch, heavy-calibre machine guns, this firepower being enhanced by the interdependent formation strategies employed. With so many guns to man, the standard crew complement was ten, including pilot, co-pilot, navigator, bombardier, flight engineer and radio operator. In combat the flight engineer would man the top turret, and the wireless operator the dorsal turret. The remaining four crew were dedicated gunners to man the ball-turret, the left and right waist positions and the tail turret.

Typical performance figures for the B-17 reflect that it was powered by four 1,200 horsepower Wright Cyclone R-1820-65 9-cylinder air-cooled engines, with Hamilton three-bladed, constant-speed, fully-feathering propellers. This combination gave it a cruising speed of 225 mph (196 knots) and permitted a ceiling of over 40,000 feet. It had a normal maximum take-off weight of 40,260 pounds – although this could be increased to 63,959 pounds – and a normal range of 3,000 miles. Its standard bomb load was 6,000 pounds, although this could be increased to 12,800 pounds, and, over a very short range, to 20,800 pounds. (For a comparison often made, the Lancaster's standard bomb load was 14,000 pounds, and it could be adapted to carry one bomb weighing 22,000 pounds.)

Fairey Battle

Although relatively impressive when it first flew in early 1936, the single-engined Fairey Battle light-bomber was already obsolete by 1939 when war broke out. Accommodating a pilot, bomb-aimer/observer and a wireless operator/air gunner, the Battle, powered by a 1,030 horsepower Rolls-Royce Merlin Mk.1 in-line engine, cruised at 210 mph (182 knots) at up to 25,000 feet and had a range of 1,000 miles. It had a bomb load of 1,000 pounds.

For defence it had a Vickers 0.303-inch calibre machine gun in a rear-cockpit mounting, and another in the starboard wing. But it was totally outclassed by the German first-line fighters, and after a series of gallantly fought, but disastrous, engagements during the German advance into France, the Battle was withdrawn as a day bomber. It continued to serve, however, in the training and target-towing roles, 2,200 having been produced.

BE2C

Geoffrey de Havilland designed the Royal Aircraft Factory's 1914 two-seater BE2C as a reconnaissance and bombing machine. The 2C was a development of the Factory's earlier BE (Blériot Experimental) models, notably introducing ailerons instead of wing-warping for lateral control. It had been designed as a stable, easy to fly machine but accordingly lacked manoeuvrability. Despite this it was chosen for mass production, a decision which was to cost the Royal Flying Corps dear as the performance of enemy types improved. Notwithstanding which the BE2C was retained on the Western Front until 1917, and only then retired to home defence and training duties.

Typical of several power sources was the 90 horsepower Royal Aircraft Factory in-line, air-cooled engine which gave the BE2C a ceiling of 10,000 feet with a working maximum speed of 72 mph (63 knots). It carried a single machine gun – unlike its predecessors from the RAF (the Factory's altogether too-confusing abbreviation) which had been unarmed – and could carry 224 pounds of bombs mounted on underwing racks.

Bell 206B Jet Ranger helicopter

The Bell 206B was held to be the world's most popular helicopter, the 2004 publicity claiming, '*First in its class in safety, this aircraft ensures its crew will be back to fly another day.*' A 400 shaft-horse-power Allison 250-C20 series turboshaft engine typically gave a top speed of 132 mph (115 knots), a cruising speed of 115 mph (100 knots), an endurance of three hours, a range of 435 miles, and seating for between four and six passengers. The maximum external weight permitted was given as 1,500 pounds.

Bristol Fighter Mk.3

The 1916 Bristol Fighter Mk.2B – from the outset 'Fighter', and never 'Scout'– reached the Western Front in April 1917. In truth, it had a disastrous baptism of fire, but once the Royal Flying Corps learnt to use it as an offensive, rather than a defensive machine, it became a telling force. Production was restarted in the post-war period when the RAF adopted the type as the standard army co-operation machine, and in 1926 all restructured Mk.2s were re-designated Mk.3s.

The two-seater biplane fighter, wooden framed, and with fabric covering, weighed 2,800 pounds when fully loaded, and had a touch-down speed of 45 mph (39 knots). A 275 horsepower Rolls-Royce Falcon 3 engine gave it a maximum speed of 123 mph (107 knots), a time to 10,000 feet of twelve minutes, a ceiling of 20,000 feet, and an endurance of three hours.

The Bristol carried a synchronised Vickers 0.303-inch calibre machine gun firing through the propeller, and at least one Lewis machine gun mounted on a Scarff Ring in the rear cockpit; additionally it could carry 240 pounds of bombs. It was not withdrawn from service until 1932.

Reims Cessna 150

The strut-braced, high-winged, tricycle-undercarriaged, two-seater Cessna 150 first flew in September 1957, after which over 30,000 were built, up to 20,000 of which were said to be still flying in 2006. Pleasant to handle, forgiving, viceless and dependable, it built up a reputation for being the most popular light aeroplane ever produced.

Typically powered by a 100 horsepower Continental 0-200A flat-four engine driving a two-bladed fixed-pitch propeller, it had an average cruising speed of 122 mph (106 knots), with 65–70 mph (56–61 knots) sufficing for virtually all manoeuvring. With a maximum take-off weight of 1,500 pounds it had an initial rate of climb of 640 feet a minute, a ceiling of 15,000 feet, and a range of 350 miles.

Boulton Paul Defiant

By 1937 most fighter designers had settled upon a fixed-gun design which required the pilot to aim his entire aircraft at the target. The Boulton Paul Defiant, in contrast, was designed to be more flexible, carrying a dedicated gunner in a moveable dorsal turret. The low-wing, all-metal, twin-crewed monoplane had four 0.303-inch calibre machine guns mounted in this turret, but notwithstanding sinking it into the fuselage the turret's weight and drag so detracted from the machine's performance that, although a more powerful engine was fitted, the Defiant was never to reach an acceptable standard, despite which nearly 1,100 were built before construction ceased in 1943.

When war broke out the German fighters soon realised that the Defiant had neither belly nor head-on protection, and in December 1940 it was withdrawn from daylight operations. Once it was re-employed as a night fighter, however, and particularly when equipped with airborne-interception radar, it was to be rather more successful. Later it was to see further service as a target tug.

With a 1,280 horsepower Rolls-Royce Merlin Mk.20 in-line engine it could cruise at 260 mph (226 knots) and climb to some 30,000 feet. At a maximum take-off weight of 8,424 pounds it had a range of 465 miles.

De Havilland DH10

The de Havilland DH10, the Amiens, had a troubled existence. Critically delayed in production until 1917 it was hardly ready for service when World War One came to an end. Even when its career did get under way it was never a success and was withdrawn from the line in 1923. Before that, however, it had served the RAF in various colonial policing roles, and more notably, helped institute the air-mail service between Egypt and Iraq. Notwithstanding which, in contrast to the majority of de Havilland ventures, it was very much a nonentity.

A three-seater, twin-engined biplane long-range day-bomber, it was fitted with twin 400 horsepower Liberty 12 engines, which, according to the contemporary *Jane's*, gave it a speed 'low down' of 128 mph (111 knots), one of 117 mph (102 knots) at 15,000 feet, and allowed it to carry ordnance weighing 1,248 pounds. Other sources add that its ceiling was 17,500 feet, and its duration six hours. For defensive armament it carried two Lewis 0.303-inch calibre machine guns, one in the nose and another amidships.

Do-It-Yourself flying apparatus

The combination of a Volkswagen engine and an aircraft propeller, cobbled together by enthusiast Mr Arthur Poulsen of Quarnford and Bosley, had little chance of becoming a viable vertical-lift flying machine, but then many pioneering enterprises in the early days of aviation had just as little science behind them. And at least this one got off the ground, and did not actually kill its would-be aviator inventor.

Europa kit aeroplane

The Europa kit aeroplane, fabricated at Kirkbymoorside, quickly built up a reputation for being dependable and enjoyable to fly. A two-seat composite monoplane whose various adaptations included a glider-wing fit, it could be swiftly de-rigged for transportation on a trailer and storage in a garage. With an average empty weight of some 820 pounds its typical power unit of a Rotax 80 or 100 horsepower engine gave it a 138–161 mph (120–140 knots) speed range and what was claimed to be comparable performance with any other trainer in the same category. The power unit fitted in G-KWIP, which crashed at Bradley, was a Rotax 912-UL piston engine.

Mignet Flying Flea

After Henri Mignet's book was published in 1934, building and flying his Flying Flea home-build aeroplane became all the rage in both France and Britain. By 1937, however, after several fatal crashes, the authorities in both countries had banned the flying of un-modified Fleas on the grounds that the design was dangerously flawed. Mignet protested that his Flea was safe; that it was only when mistakes were made in construction, or when builders used pirated plans, that the Flea was unstable. The years of the German occupation prevented him carrying on production, but he never lost faith. Accordingly, once the war was over he was back in the arena. Only notwithstanding his faith the tenor of the times was against him, and his Flying Flea became little more than a novel memory in the history of light aviation.

Performance figures vary but Mignet's own 1934 figures are based upon an Aubier-Dunne 54cc standard model engine producing 20 hp at 4,000 rpm and driving a propeller of five feet diameter, the engine revving at 1,600 rpm while at rest on the ground. Once airborne his Flea, with a tandem wing of just under twenty-feet span, climbed to 1,600 feet in 8 minutes, to 3,300 feet in 19 minutes, and 5,600 feet in 38 minutes, cruised at 65 mph (56 knots), 'flew slowly' at 50 mph (43 knots), and had a landing speed of 19 mph (17 knots). With no wind it took off in 300 feet and landed in 175 feet. And the ceiling? At the time Mignet had not tried it out: 'It has been too cold. But [estimating it from ground-level throttle opening] 13,000 feet: call it 10,000 feet if you will. It is quite enough to fly over a lot of clouds.'

De Havilland DH60G Gipsy Moth

The first of the two-seater, single-engined de Havilland Moth biplane family made its initial flight in February 1925, an early development being the DH60G Gipsy Moth which first flew in 1928 and was powered by a 100 horsepower Gipsy engine. Representative of the type's performance was a maximum speed of 105 mph (91 knots) at sea level and 100 mph (87 knots) at 5,000 feet. It cruised at 85 mph (74 knots), had an initial climb rate of 700 feet a minute, and at an all-up weight of 1.400 pounds, a ceiling of 18,000 feet. It had a range of some 300 miles. The 1928 Moth was of wooden construction, but the 1929 version, of which 124 were built for the RAF, was made of metal. Prior to this, however, several Moth variants had been utilised by the RAF, both Cirrus in-line and Genet radial-engined, some appearing at the Hendon Air Shows from 1927 to 1929.

Handley Page Hampden

The four-crewed Hampden first flew in June 1936. It was not until September 1938, however, that the RAF began taking deliveries, notwithstanding which a year later, when war was declared, ten bomber squadrons were Hampden-equipped, the machines being powered by two 1,000 horsepower, 9-cylinder, Bristol Pegasus Mark Eighteen radial engines.

But this is one of those instances mentioned in the preface to this section when propaganda-based performance figures refuse to lie dormant. So the Hampden's ceiling is frequently given as 19,000 feet, although the manufacturers themselves only claimed 15,000 feet, even while extolling their product's 'incredibly fast' 254 mph (221 knots) maximum speed. But although a 1942 source gives the cruise as 217 mph (189 knots), actual users found the workaday cruise to be nearer 130 mph (113 knots), with the least sanguine modern source encountered proffering 167 mph (145 knots).

Irreconcilable figures aside, the Hampden's Handley Page leading-edge slots did give it a landing speed of just 73 mph (64 knots), and most sources agree that at a maximum take-off weight of 18,756 pounds it had a range of 1,885 miles with half a bomb load, reducing to 1,200 miles when the full 4,000 pounds was carried. As defensive armament it mounted two forward-firing 0.303-inch calibre machine guns, with additional twin mountings in both a dorsal and a rearward-facing belly position.

The Hampden showed up poorly against German fighters, however, and just months into the war the decision was taken to restrict the type to night operations, to leaflet dropping, and to minelaying.

The Hampden was regarded as pleasant to handle, although the crew found their positions cramped, and despite its shortcomings 1,432 were produced before the type was phased out in 1943.

Handley Page Harrow

The Harrow, a four- to five-seated, twin-finned, monoplane bomber, first flew in October 1936, but being obsolescent when war broke out in 1939, initially served as a bomber-trainer, and was then re-deployed as a transport.

The type's twin 925 horsepower Bristol Pegasus Twenty radial engines powered it to a 163 mph (142 knots) cruising speed and gave it a 22,800 feet ceiling. It could carry a bomb load of 3,000 pounds and was armed with four 0.303-inch calibre machine guns: two in the tail turret and one each in nose and dorsal positions. With a maximum take-off weight of 23,000 pounds the Harrow had a range of 1,250 miles and was to make its most telling contribution by evacuating casualties during the ill-fated Arnhem operation in September 1944, its Handley Page leading-edge slots permitting it to operate from fields which were far too small for other heavy aircraft.

North American Harvard

The prototype Harvard advanced trainer first flew on 1 April, 1935, subsequent to which over 17,000 were built, a number exceeding that for any other wartime trainer. The RAF put in an early order, but the French Government too had appreciated the Harvard's value and over a hundred had been delivered to them before France fell. An untimely delivery, as it turned out, for the *Luftwaffe* then used them both for training and for familiarising those of their pilots who were to evaluate captured American machines.

Although the Harvard did not start RAF service until January 1939, it was to remain in use until 1955. An impressive tenure, although far exceeded by its working life in the South African Air Force where it was used until 1995.

Performance details for the Harvard Mk.2 typify all variants. The power unit was a 550/600 horsepower, 9-cylinder Pratt and Whitney Wasp engine, air-cooled, and driving a Hamilton two-bladed, two-position controllable-pitch propeller. Together these produced a top speed of 206 mph (179 knots) and a cruising speed of 180 mph (156 knots). The landing speed was 63 mph (55 knots) with an initial climb rate of 1,350 feet a minute. The ceiling was 23,000 feet, the range 730 miles, and the maximum weight 2,260 pounds.

Although popular, it was a demanding machine – and therefore a good advanced trainer – and required its pilot to be cognisant of both its handling qualities and its technical foibles.

Douglas Havoc A-20G, RAF Boston

The RAF far-sightedly ordered the American A-20, which they designated the Boston, before the Second World War broke out. First flown in 1938, the twin-engined A-20 would be variously employed as medium bomber, fighter-bomber, night fighter, and night intruder, and was also noteworthy as the first operational aircraft in RAF service to have a tricycle undercarriage. The crew comprised pilot, navigator and gunner.

In an early conversion the bomb-aimer's glazed station was replaced by an opaque nose which carried eight machine guns, after which the type had considerable success in night-intruder operations, lurking with intent about German airfields.

This modified version was initially designated the Havoc, but the RAF dropped this name to avoid confusion with the A-20s, already styled Havocs, which came into the theatre in July 1942 when the United States Eighth Army Air Force began A-20 operations themselves. For their especial task of ground-support operations the USAAF's A-20G models had been heavily armed, the refit including a power-operated turret.

Representative figures for the A-20G Havoc are based upon a 1,700 horsepower Wright Cyclone engine. This gave the machine a top speed of over 320 mph (278 knots) and a ceiling exceeding 20,000 feet. With a maximum take-off weight of 25,000 pounds the version had a range of 500 miles when operating as a fighter-bomber but more than 1,200 miles when acting as an escort.

Armament varied widely depending upon the role, but a typical fit was six 0.5-inch calibre machine guns in the nose, with two in the dorsal turret, and provision for carrying two 1,000-pound bombs.

Heinkel He.111

The Heinkel He.111 ('one-eleven') was extremely promising when it first flew in February 1935. Blooded with the Condor Legion in the Spanish Civil War, and later in Poland at the beginning of the Second World War, it handsomely outstripped the opposing fighters. This was not to be the case over Britain, however, when both its armament and performance proved inadequate, particularly as German fighters were unable to dwell long enough to provide meaningful support. Accordingly, from mid-September 1940, the He.111 was restricted to night operations.

Typically powered by two 1100 Junkers Jumo engines it had an average speed (collating various sources) of 250 mph (217 knots), a ceiling of 23,000 feet, and a range of 1,030 miles. Early versions had a crew of four, a bomb load of some 4,000 pounds and were armed with three 7.9 mm calibre machine-guns mounted dorsally, in the nose, and in a belly turret. When production ceased in 1944 a total of 7,399 of the type had been built.

Handley Page Heyford

Produced in 1933, the twin-engined, basically four-crewed, Heyford was a biplane-bomber of all-metal framed construction whose speedy 143 mph (124 knots) earned it the appellation 'Express'. Indeed, unlikely as it seems, a No.102 Squadron Heyford was publicly looped during the 1935 Hendon Air Show! Interestingly too, it was held – admittedly by Handley Page – that, in comparison to a retractable undercarriage, the lighter weight of the streamlined but fixed undercarriage so minimised drag that it actually enhanced the Heyford's performance. Withdrawn from first-line service in 1939 the type still gave good value as a crew trainer until 1941, being stable and pleasant to fly.

The Heyford was powered by two 575 horsepower Rolls-Royce Kestrel Mk.3 engines which gave it a ceiling of 21,000 feet, lifting up to 3,500 pounds of bombs. Its maximum permitted all-up weight was 16,900 pounds and with half its bomb load it had an operational striking range of 920 miles (' … carried a very large load of bombs for 2,000 miles': Handley Page). For defensive armament it carried three 0.303-inch calibre Lewis machine guns mounted respectively in dorsal, ventral and nose positions.

Production ended in July 1936 by which time 124 had been supplied. Although displaced by the Wellington in 1939 the Heyford was employed in training roles until mid-1941, when it was finally withdrawn from service.

Klemm Kl.35

The Klemm Kl.35 gull-winged machine, with steel-frame fuselage and wooden wings, first flew in February 1935 and was reputed to have excellent handling qualities and good visibility. Designer Klemm had set out to make a popular aeroplane that was as economical to run as a car, as easy to manufacture and maintain, and small enough to fit in a garage. As a consequence most German pilots during the 20s and 30s trained on Klemms. Interestingly, although an early and enthusiastic Nazi Party member, Klemm later fell foul of the Gestapo. Just the same, he survived the war.

The Kl.35 was powered by a 105 horsepower Hirth HM504-A2 four-cylinder air-cooled engine which gave it a maximum speed of 130 mph (113 knots) and a ceiling of 14,400 feet. It had a cruising speed of 118 mph (103 knots), and a landing speed of 48 mph (42 knots).

Lancaster and Lysander

In this Central volume these two types, the leading British heavy bomber and the short-field capability reconnaissance machine, are only mentioned with respect to spurious sites. Details of both may be found, however, on page 179 of the Southern volume of the series.

Miles Magister, RAF: Miles Hawk, civil

In 1936 the tandem-seated, low-winged Miles Hawk monoplane, metal-skinned as it was, so impressed the RAF with its suitability as an elementary trainer that a Service version was ordered. This became the Magister, with deliveries beginning in 1937. A serious spinning problem was encountered, and solved, and other modifications were made, including the provision of blind-flying equipment and a widening of the cockpit of the civilian trainer. Basically, however, the Magister remained a Hawk in uniform. Certainly, after the war, many Hawks-become-Magisters were welcomed back by flying clubs and private owners alike.

Powered by a 130 horsepower de Havilland Gipsy Major One in-line engine, the Hawk had a maximum speed of 140 mph (122 knots), a cruising speed of 123 mph (107 knots) and a range of 380 miles. It had a maximum take-off weight of 1,900 pounds and a ceiling of 18,000 feet. Boasting wheelbrakes, power-operated flaps, and a tailwheel – as opposed to a mere skid – it could be flown solo from either seat, although the front seat was preferred.

As a trainer it responded well in gusty conditions, unlike its contemporary, the Tiger Moth. On the other hand, unless controlled, the Hawk's wing would lift markedly in a crosswind. Then again there were trimming controls to master. Just two of the 'complications' that made it a good trainer. On top of that there were no vices. Only, for all its good points, it never aroused anything like the affection engendered by the Tiger Moth in (virtually) all those who had occasion to fly it.

Miles Master Marks 1 and 3

In the late 1930s it was realised that pupils would find it an unnecessarily daunting undertaking to step from Tiger Moths and Magisters into the new, high-performance Spitfires and Hurricanes. The Miles Kestrel, a private venture, seemed to be the answer, for when flown in June 1937 it showed a top speed just twenty miles an hour slower than the Hurricane, at nearly 300 mph. Accordingly the Ministry decided to adopt the new trainer, but following a pattern only too well established even at that early date, called for so many modifications that in March 1939, when the emergent Miles Master trainer first flew, it was a full hundred miles an hour slower than the Hurricane. The saving grace was that the Master's designers had ensured that the tandem-seat trainer had handling characteristics similar to those of the new fighters; in that respect, at least, easing the transition from trainer to first-line fighter.

As it was, the Master Mk.1 entered service powered by a 715 horsepower Kestrel Mk.30 in-line engine which gave it a maximum speed of 226 mph (196 knots), an initial climb rate of nearly 1,500 feet a minute, a ceiling of 28,000 feet, and a range of 500 miles. A total of 900 Mk.1s were built and a Mk.2 version followed, of which 1,799 were built.

The Master Mk.3 first flew in 1940, after which 600 were built. Powered by an 825 horsepower Pratt & Whitney Wasp Junior radial engine it had a maximum speed of 232 mph (202 knots) and a cruising speed of 170 mph (148 knots) while retaining the 85 mph (74 knots) landing speed of the Mk.1s and Mk.2s. Additionally it had a ceiling of 27,300 feet, and, at a maximum take-off weight of some 5,500 pounds, a range of 320 miles.

Noorduyn Norseman

The Canadian-manufactured, single-engined, ten-seater Noorduyn Norseman UC-64A was widely used by the United States Army Air Force as a light transport. Having first flown in 1935 it was a veteran design even in 1944, but it was rugged, adaptable, and always dependable. The latter notwithstanding, it was to gain undeserved notoriety as the aircraft type in which Major Glenn Miller, the popular bandleader, disappeared over the English Channel while en route to Paris on 15 December, 1944. (Interviewed for this series in 2004, it emerged that ex-air-gunner Mr Jack Byrom, of Ringinglow, formerly of No.149 Squadron, had been one of several aircrew to report that a low-flying aircraft, inopportunely transiting the assigned Channel ordnance-jettisoning area on the day in question, had been destroyed as the squadron let go their bombs following an abortive operation. It is now accepted that this is, indeed, how Glenn Miller died.)

The Norseman was powered by a 600 horsepower Pratt

and Whitney engine which gave it a cruising speed of 148 mph (129 knots) and a maximum speed of 162 mph (141 knots). It had a ceiling of 17,000 feet and a range of 1,150 miles.

McDonnell Douglas Phantom RF-4C

The Phantom RF-4C, whose prototype first flew in August 1963, was the unarmed photographic-reconnaissance version of the Phantom F-4C fighter, the most noticeable external difference being its longer, sharper nose. Within the modified machine, however, the armament and radar of the fighter was replaced by specialised photographic-reconnaissance equipment. This included various dedicated cameras, side-looking ground-mapping radar, infra-red imaging equipment for the reconnaissance role, a photoflash ejection system for night photography, and radar with both terrain-avoidance and terrain-following modes. Additionally there were infra-red and laser target-designators to provide slant range, and high-resolution thermal-imaging equipment.

The Phantom RF-4C was powered by two General Electric J79-GE-15 turbojets, each of 10,300 pounds static thrust, or 17,000 pounds with afterburner. This combination gave it a maximum speed of 1,459 mph (1,268 knots) at 48,000 feet – that is, Mach 2.21 (2.21 times the local speed of sound) – and 834 mph (725 knots) at sea level, or Mach 1.09. Cruising speed was 587 mph (510 knots), and landing speed 143 mph (124 knots).

The initial rate of climb varied enormously with the version, and whether or not the machine was encumbered with stores, figures varying from 28,000 to 46,000 feet a minute, and even higher. A typical service ceiling is given as 59,400 feet, a combat range of 840 miles, and a ferry range of 1,750 miles with full external fuel resources. Maximum take-off weight was some 58,000 pounds, and the maximum for engaging in combat, 39,773 pounds.

Percival Proctor Mk.3

The Proctor, a development of the four-seater 1935 Vega Gull, with flaps and dual controls, first flew in October 1939, some 1,100 being produced for the RAF and the Royal Navy. In the Proctor, the seating capacity was reduced to three, for although it was used as a communications aircraft it was also employed as a radio trainer. After the war many passed into civil hands but some continued in RAF service until 1955, notably fulfilling a taxi role for the Metropolitan Communications Squadron at Hendon.

Powered by a 210 horsepower de Havilland Gipsy Queen in-line engine, it had a maximum speed of 160 mph (139 knots), a cruising speed of 140 mph (122 knots), a range of 500 miles, and a ceiling of 14,000 feet.

Pierre Robin R1180TD Aiglon

This was a relatively short-lived variant of the 1972 Robin DR400, built in 1978. A four-seater, it was powered by a Lycoming 0-360 engine which gave it a maximum speed of some 155 mph (135 knots), a cruising speed of 136 mph (118 knots), a ceiling of 12,000 feet, and an initial rate of climb of 600 feet a minute. Handling was, by design, more stable than lively, while the canopy afforded a striking all-round view.

Supermarine Seafire

The Hurricane having been successfully adapted to a carrier-role, it was natural that the Royal Navy's attention should turn to the Spitfire. Accordingly, trials were commenced in late 1941. The narrow track of the Spitfire's undercarriage was always to cause deck-landing problems but hook-adapted Spitfire Mark Fives were soon developed as Seafire 1Bs. Not until the Seafire Mk.3 variant arrived, however, would the type have folding wings.

In truth, the Seafire was never entirely suited to carrier operations, and there were many deck-landing accidents. In particular propeller tips would strike the deck as the aircraft pitched nose-down on being arrested, a problem which was resolved in pragmatic Royal Navy style by clipping six inches off the end of all Seafire propellers as a matter of course.

Engine upgrades followed the Spitfire pattern, from the Merlin to the Griffon, the latter being tweaked yet further to enhance the take-off performance of the post-war Seafire Mk.17 development. Later versions of this mark, with its four 20 mm calibre cannon, its teardrop hood, sting-tail hook, and cut-down fuselage, had additional fuel storage, and therefore greater range.

Representative of Seafire performance then, was a maximum speed of 352 mph (306 knots), a cruising speed of 218 mph (189 knots), a ceiling of 33,800 feet, and a range of 465 miles; or 725 with a drop tank. The maximum take-off weight was 7,100 pounds.

Despite career-spanning modifications designed to maximise the Seafire's performance while minimising the weight penalty imposed by carrier-operating requirements, the type never managed to fully satisfy the Royal Navy: certainly not in the way the Spitfire did the RAF and all the other air forces which flew it. Just the same, to the Fleet Air Arm in general, the Seafire represented a marked improvement upon many types that had gone before.

Avro Shackleton Mk.3

The Avro Shackleton, which first flew in March 1949, was developed to replace the Lancaster while using many of its predecessor's tested strengths, the squadrons receiving the new type from April 1951. The maritime versions were eventually withdrawn from service in the early 1970s, but variants flew on until well into the 1990s.

During the course of its long service the Shackleton was constantly updated, not least when the tricycle undercarriage was introduced on the Mark 3 Shackleton in 1955. In 1971 the Nimrod patrol aircraft, derived from the four-jet de Havilland Comet, assumed the maritime task, although the Shackleton retained its search-and-rescue role until 1972. Even then the RAF Shackleton's operational life was extended when the type was employed as an Airborne Early Warning platform, carrying out this duty until 1991 when the Boeing E3D Sentry, with its distinctive back-mounted dish aerial, took over.

The Shackleton was typically powered by four Rolls-Royce Griffon Mk.57A in-line piston engines, each of which developed 2,455 horsepower. In addition to the Griffons some versions were power-augmented by two Rolls-Royce Viper 203 turbojets, each developing 2,500 pounds of static thrust.

In round terms the Shackleton had a maximum take-off weight of 98,000 pounds, a ceiling of 19,000 feet, a fuel capacity of 4,258 gallons, an endurance of nearly fifteen hours, and a range of some 3,500 miles. Its maximum speed was 300 mph (261 knots) and it cruised at 180–240 mph (156–209 knots) depending upon the task in hand.

Typical of its armament was two 20 mm calibre cannon in the nose, and two machine guns at the tail. It carried up to 10,000 pounds of bombs or depth charges, and was normally operated by a crew of ten. A total of 188 were built.

Douglas Skytrain C-47 modified transport/freighter variant (United States Army, C-47; RAF, Dakota)

Entering service in 1941 as a modified military variant of the civil DC-3, the C-47 Skytrain was able to accommodate heavy loads by virtue of a strengthened floor and a widened freight-cum-passenger door. Typically, two 1,200 horsepower Pratt & Whitney Twin Wasp engines gave the Skytrain a top speed of 230 mph (200 knots), a cruising speed of 207 mph (180 knots), and a stalling speed of 67 mph (58 knots). It had a range of 2,125 miles, an initial climb rate of 1,130 feet a minute, and a ceiling of 23,200 feet, its maximum take-off weight being 30,000 pounds.

Republic F-84 Thunderstreak

The swept-wing F-84 ground-support fighter-bomber was developed from the straight-winged F-84, the prototype flying in June 1950. Several engine fits then proved necessary, however, and many other modifications were called for, one of the most successful being an all-flying tail. Even then, addressing some serious handling and stability problems meant that it was 1954 before deliveries began, although 2,711 were eventually delivered. In the 1960s the type was gradually replaced by the F-100, although it lingered on with the United States National Guard until 1971.

A typical engine fit was the Wright J65-W-3, the licence-built adaptation of the British Armstrong Siddeley Sapphire, whose 7,220 pounds of thrust gave the weighty 27,000 pound Thunderstreak an initial climb rate of 7,400 feet a minute, a maximum speed of 685 mph (595 knots), and a ceiling of 44,450 feet. The limiting Mach number was M1.18 in a dive, the range some 1,900 miles, and the cruising speed 535 mph (465 knots).

Armament was six 0.5-inch calibre machine guns, one in each wing and four in the nose, and twenty-four five-inch rockets, with up to 6,000 pounds of externally carried ordnance.

V1 (*Vergeltungswaffe*) Flying Bomb

The German *Fern Ziel Geraet* (effectively 'Long-range Aiming Apparatus'), their *Vergeltungswaffe 1* ('Reprisal Weapon Number One'), was a pilotless flying bomb. It was powered by a pulse-jet engine which operated using a system of shutter-type valves whose action gave the singular sound that, as any bombarded populace quickly learnt, heralded its approach. On reaching its target area the device was rigged to dive. As the nose dipped so the fuel flow was interrupted and the engine stopped, indicating to the initiated that only moments later the bomb would explode.

The first test flight was in December 1941, with the celebrated lady pilot, Hanna Reitsch, being foremost among the test pilots who flew the piloted version during the development phase. The main assault on Britain and Belgium began in June 1944 and lasted eighty days, some being fired as late as early 1945. Regarding the total number fired, estimates vary, but in general terms it is held that of the 10,000 V1s launched against England, 7,000 landed on the mainland; a figure upheld by former WRNS Margaret Herbert, of Derby, a plotter throughout the assault.

'Our operations centre was under the Royal Naval College at Greenwich,' Margaret said in 2006. 'We'd get information from headquarters, and we'd a large table-map of the London area on which we marked where each Doodlebug came down.' Indeed, by the end of her posting that table would have been groaning under 3,876 markers!

Recording aside, the defences comprised barrage balloons, aircraft and anti-aircraft guns, but once especially adapted rangefinders became available most V1s were shot down by the guns as they crossed the coast.

As an oblique measure of the human cost to London

alone, the 'Doodlebugs' – 'Buzz-bomb' was an equally popular sobriquet – destroyed 24,000 houses and badly damaged a further 800,000. However, had secret agents not warned of the development, and had the launching sites not then been systematically bombed, the toll of both life and property would have been infinitely higher.

On firing, the V1 was propelled up a railed launching ramp by volatile hydrogen peroxide, and then accelerated to 410 mph (356 knots) by an Argus AS14 pulse-jet which developed 660 pounds of static thrust. The device was given a range of 150 miles by 750 gallons of petrol, the total weight of 4,750 pounds including just under a ton of amatol high-explosive. While normally ramp-launched against London and Antwerp from sites on the French coast, 825 V1s were carried beneath Heinkel He.111 bombers, some to be air-launched into the Peakland area.

De Havilland Vampire

The twin-boomed de Havilland Vampire, the third of Britain's jet aircraft was, like the Mosquito that preceded it, a private de Havilland venture. Again, as in the Mosquito, moulded plywood was used extensively in a composite of wood and metal, the zone from the engine intakes to the nose being predominantly aluminium-skinned wood. For a power plant the Vampire had a single centrifugal-flow Goblin turbo-jet engine whose fuel control system, being relatively unsophisticated, always demanded near-empathetic throttle handling. Just the same it could power the future 'Sir Geoffrey's' machine to over 500 mph, while to enhance that power, by minimising the losses in the jet pipe, the efflux was carried away between twin tail booms.

Although the Vampire came into service too late for the Second World War, the squadrons receiving it only from 1946, from that time on it gave a good account of itself in its several roles. Nippy, yet essentially stable and easy to fly, the Vampire, and particularly the Mk.5 fighter-bomber variant, also proved a useful advanced trainer for Flying Training Command, although the type would become more useful still after 1950 when the dual trainer version, the T.11 ('Tee Eleven'), became available.

The T.11 trainer, with its Goblin 3 centrifugal-flow, turbo-jet engine developing 3,200 pounds of static thrust, had a maximum permitted speed of 523 mph (455 knots) and a medium-level cruising speed of 265 mph (230 knots). Its maximum take-off weight was 13,380 pounds, it had a range of 730 miles, and it was to remain in RAF service until 1966. Although nominally a trainer it could mount two or four 20 mm calibre cannon, and provision was made to carry rocket projectiles or bombs.

De Havilland Venom FB (fighter bomber)

The single-seater de Havilland 112, subsequently called the Venom, first flew in September 1949. Built to succeed the de Havilland Vampire it was similar in general appearance but was, in fact, a more sophisticated design altogether. A notable introduction was a thinner, medium-sweepback wing which enabled the Venom to take advantage of the higher Mach numbers its more powerful Ghost engine could propel it to; the wing-tip tanks, meanwhile, smoothing out the airflow and imparting greater aerodynamic efficiency. The production order was subjected to severe cutbacks, but nevertheless the fighter-bomber version equipped many squadrons between 1953 and 1955 during which time it won praise for its rate of climb and its manoeuvrability at high altitudes. An updated version, the Venom FB.4, first flew in December 1953 and had an ejection seat. The Venom saw action at Suez in 1956 and in Aden in 1957, but also held the line with the Second Tactical Air Force in Germany.

Of all-metal, stressed-skin construction, the Venom was powered by a 4,850-pound thrust de Havilland Ghost 103 engine which gave it a representative maximum speed of 597 mph (519 knots) at sea level, and 557 mph (484 knots) at 30,000 feet, a rate of climb of 7,230 feet a minute, a ceiling of 48,000 feet, and a range of 1,075 miles. It had four 20 mm calibre guns in the nose and could carry 2,000 pounds of bombs.

Copyright holders authorising the use of their photographs in this volume

Bramley, Phil, *Derbyshire Times*, Chesterfield
Gordon, Bruce, Mosquito Trust, Hatfield
Guess, Barry, BAE Systems, Farnborough
Gunn, Michael A, intellectual property, Rolls-Royce; aircraft
Haigh, Richard, manager, intellectual property, Rolls-Royce; aircraft
Higton, Phyllis (daughter of Harry Gill)
Hill, Chris, *Stockport Express*
Hunt, Nicola, intellectual property rights copyright unit, MOD; most aircraft
Nokes, Judy, licensing, HMSO/Crown Copyright/MOD; most aircraft
Rigby, Stewart, *Stockport Express*
Robinson, Stewart, *Stoke Evening Sentinel*
Royal Air Force Museum; aircraft
Editor, *Sheffield Morning Telegraph*
Seal, Carol, photographic section, *Derby Evening Telegraph*
Steiner, Ralph, Mosquito Museum, Hatfield; aircraft
Temple, Julian, archivist, Vickers, Brooklands Museum, Weybridge; aircraft
Wilkinson, Roni, Pen and Sword Publishing, White Edge

Authors and websites

Barrass, Malcolm, air historian, *Air of Authority* website
Collier, Ron; with Wilkinson, Roni, *Dark Peak Aircraft Wreck* series
Earl, David W, *Hell on High Ground* series
Kedward, Brian, *Angry Skies across the Vale*
Air Britain authors

Technical and professional assistance

ASDA, Spondon, Derby, staff
Baker, Julie, Air Historical Branch, MOD
Buie, Jim, secretary, Manchester Fleet Air Arm Association
Byron, Jack, ex-No.149 Squadron air gunner (26 Ops)
Day, Graham, Air Historical Branch, MOD
Derby Local Studies and Main Libraries, Staff
Dickinson, Susan, Air Historical Branch, MOD
Elliot, Peter, Senior Keeper, RAF Museum
Forder, Nick, DH10 input
Gamble, Carol, Commonwealth War Graves Commission
Gatfield, Tom, ex-No.49 Squadron, navigator, Lancasters
Goddard, Margaret, Polish Archives, MOD Northolt
Gordon, Bruce, de Havilland Mosquito Trust, Hatfield
Kroll, Barbara, Polish Archives, MOD Northolt
Leek Local Studies Library, Staff
Macclesfield Local Studies Library, Staff
McGrath, Peter, Sheffield, ex Wellington Wop/AG (40 Ops)

Murray, Mary, police archives, Derbyshire
Public Records Office, Kew, Staff
Somay, Julie, Commonwealth War Graves Commission
Stainthorpe, Peter, Commonwealth War Graves Commission
Wallace, Ken, Wing Commander, autogiro constructor and *aviateur extraordinaire*
Whittaker, Kevin, crash-site researcher
Withers, Jackie, Commonwealth War Graves Commission
Woodside, John, air historian

Ashbourne

Chadfield, Jeff, Grange Farm, Darley Moor
Lawton, Tom, Holly Meadow Farm, Bradley

Bakewell (Chatsworth)

Robinson, David, Head Park Keeper, Chatsworth Estate
Roose, Charles, retired Estate employee, ex-RAF

Buxton

Bowler, John, Tor Gate Farm
Brittain, John, Slade Farm
Brittain-Cartlidge, Phillip, Slade Farm
Brittain-Cartlidge, Elizabeth, Slade Farm
Down, Jonathon, Rushup Farm, Sparrowpit
Farlam, Brenda, Wallnook Farm, Brandside
Groom, David, Cirencester
Hamilton, Freda, Cowdale
Heathcote, Albert, sheep farmer, formerly Saltersford Hall Farm
Jones, Miriam (née Swindell), Hill Farm
Lomas, Joe, King Sterndale
Millican, Claire, Plex Farm
Minshull, Bernard and Rosie, Goslin Bar Farm, Burbage
Mosely, Teddy, Knotlow Farm, Wormhill
Mosely, Nigel, Stich House, near Wormhill
Mycock, Fay and Roy, Colt Croft Farm
Mycock, Helen, local historian, Hayward Farm
O'Neill, Kevin, Slade Hill House
Swain, John and Margaret, Thirkelow Farm
Williams, Henry, Burbage

Chapel-en-le-Frith area

Barratt, Bill, and Carol (née Craven), Rye Flatt Farm, Combs
Barratt, George, formerly Marsh Green Farm
Collier, Wilf
Dalton, Ted and Dethick, Mary, formerly of Malcoff Farm, Chapel
Hobden, Dee, Portobello Farm, Buxworth
Hollingrake, Bill and Jean, and son, Stephen, formerly of Black Edge Farm
Jones, Alan and Margaret, Wilkin Hill Farm (Hilltop)

Loman, Stuart, Combs, gamekeeper
Lomas, Ron and Marion, Horderns Lane, Chapel
Thompson, Frank, Long Lane, Chapel
Worsley, Frank and Helen, Digleach Farm, Chapel

Chesterfield
Biggin, Ian, Unthank Lane Farm, Millthorpe
Biggin, William, farmer, Millthorpe
Bostock, Kenneth and Ruth, Heath
Bown, Sam, farmer, Captain's Barn Farm
Brailsford, Geoff and David, Honeycroft Farm
Cooper, Raymond, Old Tupton
Dart, Jack, Gladwin's Mark Farm
Dronfield, Ernest, Gladwin's Mark Farm
Dixon (née Lomas), Kathleen, Moor Farm (since, Darley Forest Grange)
Elliot, Selwyn, formerly Ordnance Survey
Fearn, David, Darley Forest Grange (formerly Moor Farm)
Green, Stan, North Wingfield
Hague, Anthony and Janet, Holmewood
Hawksworth (née Keeton), Edna, Yewcrofts Farm
Hawksworth, Peter, farmer
Houghton, Betty, Highfields, North Wingfield
Keeton, John, Yewcrofts Farm
Knight, John, farmer, formerly Brookside Farm
Needham, Peter, Church Farm, Barlow
Noble, Horace, civil engineer, Barlow
Singleton, Kari, North Wingfield
Spencer, John, Grouse Cottage Moor Farm

Curbar
Adlington, Betty (never forgetting Ken)
Fletcher, Mark and Sally, The Grouse Inn
Udall, Danny, Winsick

Derby
Butler, Jeff and Susan, Shottle Hall Cottages
Chadderton, Arthur, Cowers Lane
Easter, John, Little Eaton
Hurt, David, Carrbrook Farm
Jones, Ray, White Meadow Cottage, Brailsford
March, Mavis, Denby Common
Mills, Norman and Mavis, Hill Farm, Denby
Mottershead, Neville, DFC, Brailsford
Prince, Colin, Roston Hall Farm
Robinson, Roy, Allestree
Salt, John, Elm Farm, Little Eaton
Slater, Herbert and Mrytle, Duffield, formerly Overlane Farm
Symcox, Elizabeth, Little Eaton
Thompson, Simon and Lucy, Culland Hall, Brailsford
Wareing, Michael, Shottle Hall Cottages
Wood, Allan and Viola, Bank End Farm, Roston

Disley
Atherton, Rosemary Cordelia, Hagbank Farm
Grime, Stephen and Christine, Homestead Farm, Jacksons Edge
Makepeace, Chris, local historian
Johnson, Timothy and Miranda, The Homestead
Wheale, Ron, Jacksons Edge

Dronfield
Allonby, Tom, of Sheffield, early crash-site researcher
Broomhead, Brian and Peter, Brown Edge Farm
Fisher, Howard, Pewitt Farm
Gibbs, Nancy, Dore
Hancock, Noel, Sheephill Farm, Ringinglow
Ludlam, Jean, Hollybush Farm, South Wingfield
McArthur, Thanet House, Moorwood Moor
Marsden, Peter and Liz, of Castleton, formerly Brown Edge Farm
Wilson, Sue, of Dore

Foolow
Baggaley, Lorna, Grindleford
Bond, Les, landlord, Bull's Head
Bricklebank, Jack, of Eyam
Brooks, Ray, Great Hucklow Gliding Club
Hancock, John, farmer and Stoney Middleton butcher
Jones (née Swindell), Miriam, Hill Farm
Marples, Stewart, farmer
Morton, John, Grindleford postmaster

Hartington
DeVille, Colin, c/o Joseph Cotton Hotel
Riley, Ronald, Hartington local historian
Shipley, Alan and Valerie, Raikes Farm, Hulme End

Hope
Millward, Bill and Joy, Dale House, Hathersage Historical Society
Robinson, Eric and Noreen (née Beverley), Marsden Farm Cottages
Stamper, Robert and Dorothy, Hathersage
Wilcoxon, Mrs, Hillfoot Farm, Hathersage
Wilson, Kenneth, Greenwood Farm, Hathersage

Leek/ Cheadle
Bradbury, Ivan, Stoke
Brassington, John and Victor, Blakelow Farm
Brindley, Sheila, Upper Tean
Hulme, Kenneth John, Caverswall
Parish, Valerie, Cocking Farm, Caverswall,
Wainright, Cecil, Cheadle
Williams, Evelyn, Upper Tean

Longnor

Limer, Walter, ex-Royal Artillery
Slack, Tony and Edward, Fawside Edge
Slack, Nellie, Fawside Edge

Matlock

Barry, Kay, Matlock Golf Club, historian
Dodds, Clem, Buxton
Hole, Fred, Wayside Farm
Petts, Harold, Bull Ring, Snitterton

Monyash

Allen, Frank and Helen, Overwheal Farm
Boam, Frank, Nether Wheal Farm
Boam, Molly (Mary), landowner and retired farmer
Brough, Derek, Rake End Farm
Grigor-Taylor, Robert, Lathkil Hotel
Hollingsworth (née Kenworthy), Pat, formerly Lowfields Farm
Mycock, Bill
Mycock, Gary, Rowson Farm
Oldfield, Joe, Upper Haddon
Slater, James and Eileen, Monyash
Slater, Frank, Stanley Lodge Farm, Hucklow, formerly One Ash Farm

Parwich

Bradbury, Owen, Moor Close Farm
Chapman, Kate
Dale, Frank
Evans, Dennis, Nethergreen
Fearn, Charles, Market Rasen, formerly of Parwich
Gosling, Robert, Linda, and Daniel
Kirkham, Acer and Hilda (née Dunn)
Marriot, Simon, Major
Rushton, Jim, Mountain Ash Farm
Shields, Robert
Taylor, G, Daleside

Rotherham

Chappell, Clive G, Wath-upon-Dearne
Frost, Hedley, Treeton
Nuthall, Pat, Treeton
Stevenson, Dorothy, Treeton

Rushup Edge

Barrows, John Campion, 'Campy'
Bricklebank, Jack, Eyam
Chapman, Alan, Barber Booth
Daken, Billy, Hillside Farm
Heygi, Josef, Park Ranger, Fairholmes and Edale
Jackson, Peter, Peak Park Ranger, Glossop
Miller, Gordon, formerly Area Ranger, Edale and Kinder
Townsend, Ron, Sheffield
Worsley, Frank and Helen, Digleach Farm, Chapel

Sheffield

Arnall, Jill (née Livesey), formerly Sugworth Hall, Strines
Bailey, Maureen
Clark, Eric, Kiveton Park
Clark, Jack, Red Hill, Kiveton
Couldwell, Diane, Redmires Road
Crooks, Terence
Flynn, Patrick, Preston, former Gardener's Mate, Concord Park
Gibson, Les and Margaret, Wales
Gilmour, Sheila, Norton History Group
Hammond, Joan, North Anston
Hardy, Mary, Kiveton Park
Mills, Derek, Kiveton Park
Merifield, Brian, (RAF retd)
Pywell, Malcolm, Hackenthorpe, Greenkeeper, Concord Park
Taylor, Gordon, East Windsor, USA, formerly of Abbeyville
Taylor, Raymond, Kiveton Park
Waller, Les, Todwick
Waller, Grace and Herbert, Hardwick Farm
Waller, Phillip, Todwick
Waller, Richard, Todwick
Wheat, Nick, Holmesfield

Stockport

Wilkson, Florence, Springfield Farm
Wilkson, Roger, Springfield Farm

Wildboarclough

Ashley, Bob, Wincle
Ferns, Thomas Victor, Longnor
Borrow, Anthony, local historian, Old Post Office
Bowler, John and Sheila, Torgate Farm
Bullock, Alfred and Elsie, Golden Hill Farm, Bosley
Cantrell, Bill, son John, Clough House Farm, Macclesfield Forest
Harris, Mark, 'Bomber', ex-RAF, Shutlingsloe Farm
Johnson, Tom and Alec, Dawson Farm, Bosley
Naden (née Bullock), Evelyn, Cheddleton, formerly Golden Hill Farm
Seed, John, Shutlingsloe Farm, Land Estate Agent
Sharpley, Phillip, formerly of Crag Inn and Shutlingsloe Farm
Turnock, Len, farms Shutlingsloe Farm land

Middleton by Youlgreave

Dale, Joan, Conksbury Farm
Rowland, Colin, Middleton by Youlgreave, ex-Irish Guards
Rowland, Joan, Middleton by Youlgreave
Yates, Barry and Alison, Smerrill Grange Farm

Air Ministry. (1937) *Royal Air Force Pocket Book, AP1081*. London: HMSO

Air Ministry. (1941) *Air Navigation Volume 1, AP1234*. London: HMSO

Air Ministry. (1943) *Elementary Flying Training, AP1979A*. London: HMSO

Air Ministry. (1948) *The Rise and Fall of the German Air Force (1931 to 1945)*. London: HMSO

Air Ministry. (1954) *Flying, Volumes 1 and 2, AP129*. (Sixth edition). London: HMSO

Air Ministry. (1960) *Flying Instructor's Handbook, AP3225D*. London: HMSO

Air Ministry. (1960) *Pilot's Notes Vampire T.11*. London: HMSO

Barber, H. (1916) *The Aeroplane Speaks* London: McBride, Nast and Co. Ltd

Baring, Maurice. (1920) *RFC HQ 1914–1918*. London: Bell and Sons

Barrass, Malcolm. (2006) *Air of Authority* (RAF organisation). (www.rafweb.org)

Bennett, D.C.T. (1936) *The Complete Air Navigator*. London: Pitman

Boylan, Marshall S. (1992) *A Moorland Dedication*. Leek: William Beech

Collier, Ron; Wilkinson, Roni. (1979/1982) *Dark Peak Aircraft Wrecks*. Barnsley: Pen & Sword

Cramp, B.G. (1979) *British Midland Airways*. Hounslow: Airline Publications

Director of Flying Training RAF. (1955–1970 various) *Air Clues*. London: MOD

Fellowes, P.F.M. (1942) *Britain's Wonderful Air Force*. London: Odhams

Freidheim, E.; Taylor, S.W. (1944) *Fighters Up*. London: Nicholson Watson

Green, William; Swanborough, Gordon. (1997) *Fighters*. London: Salamander

Gunston, Bill. (1988) *Diamond Flight*. Derby: Henry Melland

Hammerton, J. (1943) *ABC of the RAF*. London: Amalgamated Press

HMSO. (1937) *RAF Pocket Handbook, 1937*. London: Air Ministry

HMSO. (1944) *Target: Germany*. London: Air Ministry

HMSO. (1942–1943) *Aircraft Recognition*. London: Sampson Clark

Jane, Fred T. (1919) *Jane's All the World's Aircraft*. London: Jane's Publishing Co.

Jordanoff, Assen. (1941) *Safety in Flight*. New York: Funk & Wagnalls

Kedward, Brian. (1996) *Angry Skies across the Vale*. Self-published: Cheltenham

Kronfeld, Robert. (1931) *Kronfeld on Soaring and Gliding* London: Hamilton

Lamplugh, A.G. (1931) *Accidents in Civil Aviation*. Royal Aeronautical Paper, Institution of Aeronautical Engineers, 29 October, 1931, London

Mignet, Henri. (1934) (ed. J.A. Chamier) *The Flying Flea, How to build and fly it*. London: Sampson Low, Marston, and Co. Ltd

Monday, David. (1994) *Hamlyn Concise Guide to British Aircraft of World War II*. London: Chancellor Press

Morris, Alan. (1968) *First of the Many, Independent Force*. London: Jarrolds

Ogilvy, David. (1977) *Bleriot to Spitfire*. Shrewsbury: Airlife

Phelps, Anthony. (1944) *I couldn't care less.* (Air Transport Auxiliary) Leicester: Harborough

Royal Flying Corps Communiqués: research in Imperial War Museum (but see three printed volumes; by Donovan: London, 1969; and Grub Street London, 1998)

Saville-Sneath, R.A. (1945) *Aircraft of the United States, Volume One*. London: Penguin

Stewart, Oliver. (1941) *The Royal Air Force in Pictures*. London: Country Life

Sturtivant, Ray; Page, Gordon. (1999) *'Air Britain Listings' series*. Old Woking: Unwin

Thetford, Owen. (1958) *Aircraft of the Royal Air Force 1918–58*. London: Putnam

Tudor, L. Thomas. (1930) *The High Peak to Sherwood*. London: Robert Scott

Winchester, Clarence. (1938) *Wonders of World Aviation, Vol 2*. London: Waverley

This section contains two major corrections, an addendum and some typographical corrections.

p.19 Avro Anson K6283, Bradnop, near Leek: Correction

Before publication the informant for this site located it, from memory, in one of the two boundary ditches of a specific field. A metal-detector search having proved negative at both, the site the informant most favoured was decided upon. After publication, however, ditching by the incumbent farmer turned up aircraft débris on the other boundary. The amended site reference is **SK 02345 55501** 337m. Apologies.

p.107 Supermarine Spitfire Mk.22 PK488, Mountain Ash Farm, north of Parwich: Correction

Writing in March 2006, Mr Charles Fearn, of Market Rasen, advised that this 1949 Spitfire crash had, in fact, occurred at Hilltop Farm, adjacent to Parwich. He then recommended me to Mr Asa Kirkham, who had been brought up at Mountain Ash Farm, and who was able to supply most details of the de Havilland Gipsy Moth which had put down on Mountain Ash Farm circa 1928 in exactly the circumstances described by Mrs Annie Walker. My error had stemmed from the fact that the RAF crash report recorded the Spitfire crash as occurring 'one and a half miles north of Parwich', so that as I was asking about a Spitfire, Mrs Walker had in mind the Moth she had seen when she was fifteen, seventy-eight years before. Again, I can only apologise to readers, and hope that the revised entry (p.183 *The Central Area*), together with a new one for the Moth (p.170 *The Central Area*), will atone for this particular error.

p.104 Supermarine Spitfire Mk.1 P9563, Hartington: Addendum

Encountered in Hartington in 2006, Mr Ronald Riley, the village's local historian, was able to supplement the account of the 1940 Spitfire crash in Hartington, published in *Peakland Air Crashes: The South*. 'I was sixteen, at the time,' he said, 'and happened to be on the roof of the cheese factory seeing to some cooling coils, when this Spitfire appeared and began to circle. He must have done this for about 15 minutes. But Arthur Tress, from the garage, remembered that, some time before, another aircraft had touched down safely in a field nearby, so he ran into the open and tried to signal the pilot to land there. After circling for a while longer, however, the pilot chose the field at the bottom of the cheese factory instead and came in from the north. He touched down all right, but then ran out of space and ploughed straight into the wall directly in front of me.' He paused. 'It was a touchy time, for who could tell when the plane might have exploded? But neither Arthur Tress nor Mr Joseph Brindley, of the cheese factory, hesitated before jumping up onto the wings to extricate the pilot. The airman wasn't hurt, just dazed. But it took them some time to realise that his harness was still secured. Once they took out the pin, though, they managed to get him out. As it happened, the aircraft didn't catch fire – but to my mind that doesn't detract from their bravery, for they weren't to know it wouldn't.' How true! And again, what a shame neither received recognition for his selfless conduct. As for the aftermath, 'The RAF', Mr Riley continued, 'sent a car for the pilot, then a tent was set up and a guard mounted overnight. And next day a Queen Mary trailer arrived and took the plane away.'

Typographical corrections

p.36 caption: delete 'interred'
p.37 mid-page: should read 'Blowoerem' Farm ['Blow over them']
p.156 para. 8 should read: 'As an historical footnote, the 1,000 or so sorely-needed Czech airmen who arrived in Britain via Poland, the French Foreign Legion, and the *Armée de l'Air*, were inducted into … '
It is hoped that other identified typographical errors, while regretted, leave the sense clear.